Texian Iliad

BATTLE OF THE ALAMO, MARCH 6, 1836

Texian Iliad

A MILITARY HISTORY OF
THE TEXAS REVOLUTION, 1835 – 1836

Stephen L. Hardin

Illustrated by Gary S. Zaboly

UNIVERSITY OF TEXAS PRESS

AUSTIN

To Mom and C.W.
for always being there . . .
my gratitude

S.L.H.

Requests for permission to reproduce material from this work should be sent to:
Permissions
University of Texas Press
P.O. Box 7819
Austin, TX 78713-7819
www.utexas.edu/utpress/about/bpermission.html

♾The paper used in this book meets the minimum requirements of
ANSI/NISO Z39.48-1992 (R1997) (Permanence of Paper).

Library of Congress Cataloging-in-Publication Data

Hardin, Stephen L., 1953–
Texian iliad : a military history of the Texas revolution, 1835–1836 /
Stephen L. Hardin ; illustrated by Gary S. Zaboly. — 1st ed.
p.   cm.
Includes bibliographical references and index.
ISBN-13: 978-0-292-73102-8 (pbk.)
ISBN-10: 0-292-73102-7
1. Texas—History—Revolution, 1835–1836—Campaigns.   I. Title.
FF390.H29   1994
976.4′03—dc20
94-1564

THUS THE NEW EPIC OF TEXAS, the chronicles so recently written and the legends so vibrantly alive with yesterday's happenings, exerts upon the tourist who wanders there the magic of a new lore and of an unmatched poetry. The names of the Milams, Travises, Fannins, and Bowies—those popular heroes of the Texian Iliad—recall to mind repeatedly and amazingly the most stalwart heroes of Homer; the fortnight of the siege of the Alamo can scarcely be paralleled by any days of the ten-year siege of Troy.

—FREDERIC GAILLARDET, 1839

WITH THE EXCEPTION of the infamous massacres of the Alamo and Goliad, and considering the Bobadil terms in which it has been spoken of, [the Texan war] is almost burlesque. —THEODORE SEDGWICK, 1844

CONTENTS

ILLUSTRATIONS

✦

✦

✛

PHOTOGRAPHS AND PORTRAITS

PREFACE

Scholarly conflicts over the Texas Revolution are at times as bitter as the war itself and almost always of longer duration. More traditional historians view it as a heroic struggle of determined Americans against overwhelming odds. Deconstructionists view it as a shameless land grab, a scheme concocted by the "slaveocracy," that marked the beginning of a particularly unpleasant phase of Manifest Destiny. The first view is boastfully romantic; the second tends to dismiss legitimate as well as fallacious elements of older interpretations.

My purpose is not to review old fights or to pick new ones. A perfunctory glance at the bibliography will reveal that much solid work has been done on the Texas revolt of 1835–1836. What was lacking was a careful analysis of the military aspects of the war. Certainly books abound on the Alamo and San Jacinto, but the glare of those shining moments has obscured the less famous, but nonetheless, important incidents. The story needs to be told in full.

Political events have been discussed only to the extent that they had a bearing on the actions of the soldiers in the field. Professor Paul Lack's recent study, *The Texas Revolutionary Experience: A Political and Social History, 1835–1836*, precludes the need for another political history of the revolt for the foreseeable future. I have, nevertheless, listed several of the earlier political treatments in the bibliography for those whose curiosity strays in that direction.

My reasons for offering a military narrative go beyond a desire to illuminate the causes of the Revolution. Students of Texas history and nineteenth-century warfare have generally failed to grasp its lessons or view the conflict within a wider context. Professor Archie P. McDonald, to cite but one, laments that "Texas has no Hannibal, no Napoleon to formulate or demonstrate great tactical or strategic truths. It contributes no infantry maneuvers or artillery innovations of lasting significance. Its only real value is moral."

Dr. McDonald is correct—to a point. Compared to the Napoleonic wars that preceded it and the Mexican and Civil wars that followed in its wake, the Texas revolt appeared trifling indeed. Even so, for the student of military history, the fact that the war was sandwiched between these pivotal events renders it all the more significant.

Tactics during the 1830s underwent a remarkable transition. Countries such as France, which had previously relied on linear tactics and smoothbore muskets, began to experiment with open order formations and skirmishers armed with rifles. Although far from being in the forefront of tactical innovation, the Texas and Mexican forces were not totally unaware of military precedents. As early as 1824, the Mexican army established *tirailleurs* in rifle companies. That same year a proportion of men in both regular and militia companies were slated as light troops. While the image of the American leatherstocking and his long rifle has been popularized to the point of stereotype, it is nonetheless true that many Texas militiamen were highly proficient with that lethal firearm. Because they lacked the training and discipline to stand in the line of battle and perform the intricate maneuvers such formations required, Americans also fought as light infantry. In Europe commanders were trying to promote individual initiative among their riflemen; on the American frontier independent action was almost second nature. The point is not that the soldiers who waged the war in Texas were trained professionals establishing doctrine, but rather that they unwittingly explored some of the same tactical modes that more sophisticated European commanders were at the same time investigating by design.

Topography played a part. Time after time, Texians, reared in the traditions of the North American woodlands, sought the protection of natural cover. When they did, they could be relatively certain that the precision of their rifles could keep the enemy at bay. Much of the war, however, was waged on the grassy prairies of the Rio Grande Plain, where trees and other natural cover were rare. Here, the Mexicans with their superior equestrian skills were formidable.

Geography also influenced the conduct of the war. By their presence in the fertile Brazos River bottom and the pine woods of East Texas, the Americans had rendered those regions cultural, as well as geographical, extensions of the North American woodlands. The plains south of the Colorado River were still predominantly the province of the *tejano* ranching culture. As cultural geographer D. W. Meinig observed, "It was not merely accidental that the two great Anglo-American disasters, at the Alamo and Goliad, took place beyond the margins of Anglo-American colonization, while their final triumph, at San Jacinto, took place deep within a country they had made their own."

I am a Texan. That fact, many insist, precludes any objective treatment of the Mexicans; I hope to convince them otherwise. A chauvinistic tone has admittedly marred many earlier studies published north of the Rio Grande. Whenever possible, Mexican sources were consulted, and I have attempted to understand and explain the monumental problems faced by the Mexican forces. The behavior of the individual *soldado* left a legacy of valor of which Mexicans should be proud and that North Americans should acknowledge.

Some friendly critics have suggested that the title of this study is hopelessly pretentious. To compare the few months of intermittent border warfare with the ten-year siege of Troy, they charge, serves only to reinforce the image of the bombastic Texan that I profess to deplore. I plead only slightly guilty. Homer's epic has its fill of heroes, but it is also replete with villains, treachery, ambition, avarice, savagery, and inhumanity. Sadly, the reader will find all of these features in the story of the Texas Revolution. It is, nevertheless, a tale that has had a profound effect on the thinking of modern Texans. The Alamo, Sam Houston, Goliad, David Crockett, and San Jacinto have become part of an iconography that has instinctive meaning for Texans and other Americans. All too often, however, the images accepted are those offered by popular culture, not primary documents. That a president from Texas during the Vietnam War should have drawn an analogy between the 1836 siege of the Alamo and the 1968 siege of Khe Sanh demonstrates the power of the myth and suggests a relevance that extends beyond the borders of the state. It is necessary, therefore, to understand the military events of 1835–1836 in realistic terms.

Recently many of the traditional heroes of the Texas Revolution have come under fire. Some have intoned, for example, that William B. Travis, a slaveholder and a young man imbued with an active libido, is not a proper "role model" for today's children and that public schools should not bear his name. The narrative that follows contains a myriad of both heroes and villains; I leave it to the reader to sort one from the other. Most participants were neither—merely common soldiers who campaigned under harsh conditions, performed their duties bravely, and tried to survive.

Whenever possible I have allowed the participants to speak for themselves. The words are sometimes raw, the syntax often confused, the spelling almost always unconventional. Through it all, however, shines their indomitable spirit.

Most of my friends who spend their days in classrooms, offices, faculty lounges, and the various other groves of academe would be uncomfortable in the company of men who fought the Texas Revolution. Many were, by the standards of our day, crude, intolerant, even racist. They were certainly harder than we are; the frontier demanded toughness. Yet their actions and their grit made it possible for milder, more cultivated men and women to follow in their wake.

One of these was Swante Palm, a Swedish immigrant and a Renaissance man whose library formed the cornerstone of the library at the University of Texas. Polished, urbane, and learned, Palm was in most ways the antithesis of the rugged citizen-soldiers of the Revolution. They did have one thing in common: a shared vision of Texas. The backwoodsmen would not have been able to articulate it as well as Palm, but they would have understood his passion. Writing from the frontier town of Austin in 1857, Palm foretold the future:

> The day will come when the cultures of the world will meet naturally here, when wisdom—unscornful of these surroundings—will look naturally upon the truths of life in this place; when life will be endowed with grace as well as with goods. Then books sent out of Texas, no less than books brought into Texas, will speak the common language of the heart, the mind and the human spirit.

I offer then, this, a book sent out of Texas. If, in telling the story of those who suffered the ordeal of the Revolution, I have captured a portion of their resoluteness, and if I have written in the "common language of the heart, the mind and the human spirit," I shall have earned my keep.

ACKNOWLEDGMENTS

At times during the preparation of this book, confronting overwhelming obstacles and impossible odds, I felt as if I had reason to identify with Alamo commander William Barret Travis. Unlike Travis, however, I was blessed with a small army of friends and associates who responded to my pleas for assistance.

I am fortunate to have had professors who nurtured my academic and personal growth. Even after I had left Southwest Texas State, Dr. James W. Pohl continued to serve as mentor and friend; his frequent calls and visits helped more than he will ever know. In Fort Worth, Dr. Grady McWhiney and Dr. Donald C. Worcester were editors whose keen eyes and steady judgment guided this study through the dissertation stage. I recall the day in Dr. McWhiney's office when he asked me about the subject of my dissertation. "I don't want to write a traditional dissertation," I blurted. "I want to write a book." Thinking for a moment, "Mac" stroked his magisterial white beard and replied, "Then I think that's what you ought to do." I will be forever grateful for his confidence in my ability and for his courage to be unconventional in a profession that is too often characterized by "foolish consistency."

Also in Fort Worth, a number of fellow graduate students read portions of the manuscript and contributed valuable comments. Among these good friends were Dr. Robert T. Maberry, Jr., Dr. Vista Kay McCroskey, Meg and Peter Hacker, and Jim Kettle. Special thanks go to my old study partner, Deborah Bloys, without whose love and guidance

I never would have survived graduate school. Deborah subsequently changed her last name to Hardin and now lives in Pflugerville, Texas, where she continues to save the author from the darker forces of his nature.

During the years of research required to complete this book, the folks at various archival repositories repeatedly offered assistance. The entire staff at the Eugene C. Barker Texas History Center at the University of Texas at Austin were eager to track down wayward documents, but Ralph Elder, John Slate, and Trudy Croes deserve special mention for their consistent good cheer. Mike Green, Donaly Brice, John Anderson, and the staff of the Archives Division at the Texas State Library were models of professional deportment. During his tenure at the General Land Office, Frank de la Teja, now a professor of history at Southwest Texas State University, proved to be a master of that agency's documents. In San Antonio, the people at the Daughters of the Republic of Texas Library at the Alamo always attempted to be helpful. Sharon Crutchfield, former director of that facility, and the late Berniece Strong, librarian, established a level of professionalism that is sorely missed.

For those of us in the pre-video-game generation, the transition from typewriter to computer has not always been a smooth one. Three friends demonstrated limitless patience in assisting me through the world of floppy disks and megabytes. Dr. Cecil Harper, Jr., a colleague at the Texas State Historical Association, helped me transfer the manuscript onto disk and offered valuable advice. My old friend Jim Green of San Marcos, Texas, kept me up to speed regarding changing technologies and offered the use of his own system for an extended period. My student Jim Burns, of Victoria, Texas, is a walking encyclopedia of computer knowledge and has made several "house calls" to assist me.

Alwyn Barr, at Texas Tech University, and James W. Pohl, military historian at Southwest Texas State University, served as readers and offered numerous suggestions that greatly improved the manuscript.

Thomas Ricks Lindley, a private researcher in Austin, Texas, has likely examined more documents relating to the Texas Revolution than has any person now living. Tom has been more than generous with the fruits of his research, sharing vital information that I never would have found on my own. This study has further benefited from countless discussions that Tom and I have had at the El Azteca Restaurant, which serves up (and I assert this without fear of contradiction) the best Mexican food in the world. Thanks also to the Guerra family, owners and managers of El Azteca, for allowing us to take up valuable table space to hold our frequent conclaves.

This book has benefited also from my long association with Kevin R. Young of San Antonio, Texas. An authority on the Mexican Army of 1836, he was the technical advisor for the film *Alamo: The Price of Freedom*. While on research trips or at professional meetings, I have routinely availed myself of Kevin's foldout sofa. I have camped out in his guest room so many times that he now calls it "my" room. More than once he has gone to work bleary-eyed after I had picked his brain until the wee hours and exhausted his supply of Dr. Pepper. Since I look forward to abusing Kevin's hospitality for years to come, I will offer my thanks in advance.

All those who view Gary S. Zaboly's superb maps and illustrations will easily discern the remarkable contribution he has made to this book. Less evident is how valuable I found his knowledgeable insight and words of encouragement.

Myriad friends have made helpful suggestions; others have unknowingly influenced the contents of this book by erudite comments, which I carefully noted. Among these are Dr. Anne Bailey, Dorcas Baumgartner, Steve Beck, Robert E. Bethea, Mike Boyd, Wallace O. Chariton, Bill Chermerka, Craig Covner, Mike Cox, Ana Carolina Castillo Crimm, Elizabeth Crook, Dr. Thomas Cutrer, Arthur Drooker, Jack "J. R." Edmonson, Tom Feely, Dr. Don B. Graham, Bill Groneman, Dora Guerra, Stephen Harrigan, Dr. Paul Andrew Hutton, Don Jank, Kenneth Kesselus, Douglas Kubicek, Dr. Paul Lack, Al Lowman, Dr. Tim Matovina, Dr. Archie P. McDonald, Ellen N. Murry, Dr. Michael Parrish, Dr. Sam D. Ratcliffe, Larry Spacik, Charles Spurlin, Frank Thompson, Dr. Ron Tyler, Eric von Schmidt, Dr. David J. Weber, Dr. Harold Weiss, and David Zucker.

Finally, my greatest appreciation is reserved for Deborah, Walker, and Savannah, who have suffered many hours of neglect while Dad was "on campaign."   —STEPHEN L. HARDIN

Illustrator's Acknowledgments

Much of the documentation regarding the Alamo's architecture and defenses is contradictory; compromise often provides the only solution to a particular problem. Although my version of the Alamo compound presented in this book occasionally resorts to informed conjectures, it also incorporates several major contributions to our knowledge of the fort's physical makeup. These new findings are

- the existence of an abatis of fallen trees in front of the palisade;
- the covering of the *entire* outer face of the north wall with a timber-and-earth outwork;
- the presence of a row of beehive ovens in the cattle pen;
- the situation of two ponds lying close to the eastern walls of the fort; and
- the location of an orchard, possibly poplar trees, just beyond the ponds. (It has yet to be determined how critical a role, if any, this terrain feature played during the siege and assault.)

Although we spent many hours of scrutiny, translation, cross-referencing, and frustration before arriving at these findings, the author and I benefited greatly from the generosity and interest of a number of scholars. Answering the call for help were Craig Covner, Bill Groneman, Thomas Ricks Lindley, and Kevin R. Young.

Craig Covner proved particularly capable at determining the fort's appearance on that cold March morning in 1836. No one else now living can so readily discuss every nook and corner, every window, every room and roof, and every nuance of adobe brick or stone within the Alamo.

The most revealing of all the published sources consulted were the "Vista y plano del Fuerte del Alamo," drawn and described by José Juan Sánchez-Navarro, reproduced in *La Guerra de Tejas; Memorias de un Soldado,* ed. Carlos Sánchez-Navarro (Mexico City 1938), and the Navarro "battle map," a somewhat cruder version of the above "plano," along with the several translations of its key, in "A Mexican View of the Texas War: Memories of a Veteran of the Two Battles of the Alamo," *The Library Chronicle of the University of Texas* 4, no. 2 (Summer 1951): 59; *A Mexican Officer's Report of the Fall of the Alamo* (Austin: University of Texas, Texana Program, 1965); and *At the Alamo: The Memories of Capt. Navarro,* trans. C. D. Huneycutt (New London, Conn.: Gold Star, 1988).

The color reproduction of the map of the Alamo and environs drawn by Mexican Engineer Colonel Ygnacio de LaBastida, which appeared on pp. 82–83 of David Nevin, *The Texans* (New York: Time-Life, 1975), provided a serviceable counterpoint to the two Navarro plans.

The plat and index attributed to Alamo engineer Green B. Jameson, drawn and described on January 18, 1836, contains information found nowhere else, even if the plat itself has been deemed spurious. The version referred to is reproduced on p. 31 of *The Alamo Long Barrack Museum*, compiled by the Daughters of the Republic of Texas (Dallas: Author, 1986).

Despite some errors and guesswork, Reuben M. Potter's outline of the fort and his key to it, as published on pp. 410–412 of Frank W. Johnson, *A History of Texas and Texans*, vol. 1 (Chicago and New York: American Historical Society, 1914), remains a primary reference on the subject.

Alamo Images: Changing Perceptions of a Texas Experience, by Susan Prendergast Schoelwer with Tom W. Gläser (Dallas: De Golyer Library and Southern Methodist University Press, 1985), offered a host of visual clues. Rexford Newcomb's *Spanish Colonial Architecture in the United States* ([1937]; reprint, New York: Dover, 1990) was especially useful. Important points were culled from articles appearing in both the *Alamo Lore and Myth Organization* newsletter and *The Alamo Journal.*

—GARY S. ZABOLY

Texian Iliad

CHAPTER I

"We Are All Captains and Have Our Views"

Retreat from Gonzales
October 2, 1835

Following the skirmish at Gonzales, this seasoned trooper glances over his shoulder to see whether the deadly Texian riflemen are in pursuit. He is happy to see they are not but realizes that service in Texas has suddenly become far more dangerous. Yet stationed in San Antonio de Béxar, the men of the Flying Company of Alamo de Parras are accustomed to the rigors of frontier garrison life. The fledgling Republic of Mexico, beset by civil strife and economic uncertainty, was hard pressed to pay, feed, uniform, and equip its soldiers adequately even in the interior. Those serving on the far-flung frontera *could expect even less, normally the dregs and hand-me-downs from an inefficient and corrupt supply system. Writing from Nacogdoches in 1828, General Manuel Mier y Terán complained: "The garrison of this fort has received nothing for seven months, and is therefore reduced to the most deplorable state." For Mexican soldiers in Texas, this "deplorable state" became a way of life, and conditions had not greatly improved by 1835.*

This cynical trooper reflects prolonged neglect. His uniform is patched and threadbare; his mount is far from a thoroughbred; and his deportment is that of one who has been dispatched to the edge of nowhere and forgotten. He has no motive to fight gringo *rebels and resents being ordered to risk his life for a cause he does not fully understand.*

His hat is of the type illustrated by the European lithographer Claudio Linati in 1828; note the wide band that obscures the crown except for about an inch at the top. The dark blue coatee had red collars and cuffs. While on campaign, troopers favored the loose-fitting blue or gray overalls reinforced with leather. A red stripe ran the full length of the outside seam of the pant leg. Boots and spurs are of a civilian pattern and are like those worn by local vaqueros.

Indeed, much of his kit reveals heavy borrowing from the Texas ranching culture. The saddle and bridle are probably the handiwork of local craftsmen. On the frontera, *one made do with whatever was available—regulation or not.*

For purposes of illustration, this trooper is well armed, but not all those who served in his unit would have been issued such a wide array of weaponry. The lance is drawn after those illustrated by Linati, and a specimen is currently on display in the Long Barracks Museum at the Alamo. The tercerola *(carbine) is a holdover from the Spanish period. Manufactured in 1815, it is actually no older than the Brown Bess muskets used by most Mexican infantrymen. Like Spanish* Cuera *(leather jacket) Dragoons from which the flying companies evolved, this trooper prefers the* espada ancha *to the longer regulation sword. The sword depicted here is drawn after one that Texas Ranger Robert Hall captured in Mexico in 1847, but a blade of this type would have been common in Texas a decade earlier. This distinctive weapon is currently housed at the Los Nogales Museum in Seguin, Texas.*

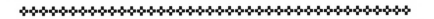

"We Are All Captains and Have Our Views"

THE AMERICAN COLONISTS OF MEXICAN TEXAS were no strangers to war: they were born to it. Most descended from America's first revolutionaries, and many had fought with Andrew Jackson in 1815 at New Orleans, where they defeated British regulars fresh from victories against Napoleon's best. But other enemies lingered closer to home. Indians harassed the frontier. And while suffering numerous losses to raiding parties, the settlers never doubted their eventual triumph.[1]

Mexico had need of such men in Texas, where the fierce and mobile Comanches, Kiowas, and Apaches discouraged settlement and made life itself a gamble. Sweeping down from their camps west of the Balcones Escarpment, Indians struck in the night, stealing horses, burning ranches, killing men, and carrying off terrified women and children. Spanish, and then Mexican, officials knew that if the region were to serve as an effective barrier against foreign intrusions, it must be populated by loyal settlers who knew how to fight. Yet despite generous offers of land, few Mexican families could be lured to Texas.[2]

Moses Austin, a former Spanish subject in upper Louisiana, proposed what appeared to be a workable solution, colonizing the area with former U.S. citizens who would become Spanish citizens and Roman Catholics. In 1821, after slight hesitation, government officials approved a grant permitting him to distribute twenty thousand acres among three hundred families. Austin's death coincided with the end of Spanish rule, but Stephen Fuller Austin set out to complete his father's work. The new Mexican rulers understood the wisdom of colonizing Texas and therefore acknowledged him as his father's heir. Soon other Anglo-Celtic empresarios established additional colonies along the fertile banks of the

Brazos River, in the piney woods of East Texas, and on the grassy plains above the Nueces River.³

At first the union was a happy one. The Mexican settlers, or *tejanos*, were happy to gain allies in their war against marauding Indians as well as opportunities for trade with the United States that had been denied them earlier. American immigrants were grateful for free land, no taxes, a liberal constitution modeled after their own, and a dispensation to retain their slaves even though Mexico had earlier abolished slavery. In 1825 empresario Green C. DeWitt reflected the spirit of cooperation by naming the capital of his colony after Rafael Gonzales, governor of Coahuila y Tejas. Mexicans reciprocated in 1831, when they provided a six-pound cannon to defend settlers against roving tribes.⁴

But by then the mood was already changing, for many U.S. citizens came to Texas uninvited. Mexican officials began to perceive these illegal immigrants to be a greater threat than the Indians. Pushed by the Panic of 1819 and pulled by the lure of free land, U.S. citizens had flocked to Texas with or without permission. Unlike those who received land grants, they felt little loyalty to Mexico. In April 1830, the Mexican congress passed a law forbidding further immigration from the United States; desirable settlers were excluded, but the flood of illegal squatters continued, thereby aggravating the situation. Colonists were alarmed when President-General Antonio López de Santa Anna overthrew the constitutional government and jettisoned the Federal Constitution of 1824. He ordered all illegal settlers expelled, and all Texians (as they now preferred to call themselves) disarmed. Austin rode to Mexico City to seek separate statehood for Texas. Discouraged at the lack of progress, he wrote an intemperate letter to the *cabildo* of San Antonio de Béxar urging it to act without government permission. Government officials intercepted the missive, and angered by what appeared to be sedition, President Valentín Gómez Farías had Austin arrested. Upon his release two years later, Austin returned to Texas convinced that resistance to centralist tyranny was the colonists' only recourse. By that time, Santa Anna had annulled all constitutional restraints and assumed dictatorial powers. In May 1835, when Mexican federalists in Zacatecas rose in revolt, the self-appointed "Napoleon of the West" crushed them with a ruthlessness that was to become his trademark. Upon defeating the rebels, Santa Anna rewarded his centralist soldiers by allowing them two days of rape and pillage in Zacatecas; more than two thousand defenseless noncombatants were killed in that orgy of destruction. Texians received reports of the rape of Zacatecas with dismay and foreboding.[5]

Nevertheless, prior to September 1835, the citizens of DeWitt's Colony had been staunch supporters of the Mexican government. On the tenth day of that month, however, a Mexican soldier entered Adam Zumwalt's storeroom and with little or no justification bludgeoned Jesse McCoy with the butt of his Brown Bess musket. This act of military brutality appeared to have altered the sentiments of the DeWitt colonists. Tales of centralist maliciousness, formerly dismissed as war party propaganda, seemed to have been authenticated. Suspicions were further confirmed when Colonel Domingo Ugartechea, military commander at San Antonio de Béxar, recalled the Gonzales cannon. Ugartechea could not have foreseen the consequences of that fatal command.[6]

The cannon became a point of honor and an unlikely rallying symbol. Gonzales citizens had no intention of handing over the weapon at a time of growing tension between Texians and the Mexican government, especially since McCoy's beating, and they escorted out of town the squad sent to pick it up.[7]

Angered by the Texian action, Colonel Ugartechea sent Lieutenant Francisco Castañeda and a hundred dragoons to redeem the cannon. Once Ugartechea had ordered its return, it became a matter of principle; his demands must be enforced. Ugartechea nevertheless ordered Castañeda to demand the cannon but if possible to avoid confrontation. Late in September 1835, presidial troopers left Béxar, as most settlers now called San Antonio, on what seemed a routine mission, making their way toward the tiny settlement on the banks of the Guadalupe.[8]

When Castañeda's troops arrived on September 29, only eighteen Texians stood ready to oppose them. The settlers had removed the ferry and all the boats to the east bank of the rain-swollen stream. Gonzales pickets and the swift current prevented the dragoons from fording. Shouting across the torrent, Castañeda informed the armed citizens that he carried a dispatch for the *alcalde*. The defenders replied that they would allow one courier to swim across.[9]

For once the rigid Mexican bureaucracy aided the settlers. Upon reading the message, Captain Albert Martin, leader of the Gonzales eighteen, replied that Alcalde Andrew Ponton was out of town; until he returned Castañeda must wait on his side of the river. Martin did not say so, but the Texians were determined not to surrender the cannon. In fact, as soon as he learned of the Mexican demand, Martin sent three men to bury the gun. The Texians needed time to assemble more men, and they gained it by stalling. Blocked by the river, the colonists, and the Mexican penchant for well-ordered procedure, Castañeda pitched camp about three hundred yards from the contested crossing, atop DeWitt's Mound, the highest ground in the area.[10]

Back in Béxar, a Gonzales doctor with the unlikely name of Launcelot Smither attempted to intercede as a self-appointed peacemaker. While in San Antonio on private business, he had heard of his neighbors' refusal to hand over the cannon and "immediately remonstrated" to Ugartechea. The colonel listened to his pleas, then told Smither that, if he would ride to Gonzales and persuade the settlers to comply, he would order his soldiers not to take hostile action. Accompanied by a Mexican sergeant and two troopers, Smither rode out toward Castañeda's camp on the Guadalupe.[11]

While Dr. Smither and his escort were riding to prevent bloodshed, messengers from Gonzales galloped to surrounding settlements calling volunteers to battle. A Fayette militia company under Colonel John Henry Moore responded. Other detachments came from Columbus, but they had been unable to choose a captain and were commanded in committee fashion by Edward Burleson, Robert M. Coleman, and Joseph Washington Elliot Wallace. Writing to San Felipe resident James B. Miller, Coleman reported, "We have as yet no head [but] there will be one chose to day." Even so, Coleman, who would later be an insubordinate thorn in the side of General Sam Houston, did not appear overly concerned. "We are all captains and have our views," he affirmed. Among egalitarian volunteers, an officer was merely first among equals, a man who displayed "natural" leadership.[12]

In keeping with U.S. militia tradition, the assembled volunteers elected their officers. Captain Martin held titular command of the Gonzales contingent, but the reinforcements, unwilling to serve an officer they had not chosen, "required a reorganization." When the results of the election were tallied, Moore emerged as colonel, Wallace as lieutenant colonel, and Burleson as major.[13]

In the meantime, Dr. Smither and his escort had traveled from Béxar to the Mexican camp in the "shortest time that distance could be rode." Once there he found a frustrated Castañeda; what had begun as a routine mission had developed into the makings of a conflict, and one for which the junior officer did not wish to assume responsibility. Three mounted Texians were currently scouting his position, and he asked Smither to take these men a message: he had no wish to fight settlers; he wanted only to talk with their commander, but his requests for communications had been repeatedly denied.[14]

As Smither approached the Texian outriders, he recognized one of them as Captain Matthew ("Old Paint") Caldwell, a noted ranger captain and Indian fighter. The doctor explained Castañeda's position, giving Caldwell "all the particulars." Caldwell told Smither to return to the Mexican camp and remain there until dawn. He further directed Smither to assure Castañeda that he would not be molested that night and that, if that officer would come to Gonzales with Smither the next morning, "he should have any communication he wished" and would be "treated with all the respect of a gentleman." Smither returned to Castañeda with Caldwell's expressions of goodwill.[15]

Despite those assurances, the settlers prepared for action. Moore had called a council of war, although there had been no declaration of hostilities, and Castañeda seemed content to remain on his side of the river. True, he had demanded the cannon, but thus far he had not attempted to take it by force. Moore and his council ultimately reached a decision, not for political or military reasons, but according to the dictates of homespun practicality. They determined that it would not do "to bear their own expenses and to ride the distance they had merely to meet the enemy and return home without a fight." Good men had been summoned to meet the foe, and if the Mexicans would not attack, the Texians would carry the fight to them. It remains uncertain whether they were aware of Caldwell's promise to Castañeda when they made the decision to attack, but at that juncture any promise to a *centralista* would have meant little.[16]

Once the Texian officers determined their course of action, the men prepared for battle. A squad dug up the cannon and mounted it atop a pair of cart wheels. Lacking cannon balls, the townsmen gathered metal scraps to substitute for canister. The volunteers also readied their long rifles, shotguns, and even fowling pieces.[17]

Nor were spiritual considerations overlooked. The Reverend W. P. Smith, a Methodist preacher, delivered a sermon replete with references to the American Revolution. He reminded the congregation that "the same blood that animated the hearts of our ancestors in '76 still flows in our veins." Smith assured the men that, as one of Jackson's New Orleans veterans, he had examined the battle plan and judged it sound.

On the frontier, any combat experience apparently made a man an authority on tactics, but veterans of New Orleans were held in special esteem. Southerners celebrated January 8, the anniversary of Jackson's victory, with every bit as much fervor as July 4. Many Texians had friends or relatives who had fought behind the cotton bales, and their papers are replete with references to that contest, which seemed to validate one of the prevailing tenets of Jacksonian Democracy. After all, was not it there that the "unerring aim" of volunteer riflemen had smashed the serried ranks of British regulars?

Actually, no. Most of the militiamen were not armed with rifles. Still, even if they had been, the fog of gunpowder smoke shrouding the field after repeated volleys would have prevented individual-aimed fire. The British always insisted that U.S. artillery accounted for the majority of their casualties on that terrible day. Moreover, modern students of the battle maintain that Major General Sir Edward Pakenham bungled his assault by advancing his infantry only to halt them within range of Jackson's guns. Nevertheless, such inconvenient realities failed to jibe with treasured canards regarding the superiority of the "common man," so Americans simply ignored them. Thus, with rifles loaded, jugs in hand, and God on their side, the Texian militia sallied forth to meet the Mexicans.[18]

Actually, both forces were on the move. A Coushatta Indian entered the Mexican camp and informed Castañeda that the Texians now numbered at least 140 men and more were expected. Knowing he could not force the guarded crossing, Castañeda abandoned DeWitt's Mound and marched his troops in search of another place not so well defended, where he could "cross without any embarrassment." Nightfall of October 1 found the troopers camped about seven miles farther upriver. The Texians began to cross at the ferry about seven o'clock that evening. Only 50 of Moore's 180 men were mounted. Once across the river, the group made its way toward the Mexican camp. Around midnight a thick fog slowed the Texians, but they stumbled forward in the darkness. At three o'clock, as they stealthily approached the camp, the yapping of a dog, followed by the report of a Mexican carbine, shattered the silence, costing the rebels the element of surprise. When the vanguards exchanged fire, a Texian horse reared and threw its rider. The cursing horseman arose from the hard ground, nursing his bloody nose. Whether or not he was proud of the fact, he was the first casualty of the Texas Revolution.[19]

Both commanders were unsure of how to proceed. Moore ordered his men to take cover in a stand of trees along the riverbank until the rising sun cleared away the fog. Since the morning was "dark and cloudy," Castañeda could not determine the number of militiamen "lying in ambush down next to the river." The Mexican commander, incensed that the Texians had broken their word, moved his troops to a slight rise about three hundred yards to his rear. While awaiting the dawn, Texians whiled away the time feasting on watermelons foraged from a nearby patch.[20]

The light of a new day, October 2, found both sides in a defensive position. The Texians discovered that they stood on the farm of Ezekiel Williams. A rail fence Williams had erected to keep livestock out of his corn patch blocked their cannon's field of fire; Moore ordered it knocked down. The militiamen checked their powder as the mist began to clear. Around six o'clock, they ventured out of their cover and began sniping at the Mexicans on the hill. Castañeda responded by ordering Lieutenant Gregorio Perez to attack with forty mounted troopers; the remainder of the command stood in reserve. In the face of the Mexican cavalry charge, the Texians quickly fell back to the cover of the wooded riverbank and fired a volley, wounding a Mexican private. Unable to penetrate the treeline, the horsemen returned to high ground "to wait for the fog to dissipate so that we could work."[21]

As the Texians listened and waited, they heard the steady staccato of galloping hooves accompanied by an American shouting, "Don't shoot, don't shoot. I have a message." Gonzales men recognized the voice of Dr. Launcelot Smither. Earlier, when the sentries were attacked, Castañeda had summoned Smither and demanded an explanation. The doctor could only reply that he had merely repeated what Caldwell had told him. Castañeda angrily placed Smither under guard and confiscated his mules, money, and belongings. But when the fog broke, Castañeda needed an English-speaking envoy more than a prisoner and dispatched Smither with a message to the rebel leader.[22]

The hapless doctor conveyed Castañeda's request for a parley, but his problems were far from finished. Smither seemed too friendly toward the Mexicans to suit Colonel Moore, so he ordered him to the rear under arrest. Having been taken prisoner by both sides that morning while serving the cause of peace, the doctor was understandably testy. Since the Mexicans still retained his mules, money, and clothes, he asked if he might at least go forward with a flag of truce to request their return.

Smither later complained that "Moore said I could go ten paces in front and see but I could not go up." Under the watchful eyes of the indignant doctor, the two commanders met on neutral ground midway between their forces. Castañeda asked why he had been attacked. Moore replied that the Mexican troops were acting on behalf of the usurper Santa Anna and were defying constitutional authority. The Mexican lieutenant answered that his orders were only to request the cannon, not seize it; that he had no wish to fight American colonists; and finally, that he was also a republican. Moore fired back that, if Castañeda were a true federalist, he wore the wrong uniform and fought on the wrong side; if he were sincere, he and his troopers should join the Texians in their fight for the Constitution of 1824. Taken aback by this shocking invitation to mutiny, Castañeda responded that as a soldier he was obliged to obey orders. With nothing more to say, the antagonists returned to their respective commands.[23]

Upon Moore's return, Lieutenant Colonel Wallace ordered artilleryman J. C. Neill to fire the gun toward the Mexicans clustered on the hill, and the first cannon shot of the revolution echoed along the Guadalupe. The Texians had defiantly raised a white banner. Painted in black was an image of the disputed cannon barrel; underneath appeared the challenge: "COME AND TAKE IT." The crack of Kentucky rifles followed the boom of the cannon. Wild shouts contributed to the cacophony as Moore led his men in a spirited charge. But the Texians did not close with the enemy. Mindful of his orders, Castañeda prudently quit the field and withdrew toward Béxar. In his report to Ugartechea, the lieutenant stated that "since the orders from your Lordship were for me to withdraw without compromising the honor of Mexican arms, I did so." Outnumbered and outgunned as he was, it would have been difficult for Castañeda to have remained on the field without "compromising the honor of Mexican arms." By the time rebel cannoneers were able to load for a second shot, the Mexicans had departed.[24]

The "Lexington of Texas" was not a battle; it was not even much of a skirmish. Only later did historians label it the "Battle" of Gonzales. Unpretentious frontiersmen who fought there mostly remembered it as "the fight at Williams's place." The encounter resembled a shoving match more than a pitched battle.[25]

Still, some elements of the melee merit consideration. The Anglo settlers fought as light infantry; the Mexicans as dismounted dragoons and on horseback. In terms of weaponry, Texian accounts refer to rifles, presumably of the Kentucky type, but some had shotguns and fowling pieces. The Mexican cavalrymen were armed with surplus Pagent carbines, which, while good firearms, lacked the range and accuracy of the long rifles. Unable to match the range of the Texian weapons with his inaccurate carbines, Castañeda had wisely ordered a withdrawal. Moore, unwilling to have his horsemen pursue a detachment twice their number, could only watch as the enemy rode away. That the Texians took "position . . . in the vicinity of a skirt of timber" is also significant. Schooled in the tactics of the woodlands, North American frontiersmen were accustomed to fighting behind natural cover. Despite Preacher Smith's bland assurances, the tactics employed were painfully amateurish. At no time did Moore attempt to sever Castañeda's lines of communication, an assignment for which his horsemen would have been well suited. After stumbling onto the Mexican sentries, Moore never tried to turn the flanks. Indeed, the screaming, headlong assault that comprised the fight resembled nothing more than a wild Highland charge.[26]

Militarily, the clash outside Gonzales accomplished little, yet its political significance was immeasurable. Accounts differ, but apparently the Mexicans suffered few casualties, with no more than one or two killed. The fight did not last long enough for there to have been more. Total Texian casualties: one bloody nose. The important fact remained, however, that shots had been fired; blood had been shed; a fatal step had been taken. There could be no turning back. Spreading throughout Texas, the news brought recruits like the big Pennsylvania Dutchman Conrad Rohrer and North Carolina blacksmith Noah Smithwick. Those Texians who sped toward the Guadalupe in the days after October 2 were all in agreement that they were ready to fight, even though they had not agreed on their cause. In his dotage, Smithwick reportedly recalled: "Some were for independence, some were for the Constitution of 1824; and some were for anything, just so long it was a row."[27]

While the militiamen in Gonzales gloried in their perceived victory, another expedition was being organized at the mouth of the Colorado River in the coastal town of Matagorda. The slowness of communications and the intransigence of willful frontiersmen prevented any central strategic planning. Still, some action, coordinated or not, seemed in order, so the planters around Matagorda mustered a militia company to oppose the Mexicans.[28]

Texian volunteers, convinced that they were responding to a threat against their liberty, had seen their worst fears realized in mid-September

1835, when Mexican General Martín Perfecto de Cós landed a punitive force of five hundred troops at Copano Bay. Cós, who was Santa Anna's brother-in-law, had been ordered to expel troublemakers and to disarm all colonists. This threat of being stripped of their weapons alienated not only peaceful old colonists but also a number of *tejanos*, many of whom were staunch federalists. In a letter to Henry Rueg, the political chief of Nacogdoches who had written an inflammatory proclamation, Cós made his position clear: "The plans of the revolutionists of Texas are well known to this commandancy; and it is quite useless and vain to cover them with a hypocritical adherence to the federal constitution. The constitution by which all Mexicans may be governed is the constitution which the colonists of Texas must *obey*, no matter on what *principles* it may be formed." The obdurate Cós misjudged the degree to which Texians would insist that those principals be federalist.[29]

Reflecting the democratic spirit that Cós had so casually dismissed, on October 6, 1835, Matagorda volunteers met at the home of Captain Sylvanus Hatch to elect leaders. The twenty-man company had soon named provisional officers: Mississippian George Morse Collinsworth as captain; Dr. William Carleton as first lieutenant; and D. C. Collinsworth as second lieutenant. Volunteers included Samuel McCulloch, a freed slave formerly owned by Captain Collinsworth. At the meeting, the men decided to attack the Mexican garrison at the *presidio* of La Bahía outside Goliad, and they set out that same night. On the march, the men informed the officers that while the Collinsworths were still acceptable, they had decided to replace Dr. Carleton with James W. Moore. Officers were "provisional" indeed.[30]

At first the expedition against La Bahía took on the nature of a kidnapping plot rather than a military operation. It was rumored that Cós had marched to Goliad with a military chest containing at least $50,000. Collinsworth and his band hoped to seize the money or else capture General Cós and hold him for ransom.[31]

On the way, other contingents and individuals joined Collinsworth's original twenty. Men who had learned of the fighting—or the prospect of securing Mexican silver—were eager to share in the adventure. Encouraged by the additional recruits, Collinsworth sent word to surrounding settlements, inviting anyone who wanted to join him to assemble on the Guadalupe River outside Victoria. Settlers from throughout the coastal prairies responded to the call. On October 7, at

the Victoria rendezvous, the party rested while local men and others enlisted in the rebel ranks. *Tejanos* José Antonio Padilla, Sylvestre de León,
Plácido Benavides, and Mariano Carbajal joined the expedition at the
head of about thirty *vaqueros*. Because Collinsworth failed to keep accurate muster roles, the exact number of men under his command is unknown, but he may have had as many as 125 by the time the expedition
reached La Bahía.[32]

While the company rested in Victoria, news arrived that the officers
greeted with mixed feelings. General Cós had already left for Béxar with
his war chest; the kidnapping scheme would have to be abandoned. But
while Texian financial hopes lay in ruins, the military situation looked
promising, for Cós had not reinforced the garrison at the *presidio* of
La Bahía.[33]

The news that Cós had departed made it necessary to alter the purpose of the expedition. The men drafted a document headed, "Compact
of Volunteers under Collinsworth, dated Victoria, October 9, 1835."
The forty-nine signatories expressed their loyalty to the federal government and attempted to quiet the fears of local *tejanos*. "The volunteers . . . declare in a clear and unequivocal manner, their united and
unalterable resolution to give ample and complete protection to the
citizens of this town, and to those also of every other which may enter—
requiring only, that, the citizens of said towns stand firm to the Republican institutions of the Constitution of 1824." The document ended
with words familiar to U.S. citizens in the group: "For the redemption
of this resolution, we pledge our lives, our property, and our sacred
honor."[34]

Having agreed that their purpose was to defend the constitution, the
members of the expedition resumed their march on October 9 in two
columns. A small vanguard pushed ahead well in advance of the main
body under Collinsworth. Eight miles outside Goliad, the main column
halted to rest and reconnoiter. Before attacking, Collinsworth needed to
know the strength of the Mexican garrison at La Bahía, and several Hispanic citizens of Goliad, or *labadeños*, volunteered the necessary information. These local *tejanos* not only kept the impending attack secret
but served as guides.[35]

From the *labadeños*, Texian commanders learned of the fort's vulner-
ability. Cós had not reinforced the garrison commanded by Lieutenant
Colonel Francisco Sandoval. It consisted of Captain Manuel Sabriego,

Ensign Antonio de la Garza, Cadet Juan de la Garza, and about fifty enlisted men—not enough to defend even the perimeter of the *presidio*. Cós, of course, had anticipated no attack.[36]

As the Texians made their way toward the fort, a fortunate accident brought them a valuable recruit. In the darkness, the main body missed the road and became entangled in a mesquite thicket. While attempting to find their way out, one of the men sighted a person crouching under one of the trees. When hailed, the figure answered, "My name is Milam." He was Benjamin Rush Milam, a native of Kentucky and one of the first Americans to trade and settle in Spanish Texas. In 1819 he joined an ill-fated filibustering expedition under General José Felix Trespalacios and Dr. James Long. In 1822 he was captured and imprisoned by Mexican officials. When, however, Mexico adopted a federal constitution, Milam joined the Mexican army, became a Mexican citizen, and sought an empresario grant in Texas. Returning to Texas, he assisted Arthur G. Wavell in settling American colonists along the Red River. In 1835 Milam traveled to Monclova, requesting a land commissioner who could grant legal titles to the settlers in the Red River area, but on his return trip he was arrested. He escaped after a stint in a Monterrey jail and had just ridden over four hundred miles when Collinsworth's contingent found him. Delighted to be reunited with fellow Texians, he joined the ranks as a private.[37]

After the detour through the brush, the main body finally reached the lower ford of the San Antonio River about a mile south of Goliad and rejoined the vanguard. Collinsworth sent a deputation to the civil authorities demanding surrender of the town. At approximately eleven o'clock on the night of October 9, the envoys returned with the *alcalde's* answer: they would not surrender without a fight. Either not all *labadeños* were federalists, or the Goliad officials thought it too early to take sides in an uncertain conflict. Collinsworth was not upset, for if the town's city fathers were not responsive, neither were they openly hostile. The attitude of the *tejanos* was understandable; they could not determine which side was likely to win and declined to expose themselves to retaliation by siding with the federalists.[38]

In the early morning darkness of October 10, the Texians assaulted the *presidio* of La Bahía. With axes provided by local *tejanos*, they broke through the door of Sandoval's quarters, then accepted his surrender. Hearing the commotion, the Mexican soldiers fired from their barracks, and Samuel McCulloch, the freedman, took a bullet in the shoulder. In the gloom, the flashes of the garrison's muskets served as targets for the rebel riflemen. During a lull in the shooting, a Texian spokesman called on the enemy to surrender. The Mexicans asked for terms. The insurgent interpreter angrily replied that the colonists would "massacre everyone of you, unless you come out immediately and surrender. Come out—come out quick!" A Hispanic voice responded: "Oh, do for God's sake keep them back—we will come out and surrender immediately." In less than thirty minutes, the *presidio* of La Bahía had been won.[39]

The capture of the fort gave the insurgent federalists a crucial strategic advantage and a windfall of much needed provisions. With Goliad under rebel control, Cós was cut off from communication with Copano Bay, the nearest port through which he could obtain supplies and reinforcements. Unable to reach Cós by sea, the centralists could send him supplies only by the long and difficult overland route across the deserts of northern Mexico. In the fort, Collinsworth found a large number of muskets, but most had been discarded as unfit for service. In a "Report of Arms Captured at Goliad," settler Ira Ingram listed: "200 stands of Muskets and Carbins—some of which Might be made Serviceable by small repairs but the greater part are broken and entirely useless." He also mentioned "44 Lance Heads and From 100 to 200 Bayonett [that] will be very useful in case of a charge."[40]

Collinsworth treated the Mexican prisoners courteously. Ensign de la Garza, who had suffered a painful wound, was given the freedom of the town. The other captive officers were sent to Gonzales for disposal by *empresario* Stephen F. Austin, who received them cordially. Captain Sabriego, who was married to a *labadeña*, convinced Austin that he was a dedicated federalist and was released to rejoin his wife and family at Goliad. Austin sent the other two Mexican officers to San Felipe with the admonition that he wanted "them treated as Gentlemen and that their situation should be made as agreeable and comfortable as possible.[41]

Back at Gonzales, confidence was high as the call "On to Béxar" sounded throughout the Mexican camp. A majority of the men were not devotees of poetry, yet all could appreciate the sentiment of N. T. Byars's verse:

> Boys, rub your steels and pick your flints,
> Me thinks I hear some friendly hints
> That we from Texas shall be driven—
> Our lands to Spanish soldiers given.[42]

17

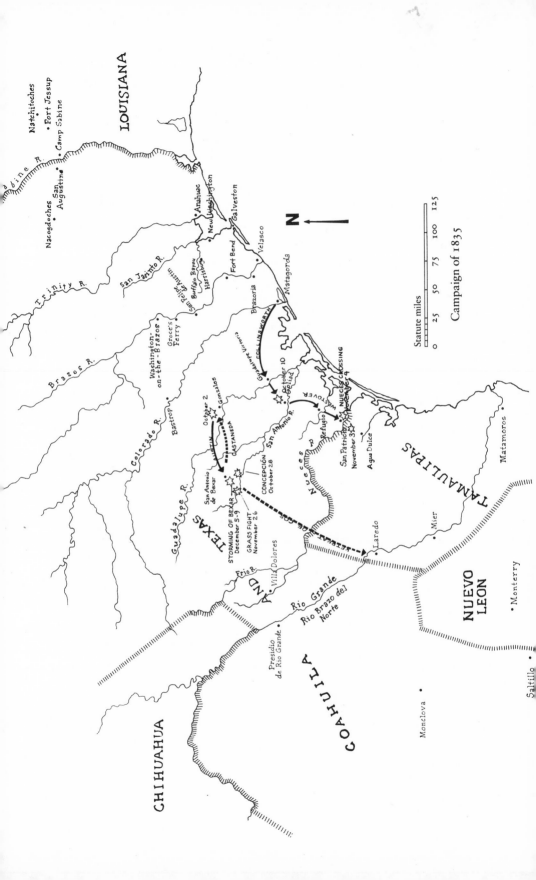

N

Statute miles

0 25 50 75 100 125

Campaign of 1835

LOUISIANA

Natchitoches
Fort Jessup
Camp Sabine
Sabine R.
Nacogdoches
San Augustine
Anahuac
New Washington
Galveston

Trinity R.
San Jacinto R.
Buffalo Bayou
Harrisburg
Fort Bend
Velasco
Matagorda

Brazos R.
San Felipe de Austin
Groce's Ferry
Washington-on-the-Brazos
Brazoria

Colorado R.
Bastrop
COL. LINSWORTH
Guadalupe Victoria
October 10
Goliad
Guadalupe R.
October 2
Gonzales
CASTANEDA
San Antonio R.
WESTOVER
NUECES CROSSING
November 4
Refugio
TEXAS
San Antonio de Bexar
CONCEPCIÓN
October 28
San Patricio
November 3
Agua Dulce
STORMING OF BEXAR
December 5-9
GRASS FIGHT
November 26
Nueces R.
Frio R.
Villa Dolores

Laredo
Mier

Rio Grande
Rio Brazo del Norte
Presidio de Rio Grande

COAHUILA

ANDA

CHIHUAHUA

Monclova

NUEVO LEON

Monterry

Matamoros

TAMAULIPAS

Saltillo

The American settlers were eager to continue the conflict. The *New York Star* described the volunteers who flocked to fill rebel ranks as "mostly muscular, powerful men, and great marksmen; and whether at a distance with a rifle, or in close combat, they will be terrible." Reflecting this attitude of supreme self-assurance, Gonzales veteran David B. Macomb crowed, "The Anglo-American spirit appears in everything we do; quick, intelligent, and comprehensive; and while such men are fighting for their rights, they may possibly be overpowered by numbers, but if whipped, they won't stay whipped." Although at the time it appeared idle bravado, subsequent events would prove his words prophetic.[43]

CHAPTER 2

"Not Withstanding Peculiar Circumstances"

GARY ZABOLY
© 1993

2. TEXIAN LEATHER STOCKING

Battle of Concepción
October 28, 1835

In her book Texas *(1836), Mary Austin Holley conceded: "The character of Leather Stocking is not uncommon in Texas. Many persons employ an individual in the business of hunting . . . and thus are constantly supplied with provisions of every description. . . . The dress of these hunters is generally deer-skin. Hence the appropriate name,* Leather Stocking.*"*
Movies and novels have advanced the image of the buckskin-clad rustic with long rifle and coonskin cap to such a degree that he has become a stock popular culture caricature. While these "Leather Stockings" attracted much comment from their more conventionally attired comrades, they remained a distinct minority. That said, however, it is also true that "buckskinners," as illustrated here, saw action in every battle of the Texas Revolution. Following the fighting at Concepción, this trans-Appalachian frontiersman inspects a battlefield trophy — a Mexican officer's ornate dress sword.
His hunting coat is made of buckskin; his leather leggings are gathered under his knees by Indian garters. The accuracy of his Kentucky long rifle has accounted for the many casualties among the enemy officers. This young Leather Stocking straps his hunting bag and powderhorn over his left shoulder; a sheathed patch knife is attached to the strap. A larger hunting knife, with antler grip, hangs from his belt. A bone powder measure swings to the right of a small priming horn, with a leather bullet pouch on the left. Between his brass belt buckle and powder horn, a vent pick and brush to remove clogged powder residue can be seen. A wooden loading block, still holding three patched and greased rifle balls, is also attached to the strap of the hunting bag. A loading block allowed a rifleman to reload quickly, without having to fumble for individual bullets. Not content with the more banal coonskin cap, this wild soul sports pantherskin headgear. A checkered linsey-woolsey shirt is worn beneath the hunting coat, and leather moccasins constitute his footwear.
A Mexican cartridge box lies discarded at his feet. Texians realized that the Mexican cartridges would not fit the smaller bores of their hunt-

ing rifles but had hoped that they could use the powder contained within. Yet when the rebels inspected the captured powder, they "found it little better than pounded charcoal" and "rejected it as altogether useless." Experienced marksmen preferred gunpowder manufactured by the Wilmington, Delaware, firm of E. I. du Pont de Nemours & Company. "Compared with the double Dupont," one insurgent veteran of Concepción reported, "it was evident that we had vastly the advantage over our enemy in this particular. We therefore emptied all the cartridges, and saved only the bullets."

"Not Withstanding Peculiar Circumstances"

WITH COURAGE, CONFIDENCE, AND RESOLVE fortified by generous amounts of corn liquor, the Texians of the "Army of the People" prepared to challenge the Mexican battalions in San Antonio de Béxar. Perhaps such self-assurance was justified. They had, after all, already whipped Mexican contingents at Gonzales and La Bahía. Additionally, rebels holding Goliad blocked delivery of provisions from the coast, presenting Cós and his soldiers in Béxar with serious logistical problems. The only line of communication with San Antonio was the long overland route from San Luis Potosí, more than four hundred miles within the interior.[1]

General Cós, furthermore, faced more than supply problems. He also suffered a crucial deficiency of human material. Traditionally, the Mexican army had not assigned their best men to the borderlands. Indeed, many were convicts who had been given the cruel choice of prison or Texas. Far from Mexico City, the hapless border garrisons were the last to be considered, thus experiencing constant shortages of uniforms, good officers, money, and not surprisingly, morale. As principal military commandant of Coahuila and Texas, Colonel Ugartechea routinely requested money and supplies as well as more and better men. The answer, however, had always been the same: the revolt in Zacatecas had drained all available resources. Some measure of consolation seemed to be forthcoming on September 20, 1835, when Cós had landed at Copano Bay with reinforcements. When added to the skeleton garrisons already in the province, the total number of combat troops available to Cós would never have exceeded 647 effectives. With that meager total, he was expected to quell over thirty thousand American settlers who would arm "even the children" to fight the *centralistas*.[2]

By October 11, 1835, Texians had assembled around Gonzales to elect officers and to consider tactical problems of their own. Demonstrating a rare solidarity, the rebels unanimously elected *empresario* Stephen F. Austin as their commander. General Austin had almost no formal military training but had led many forays against hostile Indians; more important, he was widely respected for his solid judgment. He was aware that his army faced tremendous obstacles. Cós had fortified San Antonio; behind barricades his troops manned more than twenty cannon. He also had a highly effective cavalry. Apprehensive of enemy horsemen, one Texian explained: "The enemy have a well appointed cavalry, who are volunteers. The infantry is composed of convicts, who are placed in the army as a punishment for their crimes. Our riflemen," he added, "are a deadly species of troops . . . but in the prairies they will be powerless against cavalry." Another adviser warned Austin that the Mexicans had "artillery, cavalry, muskets, bayonets, lances, against all of these you present a band (perhaps brave to a fault) of untrained militia, with such arms as could be produced in an emergency." Consequently, he advised, Austin should "fight [the enemy] from the Brush all the time."[3]

Ignoring the obvious lack of materiel and experience, the Texians marched out of Gonzales toward Béxar on October 12 in an assortment of civilian and military garb. Austin's men lacked even the most basic equipage: "In lieu of a canteen, each man carried a Spanish gourd, . . . having two round bowls, each holding a quart, connected by a short neck, apparently designed for adjusting a strap about." Truly, the men marching on Béxar lacked nearly everything but determination. As one of them admitted, their army presented "a fantastic military array to a casual observer, but the one great purpose animating every heart clothed us in a uniform more perfect in our eyes than was ever donned by regulars on dress parade."[4]

Although insurgents armed with Kentucky long rifles were deadly, not all Texians owned such weapons, and even those who did lacked gunpowder and shot. Some preferred the mutilating short-range blast of a shotgun to the surgical long-range precision of the rifle. Many, however, arrived with no weapon whatsoever. On October 4, 1835, only two days after the clash at Gonzales, Austin complained that "we have more men than guns." Yet given the critical shortage of powder and lead, the dearth of firearms was almost irrelevant. Without ammunition the best of weapons was useless.[5]

Especially aware of the inexperience of his horsemen, Austin knew that he needed the kind of intelligence that only mounted reconnaissance patrols could provide. His "cavalry" consisted of the self-styled Gonzales Lancers, an improvised company armed with hastily contrived cane poles topped with sharpened steel files and astride "half-broke mustangs" and "methodical mules." As his novice lancers employed their new weapons to playfully prod sluggish oxen, Austin was painfully aware that his mounted contingent would be totally outclassed by a squadron of first-rate Mexican cavalry. Even though most horsemen soon abandoned their lances for the more familiar rifles, the Gonzales Lancers represented one of the first attempts to adapt to the methods practiced on the Hispanic prairies.[6]

On the march through unfamiliar country, Austin named Captain Ben Milam commander of a mounted spy company to reconnoiter the approach to Cibolo Creek. This proved a wise precaution, for when the army pitched camp on the banks of the stream two days later, Milam's scouts discovered the trail of a hundred enemy cavalrymen only ten miles from the campsite. When an encounter seemed likely, Austin dispatched other scouting parties to locate the enemy. On October 15, one of these under a Lieutenant Bull was attacked by a ten-man Mexican cavalry patrol. Bull gave ground until the Mexicans were within fifty yards, then halted his squad, wheeled on the advancing horsemen, and discharged a point-blank volley. Surprised and unnerved, the Mexican dragoons fled in disorder. Bull's men pursued for two miles but were unable to overtake them. When the Texians pulled up, the Mexicans fell back into Béxar. General Austin's aide, William T. Austin, noted that "this little skirmish . . . had a very happy effect in the army, it being the first meeting had with the enimy since the army left Gonzales the result was regarded as a favorable omen & it afforded a subject of exultation which was by no means out of place at that moment."[7]

When the Texians reached the outskirts of Béxar, the full extent of their tactical problems came into sharper focus. On October 19, they had marched from Cibolo Creek and had reached Salado Creek by daylight the next morning. From Camp Salado, five miles east of San Antonio, Austin could make out the Mexican fortifications. To assault enemy breastworks with his inferior numbers would be foolish; to do so without artillery would be suicidal.[8]

But there were hopeful signs as well. On October 15, the same day as the Cibolo skirmish, Victoria *alcalde* Plácido Benavides joined the federalist cause with about thirty mounted *rancheros*. On October 22, *tejano* Juan Seguín rode into camp with word that many Mexican citizens of Béxar—*bexareños*—supported the revolt, and some were even eager to serve in Texian ranks. Austin then appointed Seguín a captain and authorized him to raise a company of *vaqueros* who would provide "essential service" as mounted troopers. William T. Austin elaborated on their contributions: "These mexicans being well acquainted with the country, were of important service as express riders, guides to foraging parties, &c." *Tejanos* thus brought much needed range skills to the rebel army, rendering it a blend of two frontier traditions. For Anglo-Celtic Americans out of their element, such assistance was critical.[9]

Even with *bexareño* aid, Austin still considered a frontal assault to be out of the question; a slow, strangling siege seemed the only option. Austin wrote to Goliad commander Philip Dimitt on October 23 expressing his intentions to "commence such operations on the town as to . . . shut in the force now there" so that "it will be obliged to surrender for want of provisions."[10]

Needing more horsemen to patrol the perimeter of the town, Austin continued efforts to upgrade his mounted arm. On October 26, the general called on Colonel John H. Moore, the hero of Gonzales, to organize a cavalry company.

The next day Austin authorized Lieutenant William Barret Travis to raise a volunteer mounted company but stipulated that it would number no less than fifty but not more than eighty men. The Texian commander had definite views regarding weaponry, for he ordered that Moore's troopers be equipped with "double barrel shot guns and pistols," likewise every man who rode with Travis was "to be armed with a double barrel gun and a brace of pistols."[11]

Because Mission Espada was too far from Béxar to serve effectively as a base of operations, the Texians sought a new position closer to the town. A proper site, however, proved difficult to find. It had to be near Béxar, yet defensible against a sortie; in a position to block enemy communications, yet accessible to the reinforcements arriving daily. Pinpointing such a location would require a search party that might have to fight as well as reconnoiter. To command such a force would require men of sound judgment as well as courage. For the task, Austin selected James Bowie, James W. Fannin, and Andrew Briscoe.[12]

Bowie and Fannin had actually proposed the plan to Austin originally. On October 24, the two men wrote to Austin urging "the necessity of some movement, which will bring us nearer together, and shut in the enemy, and either starve them out, whip them out, or dishearten and beat them in small parties."[13]

Austin had chosen three natural leaders. Bowie was already famous throughout the trans-Mississippi frontier, where both he and his deadly blade had achieved sinister reputations. Arriving in Texas in 1828, he married into a wealthy Béxar family. After losing his wife to cholera in 1833, Bowie took to the bottle. But when war broke out against Santa Anna's *centralistas*, he seemed in fine form, revitalized by the likelihood of a good fight. Frontiersmen respected the forty-year-old Bowie as a seasoned Indian fighter and barroom brawler; no stranger to killing, his cold eyes and steady manner commanded deference.[14]

Georgian James W. Fannin was a promising young officer but also something of a dilettante. He had entered West Point in 1821 but withdrew after only two years. Bringing his family to Texas in 1834, he made his living as a slave trader but dabbled in politics. Because Fannin was one of the few men in Texas with any formal military training, many deferred to him in martial matters. But although the captain assumed an attitude of authority, he had never commanded troops in combat.[15]

At age twenty-five, Mississippian Andrew Briscoe embodied the spirit of revolt. In 1835 he had opened a store in Anahuac, where he became embroiled in the growing conflict between American settlers and Mexican authorities. Soon afterward he was arrested for his outspoken views, but a mob led by William Barret Travis, the same man who was now busily organizing a troop of Texian horse, stormed the jail and secured his release. Briscoe's reputation as a firebrand prompted the volunteers from Liberty to elect him captain.[16]

With Bowie in tactical command, the ninety-two-man reconnaissance, consisting primarily of the companies of Fannin and Briscoe, supplemented by those of Robert Coleman, Michael Goheen, and Valentine Bennet, departed Mission Espada on October 27 and rode up the San Antonio River. Bowie's old friend, Juan Seguín, and some of his *ranchero* cavalry appear to have acted as guides. The party examined the Mission San Juan Capistrano and then continued upriver to Mission San José y San Miguel de Aguayo; both proved indefensible. At nightfall they arrived at Mission Purísima Concepción, where they found the spot they sought. Enclosed in a bend of the San Antonio River, it was five hundred yards above the mission and for defensive purposes seemed ideal. The U-shaped bend formed a natural cul-de-sac, with the distance across its mouth measuring about one hundred yards. The timber-lined riverbank formed a natural bulwark, as the water was six to ten feet below the level of the surrounding plain. The land within the arch was level and clear except for a few scattered mesquite trees, a near perfect field of fire for Texian rifles.[17]

Before Bowie left Mission Espada that morning, Austin ordered him to reconnoiter only "so far as time and circumstances will permit," but it had taken him all day to find a suitable position. Colonel Bowie was supposed to have reported "with as little delay as possible, so as to give time to the army to march and take up a position before night." But both time and circumstances had proven inadequate. Since it was too late for his command to return to Espada, Bowie pitched camp. He did not want to risk losing this choice ground even if it meant disobeying Austin's explicit instructions. Bowie dispatched a rider to Espada to inform Austin of his decision to stay the night.

When Bowie's messenger arrived at nine o'clock that night with the news, General Austin was enraged. This was just the type of situation that he had tried to avoid. His army was split and liable to be defeated piecemeal. Fearing such an attack on Bowie's isolated patrol, Austin summoned his officers and instructed them to have their men ready to move out at first light.[18]

Bowie, aware that his detachment was closer to the enemy than to Austin's main force, prepared to meet a surprise attack. The men tethered their mounts, the officers posted pickets, and Bowie stationed a lookout in the mission bell tower. Those not on guard duty slept beside their weapons. These precautions were negated, however, by an early morning ground fog that shrouded the area and reduced visibility to only a few feet. Sentries could see little through the ominous haze.[19]

Such safeguards were timely, for General Cós had learned of the separated detachment and was preparing to crush it. Some of the Texians believed that a priest from Mission Concepción had gone to the Mexicans with the information. Whatever his source, Cós roused his men for battle. Hidden by the heavy fog, approximately three hundred Mexican dragoons and one hundred infantry quietly approached the vulnerable rebels encamped above Concepción.[20]

A clash was not long in coming. As rifleman Creed Taylor approached the Texian picket post near the mission, sentry Henry Karnes cautioned silence; he thought he had heard hoofbeats. While the two men listened and watched, a single musket shot shattered the silence. A loud crack followed a second report; then Karnes exclaimed: "Boys, the scoundrels have shot off my powder horn!" Regaining his composure, along with his powder horn, Karnes fired his pistol toward the enemy as he rejoined the other sentries. Together they fell back on the rest of the command, which had been alerted by the sporadic firing.[21]

The Texians quickly prepared to receive the enemy. The men secured their horses below the bank. The night before, Bowie had split his command into two divisions. Now he positioned them in an angle, one along the left bank of the curve and the other across the bottom, to consolidate the men and prevent them from shooting one another in a crossfire. Seeing the dragoons approaching through the dissipating fog, Bowie shouted, "Keep under cover, boys, and reserve your fire; we haven't a man to spare." Taylor later recalled that "along our front the brush was in our way and at other points the declivity [of the riverbank] was too steep for a foothold. With our hunting knives we soon cleared away the bushes and along the steep places we cut steps so that we could ascend, fire, fall back, and reload under cover."[22]

After the period of initial skirmishing, the main battle began about eight that morning. Mexican infantry advanced behind two field cannon and unleashed "one continued blaze of fire." Texians reciprocated. Since they were short of ammunition, their shots were "more slowly delivered, but with good aim and deadly effect." Shielded by the bank, Texian Noah Smithwick remembered that enemy "grapeshot and canister thrashed through the pecan trees overhead, raining a shower of ripe nuts down on us, and I saw men picking them up and eating them with as little concern as if they were being shaken down by a norther."[23]

Skillful fire from Texian long rifles quickly thinned Mexican ranks. Taylor praised the marksmanship of frontier snipers who obeyed Bowie's orders to "be cool and deliberate and to waste no powder and balls, but to shoot to hit." Smithwick, never one to express admiration for his Mexican adversaries, also noted the withering fire. "Our long rifles—and I thought I had never heard rifles crack so keen, after the dull roar of the cannon—mowed down the Mexicans at a rate that well might have made braver hearts than those encased in their shriveled little bodies recoil." The Mexicans told a different story. General Vicente Filisola, for example, reported the steadfastness of *soldados* who had received "several bullets" but nonetheless staggered toward the Texians and "sought with their bayonets in their last moments to avenge . . . their lives and the insults to their country."[24]

Texian sharpshooters made the Mexican gunners special targets and soon silenced the "dull roar" of the artillery. "The cannon," reported Bowie, "was cleared as if by magic." Smithwick boasted that "three times we picked off the gunners, the last one with a lighted match in his hand." In the face of such deadly fire, not even the bravest artilleryman dared approach the fieldpiece.[25]

Despite the heavy fusillade of Mexican musketry, the Texians were virtually unscathed. One marveled at the "harmlessness" of Mexican firepower. "We wondered," he elaborated, "to see that their balls often fell short of us." Even when on target, the Mexican fire was at times ineffective, for several of the Texians were "struck by balls which were far too spent to break the skin, and only caused an unpleasant bruise." One of the Texians, Pen Jarvis, was saved from serious injury when an enemy bullet struck the broad blade of his Bowie knife. Thereafter, he was known to his comrades as "Bowie-Knife" Jarvis.[26]

Although Bowie had originally placed his men in an angle along the left side of the bend, many now maneuvered around the curve. The riflemen secured both arms of the bank, Smithwick explained, so as "to get them in a cross fire." Most were experienced frontier hunters who positioned themselves anywhere they could to get off a good shot.[27]

This independent spirit produced the only Texian casualty. When Bowie shifted his forces to relieve a point where the Mexicans were concentrating their attack, a contingent led by Robert Coleman rushed to the aid of their beleaguered comrades. They had been cautioned to keep under the cover of the embankment and the trees and not to expose themselves needlessly. Yet while making their way across the open space along the sheltered bank, Richard Andrews brashly cut across the open space above the bluff. As the shocked Texians yelled for him to take cover, every Mexican within range cut loose with their cannon and a "shower of bullets." Andrews dropped, shot in the gut. He paid a cruel price for his bravado. A grapeshot had penetrated his right side, lacerated his bowels, and exited through his left side.[28]

As Andrews lay moaning, the Mexicans pressed their attack but were unable to cross the open field without being struck down by Texas rifles. Facing additional fire power from Coleman's men, the Mexicans floundered before Fannin's portion of the line, where they had focused their efforts.[29]

The infantry stolidly pressed forward, but their smoothbore Brown Bess muskets were ineffective against the Texian long rifles in this type of snipe-and-hide combat. In European conflicts, it had mattered little if muskets had a maximum effective range of only seventy yards because the enemy's muskets were no more powerful. On formal European battlefields, serried ranks traded close range volleys until one or the other gave ground. In Texas, however, a sniper with his long rifle could kill at over two hundred yards. General Cós's superior numbers could not overwhelm the Texian line if his men could not come within the striking range of their muskets, a fact not lost on his exposed soldiers.[30]

Demoralized, the Mexicans began to fall back, first as individuals, then as squads, and finally as whole companies. The dispirited *soldados* fled as Bowie led a headlong charge upon the cannon and a battle standard abandoned in the hasty retreat. The *soldados* became even more discouraged when the Texians turned the artillery and peppered them with their own grapeshot. Fire from the captured ordnance killed the mule driver atop a caisson, and as he tumbled to the ground, the team careened through the shattered Mexican ranks.[31]

Austin and the rest of the Texas army, with the cavalry in advance, arrived about thirty minutes after the Mexicans had quit the field. On the morning of October 28, upon hearing distant shots, Austin had assembled his men and hurried toward the sound of the guns. Although the general had posted the newly mounted company of Lieutenant William Barret Travis well ahead of his infantry column, he had ordered the cavalry to delay any attack until the main force arrived. But upon reaching the field, Travis saw the enemy fleeing in the distance; the twenty-six-year-old cavalier was not one to pass by such an opportunity. At the head of his troop, Travis led a charge upon the already broken enemy scurrying back into Béxar.[32]

General Austin, excited by this easy victory and aware that the Mexicans were temporarily stunned, rode about shouting: "The Army must follow them right into the town!" Others knew better. Bowie, Fannin, and Briscoe, realizing such action would be disastrous, strongly objected. They had just observed the carnage created by determined infantry in a strong defensive position and had no wish to see that situation reversed. Bowie, who had left Béxar only a few days before, reminded Austin of the town's fortifications. He insisted that Texians could never penetrate the breastworks without cannon, especially in the face of enemy artillery. Their arguments finally convinced Austin, who reluctantly withdrew his order for an immediate assault.[33]

The day's fighting ended, the victors searched the field for spoils but found only the answer to a question that many had pondered during the battle. Plundering the enemy dead of their cartridge boxes, they were sorely disappointed. As one veteran noted: "On examining the powder, we found it little better than pounded charcoal, and after a trial, rejected it as all together useless. It was by far the worst powder I ever saw, and burnt so badly that we could clearly account for the inefficacy of the enemy's fire." When compared with the excellent du Pont powder that the Texians used, "it was evident," he added, "that we had vastly the advantage over our enemy in this particular." The Texians, therefore, emptied the cartridges but kept the bullets.[34]

The brief action had exacted numerous casualties. The Mexicans had lost about seventy-six killed or wounded, "among them," according to Bowie, "many promising officers." Richard Andrews had been the only Texian lost, but the circumstances of his death were especially gruesome. Creed Taylor recalled that "he lingered for several hours suffering the most agonizing torture, begging all the while to be relieved, and the poor fellow would place a finger on each of the bullet holes and try to tear them open in frantic efforts to alleviate his sufferings."[35]

Could Cós have avoided such a costly defeat? Probably. His deployment on that day seemed mulish and unimaginative. Underestimating the accuracy of American long rifles, he had hoped to overwhelm the Texians by concentrating his mass on Bowie's right and then rolling up the entire line. Not a bad plan, but Cós's troops were gunned down before they could bring sufficient weight upon the Texian flank. Perhaps Cós may be forgiven that oversight; after all, nothing in his military experience had prepared him for the effects of such weapons. Even so, charging blindly into a cul-de-sac would have been ill advised even if the enemy had been armed only with smoothbore muskets. No general worthy of his epaulets ever assaulted any defensive position without a thorough reconnaissance.[36]

If Mexican tactics were faulty, Bowie's, despite their success, were hardly any better. Military theorists since the time of Caesar warned against the folly of deploying with a river at one's rear, for in the event of a reverse there could be no retreat. Had Bowie faced an adversary with more acumen or experience than Cós, the outcome might have been quite different. A good general would have pinned down the Texians with a feint attack to the front while sending companies of skirmishers around both flanks. Once in position, Mexican infantrymen could have converged on the rebels in a pincer maneuver. In such a scenario, numbers might have prevailed, for, arrayed in line, few of the Texians would have been able to concentrate their fire against the flanks. With artillery on their front, infantry on both flanks, and a river at their rear, Bowie's men could have been obliterated. That Cós was too inept to do so brought no credit to Bowie. Although victorious, Bowie was more lucky than capable. He had demonstrated the traits of a riverboat gambler rather than those of an able commander during the campaign. Throughout his life, and again at Concepción, courage and luck had always seen Jim Bowie through rough scrapes. The following March, in an old mission some two miles from the site of this victory, he would discover the limits of both.[37]

Despite the insubordination and mistakes that preceded the battle, General Austin praised the "brilliancy" of the victory. He seemed to have chided Lieutenant Travis for his unrestrained and unauthorized charge. While not dissatisfied with the results, Austin informed the young lieutenant that he should have given "notice to the Army as would have been proper." Austin could not remain angry long; for a troop that had been mounted only one day, Travis's men had performed remarkably well. Austin also seems to have forgotten his anger with Bowie for staying the night and splitting the command against orders. The large number of Mexican bodies littering the field argued in favor of Bowie's decision.[38]

The relative ease of the victory at Concepción instilled in the Texians a reliance on their long rifles and a contempt for their enemies. Expressing the view held by most Texians at the time, one veteran wrote that "not withstanding the peculiar circumstances under which it took place, . . . [Concepción] proved the fact that Texians with their rifles and pistols were decidedly formidable . . . sufficiently so to cope with Mexican troops even with greatly superior numbers." The battle "had a tendency to inspire the men with a degree of confidence in their efficiency that previously did not exist, and it also had the effect to depress & alarm the Mexican troops and bring them to a more respectful consideration of the importance of Texian volunteers than was previously entertained." Texian self-assurance was matched only by the disdain with which they regarded their Mexican adversaries. Estimations that, in both cases, subsequent events proved undeserved.[39]

❖❖

CHAPTER 3

"We Flogged Them Like Hell"

❖❖

✤

3. TROOPER, MEXICAN LIGHT CAVALRY

Atascocito Road
October 1835

Exhausted and dusty following a hard ride, this trooper dismounts only to land in one of the unavoidable hazards of cavalry service. Nevertheless, the oldest maxim of the horse soldier prevails: the health and comfort of the mount come before that of the rider. Thus, only when his horse is happily engaged in dining from a nosebag does its rider pause to clean his boots. Observe that the horse's tail is not only cropped but also tied up and secured by a crupper — a practice documented by Linati and other contemporary observers.

The light cavalry uniform, one of the most elegant in the Mexican army, closely reflects European patterns. This trooper boasts a dark blue coatee fastened with white metal buttons; the piping around the collar and epaulets are red. Both carbine strap and cartridge box strap are white leather. The white metal insignia that graces the cartridge box strap seems to have been a unique distinction of the light cavalry. The heavy leather gauntlets are patently nonregulation but highly utilitarian.

The campaign overalls — medium blue with a red seam stripe — are similar to those worn throughout the Napoleonic wars. Called the cha-rivari in French, this sturdy garment was reinforced by leather, chamois, buckskin, or suede. These overalls were sewn together from the inseams to the instep of the pant leg and left open to be buttoned up the outer seam. The drop flap allowed the busy trooper to answer nature's call without dropping his overalls, an involved task with all those seam buttons. A leather strap fastens the overalls under the boots.

Small tin-plated iron spurs are not strapped on in the conventional method but rather are screwed directly into the wooden heel; the heels themselves are reinforced by a horseshoe tap that is secured by four tiny screws.

The comb of his helmet is adorned with a mane of black horsehair; the bands of the pompon reflect the national colors — (back to front) green, white, and red. The turban and peak are constructed of hard black leather. The comb and plate are fashioned of stamped white metal, as is the peak edging. The chin straps are each formed in two parts, the strap itself and the rosette or boss. The rosette is secured to the turban by clips. The strap is composed of as many as fifteen individual scales to allow maximum flexibility. Note the plume socket attached to the left side of the turban. Even so, plumes were rarely worn on campaign.

Weapons are the lance, a saber, and the Pagent carbine, a British surplus item. The short-barreled carbine, a lighter version of the infantry musket, enabled the light cavalryman to perform as a skirmisher, firing either from the saddle or dismounted.

3

"We Flogged Them Like Hell"

WHILE GENERAL AUSTIN AND THE TEXIAN ARMY were camping out-side Béxar celebrating their victory at Concepción, Philip Dimitt, com-mander of the rebel garrison at Goliad, proposed a drive against the Mexican post of Lipantitlán. As early as October 15, Dimitt had written Austin urging the reduction of that post. Its capture, he argued, would secure the frontier, provide a vital station for defense, create instability among the centralists, and encourage Mexican federalists. Dimitt also suggested an offensive against Matamoros, which he believed would pro-duce "the most important consequences to the present and future repose of Texas."[1]

Dimitt overstated his case, perhaps out of enthusiasm, but his plan had merit. Positioned on the west bank of the Nueces River along the Atascosito Road, Fort Lipantitlán could serve as a springboard for a Mexican relief column sent to retake Goliad or to break the siege of Béxar. The threat to Goliad posed the greatest danger for the Texians, since its recovery would restore the Mexicans' link to the vital port at Copano Bay. Eliminating the centralist garrison at Lipantitlán would also permit the predominantly federalist citizens of nearby San Patricio to form a local government and to organize a militia. The fort reportedly housed the cannon, a supply of small arms and ammunition, and a "Valuable caballada" (horse herd), all much needed by the rebels. On October 10 and 11, Dimitt had sent two young Irishmen, John Williams and John Toole, to San Patricio with dispatches for the town's federalist leaders. Soldiers at Lipantitlán had intercepted them and now held them prisoners within the compound. Dimitt yearned to storm the place and rescue his captured couriers.[2]

But first he sought intelligence regarding the enemy's strength. On October 20, he informed General Austin that a reconnaissance, just returned from Lipantitlán, had reported that the Mexican troops had taken the cannon inside their compound and were working around the clock to improve the defenses. Dimitt had also received word that two hundred Mexican cavalrymen were on their way to reinforce the garrison on the Nueces. In their wake rode an additional two to three hundred enemy horsemen from Matamoros. Their reported mission: the recapture of Goliad. More than ever, the security of Goliad required the Texians to take Lipantitlán before it was reinforced.[3]

On October 27, 1835, Dimitt wrote Austin again to report the transfer of Williams and Toole from Lipantitlán to confinement in Matamoros. The men of Goliad believed that their delay had doomed two comrades to a "distant dungeon, there to linger out a mere fragment of existence." Quick and forceful action might have saved them. Now they were beyond help, beyond hope. The Goliad garrison was especially angered as they recalled the clemency shown the Mexican prisoners taken during George Collingsworth's capture of La Bahía on October 9. "The men under my command," Dimitt reported, "are clamorous for retaliation, either by clothing with suits of iron, those in our power; or by marching immediately against the garrison [of Lipantitlán] and reducing it to unconditional submission, or putting it to the sword."[4]

Dimitt dispatched an expedition to capture Fort Lipantitlán. From Goliad he wrote Austin on October 30, "I have ordered a detachment of 35 men, under the command of Adjutant Ira Westover, to proceed forthwith to Le Panteclan [Lipantitlán], the garrison on the Nueces, reduce and burn it. The arms and Ammunition if possible, will be brought off and, if practicable, the public horses taken, and driven to this place."[5]

It was one thing to know that a campaign was necessary, another to find the means of supplying it. Westover's force could not even have left Goliad if federalist *tejanos* had not provided horses and food. The *rancheros* of Goliad furnished twenty mounts for the expedition, while those of Guadalupe Victoria donated thirty head of cattle. The contributions of insurgent Texas Mexicans were as crucial to this operation as they were to others.[6]

Ira J. Westover of Refugio led the column; it would be stretching the point to claim that he commanded it. True, Dimitt had named him commander, with First Lieutenant John P. Borden and Sergeant William Braken as his subordinates, but John J. Linn, Major James Kerr, and

Colonel James Power accompanied him as a self-appointed advisory committee. Westover would find their advice hard to ignore. All three had been elected delegates to the Consultation at San Felipe but had postponed their political duties to participate in what promised to be a fine shooting scrape. After all, Texas politicians could always find time to bicker over the latest predicament, but a good fight waited for no man. On October 31, Westover, an artilleryman by training, rode out of Goliad with fewer than forty mounted riflemen. In case he ran into difficulties, Kerr and Linn rode at his elbow.[7]

The force took an indirect approach to Lipantitlán. Instead of heading southwest toward the enemy, Westover and his party rode southeast toward Refugio, where they were joined by a few locals and Colonel Power, the third member of the advisory triumvirate. Francisco de la Portilla, Power's brother-in-law, served as a guide on the lower road to San Patricio. While Mexican dragoons patrolled the Atascosito Road north of town, the insurgents approached from the east.[8]

At almost the same time, the Mexican troops at Lipantitlán had launched an offensive of their own. On October 11, post commander Captain Don Nicolás Rodriguez had received orders from General Cós to harass the rebels at Goliad, no doubt to relieve the growing pressure on Béxar. With him was Captain Manuel Sabriego, who had been captured at La Bahía during the assault of October 9 and paroled by Austin because of his avowed federalist loyalties. Immediately upon his release, Sabriego had ridden to Matamoros to give a full report to government officials. He soon returned to the Goliad-Lipantitlán area and surreptitiously organized an espionage and intelligence network. Dimitt, aware of Sabriego's duplicity and chicanery, was eager to capture or—preferably—to kill him, one of the primary goals of the raid on Lipantitlán. Ironically, Rodriguez, Sabriego, and the bulk of the Mexican garrison departed Lipantitlán for Goliad on October 31, the same day that Westover's party left Goliad for Lipantitlán. If they had met en route, the more numerous Mexican dragoons would have had the advantage.[9]

Arriving at San Patricio on November 3, Westover learned that most of the enemy "were out in persuit of us" and pushed ahead to capture the fort before the garrison returned. The Texians reached Lipantitlán about half an hour after sundown, and the next act of the rapidly developing comic opera ensued. Many Irish citizens of San Patricio sympathized with the centralists; therefore, Westover arrested one, a James O'Riley, for "aiding and assisting the enemy." Once at the fort, however, the cagey O'Riley offered to enter and persuade the skeleton garrison to surrender, provided that Westover guarantee his personal safety. Although the Texians had boasted earlier of accepting nothing less than "unconditional submission," the prospects of assaulting breastworks apparently made them less "clamorous for retaliation." Perhaps it was best to let O'Riley talk the Mexicans out of their fort. He must have been persuasive, or maybe the twenty-seven defenders considered the odds against them too great. More likely, the surrender terms were just too good to refuse. Whatever their reasons, at about eleven o'clock that night those remaining inside Lipantitlán agreed to the terms offered. The conditions were exceedingly generous. Upon surrendering, the centralists were to be released immediately on the promise that they would not take up arms for the remainder of the conflict. With these terms accepted, the rebels walked into Lipantitlán unopposed. Not one shot had been fired.[10]

The enemy compound failed to impress the Texians. Lipantitlán was certainly no fort; it might charitably be described as an armed camp, but Irish Texian John J. Linn was not in a charitable mood. Was this the "'formidable' fortress" for which he had forsaken a warm bed in San Felipe? "The 'fort' was a single embankment of earth," he recalled, "lined within by fence-rails to hold the dirt in place, and would have answered tolerably well, perhaps, for a second-rate hog pen." Equally deficient was the armament, which "consisted of two four-pounded cannon, eight 'escopets' or old Spanish guns, and three or four pounds of powder; but no balls for the guns were discovered." Small wonder the Mexican garrison had surrendered so readily.[11]

Westover's men took a well-deserved rest after their forced march. Returning to San Patricio, they "remained in quiet possession of the town." The next morning, November 4, the Texians burned the wooden huts adjoining the compound and with only limited success dismantled the earthen embankments that constituted the walls. Finally, around three o'clock, having done all the damage they could, the men rounded up fourteen of the "public" horses, secured the two cannon, and prepared to return to Goliad.[12]

Captain Rodriguez, meanwhile, had nearly reached Goliad when one of Sabriego's spies galloped up with news that the enemy had taken possession of Lipantitlán. Surprised and embarrassed, the captain ordered an abrupt about-face and led his column southward. Whipping horses into a lather, his force of about sixty Mexicans and ten Irish supporters from San Patricio reached the outskirts of their former post around four o'clock that afternoon.[13]

Westover, spotting Mexican outriders scouting the Texian position, posted half of his men on the east bank of the Nueces to intercept the enemy. The riflemen crossed the stream and formed a battle line among a grove of timber.[14]

Rodriguez had lost any chance of surprise, and with the Texians ensconced in the woods, his cavalry was useless; ordering his dragoons to dismount, he deployed for an assault. Westover described how "the enemy came up in front and made a move from their centre around our flanks on the river leaving a few men under cover of a mote in front. The enemy on our right flank dismounted and took the advantage of the timber led on by nine of the Irish of San Patricia."[15]

The action at Nueces Crossing was a replay of Concepción on a smaller scale. The Mexicans opened fire at two hundred yards, but their Pagent carbines and Brown Bess muskets were useless at such a distance. Not so the Texians' long rifles. Westover's snipers drew blood; "those on the opposite bank of the river were enabled to operate on the flanks of the enemy above and below the crossing which they did with fine effect."[16]

The Mexicans and their Irish allies pressed forward. Linn expressed admiration for one Mexican officer, "a brave fellow—[he] stood on the declivity of a slight elevation and fired guns at us as fast as his men could load and hand them to him." Major James Kerr made this officer his "special target . . . and succeeded in wounding the cool fellow, who was borne from the field by two of his comrades." Three of the nine Irishmen who were in the forefront of the attack were also brought down by Texian fire.[17]

Yet the antagonist the Texians sought most eluded them. When the fighting began, Sabriego bolted for Matamoros. He may have gone for reinforcements, but more likely he feared the vengeance of those he had deceived.[18]

The inaccurate Mexican fire claimed but one victim. Sergeant William Bracken had just shot down an enemy soldier and was reloading. He never finished. A half-ounce slug struck his right hand, "sweeping away three fingers." Continuing on its path, it fractured his left hand as well. Bracken enjoyed the dubious distinction of being the only insurgent wounded at Nueces Crossing.[19]

After half an hour of combat, Captain Rodriguez withdrew with heavy losses. In a letter to James Fannin, rebel rifleman A. H. Jones crowed that forty Texians had taken on "70 odd of the enemy" and "flogged them like hell." He explained that the Mexicans "admitted 3 killed and about 14 wounded, several mortally," but that "information since says 5 killed, 17 wounded, and 20 missing." Jones added that "the best of the story is yet to come—by some means about 20 of the Irish in that quarter had been induced to join the enemy—among them the alcalda, Judge, and Sheriff—all three were badly wounded."[20]

The victors of Nueces Crossing had little time to rejoice; toward nightfall a heavy rain heralded the approach of a blue norther. Captain Westover, with remarkable understatement, recalled that his men were "very much chilled." Linn, with equal aplomb, remembered the norther being the "reverse of agreeable." With night approaching and no draft animals available, Westover's three-man advisory board counseled "the propriety of throwing the Artillery in the river and it was accordingly done." Seeking shelter from the storm, the expedition headed for San Patricio, where the citizens "hospitably vied with one another in their efforts to make us comfortable." The hapless Mexicans spent a harrowing night exposed to the cold rain and the pitiful pleas of their wounded.[21]

At dawn, Captain Rodriguez, who had no surgeon, dispatched a messenger under a white flag to request a truce and permission to send in his wounded. Westover readily assented, and the injured Mexicans hobbled or were carried into San Patricio. Linn was dismayed to learn that among them was an old friend, Lieutenant Marcellino García, and did everything he could to ease García's pain during his few remaining hours. The dying Mexican, in a final magnanimous gesture, gave Linn his horse. "With his last breath," García, a federalist, "deplored the unhappy relations existing between Texas and the mother-country in consequence of Santa Anna's ambitious purposes." He further admitted that he was "at heart a sympathizer with the Texians; but being an officer of the regular service, had no option in the premises." Fighting men on both sides mourned García as he was buried with the full honors of war.[22]

After García's funeral, Westover sent a courier to Captain Rodriguez requesting his attendance at "another pleasant meeting." He, like General Cós, had learned a costly lesson and politely declined. His men, he apologized, were ill equipped to match "the Texas rifles and could not accept the invitation." Already bloodied in one encounter and cut off from his base in San Patricio, Captain Rodriguez and his men fell back to Matamoros.²³

With no Mexicans to fight, the Texians returned to Goliad. Upon their arrival on November 12, however, Westover found Dimitt displeased with his conduct. Writing to Austin the next day, Dimitt complained that "Westover obeyed no part of the order under which he acted." Just what that order was is unknown, since no written commands were ever found. Dimitt probably issued verbal instructions before Westover left for Refugio on October 31. Westover, indignant at his reception, refused to provide a written account to his commander, preferring to report directly to General Sam Houston. In his letter of November 15, Westover praised the courage of his men, extolled the "signal service" of Kerr, Linn, and Power (with whom he gladly shared the responsibility for jettisoning the captured cannon), and claimed a complete triumph.²⁴

Sweeping aside the bravery, the blood, and the braggadocio, what had the expedition actually accomplished? On the surface, precious little. The "fort" was taken but Sabriego, Rodriguez, and most of the garrison had escaped to Matamoros. Even those who had surrendered had been released. A few wooden shacks had been burned, but the dirt embankment had proved largely indestructible. The enemy ordnance that had fallen into Texian hands had been dumped in the Nueces. The captured muskets and the small supply of ammunition taken proved useless; the disgusted rebels threw most of those into the river as well. Fourteen captured horses were driven to Goliad, but the Mexicans had ridden off to Matamoros with a much larger number. It appeared to Dimitt that Westover, having taken Lipantitlán and driven off the enemy, had returned to Goliad and left the unlucky federalists of San Patricio to fend for themselves.²⁵

Such a casual assessment was, however, unfair to Westover and his men. Politically, the venture was significant, for in the absence of the centralist garrison, the San Patricio federalists regained control of the municipal government, declared support for the Constitution of 1824, elected representatives to the Consultation, and organized a militia. Militarily the operation had been equally successful. Westover's untrained volunteers had repulsed an enemy contingent that outnumbered them almost two to one. Additionally, and most important strategically, General Cós had been denied the last link of communication between Béxar and the Mexican interior. Westover obviously lacked a sufficiency either of men or supplies to garrison Lipantitlán. Furthermore, as far as is known, he had never been ordered to occupy the post.[26]

It was clear, however, that Lipantitlán had to be garrisoned if San Patricio were to remain in the federalist fold. Less than a month after Westover's departure, John Turner, a worried San Patricio federalist, wrote Dimitt: "We have neither men nor means to withstand any force that may be sent against us, as the people here are still divided." Captain Rodriguez, he continued, had written town leaders promising a prompt return. If they joined his ranks, all would be forgiven. If not, "the vengeance of the Mexican army" would be unleashed upon the forlorn civilians of San Patricio. In a postscript, Turner reemphasized the plight of the town. "Please not to be mistaken in our situation, we have neither men nor bread, & no place to procure some without it comes from your quarter; as there is none to be had here at any price, and our men are too few to spare, to send in pursuit of it."[27]

The citizens of San Patricio were, indeed, exposed to peril, and as it happened, the centralists did reoccupy the settlement. But none of that was Westover's fault. The town was simply too far from Goliad, and the rebels were too few to protect it. Nevertheless, Westover had carried out his assignment as he had understood it. The venture had not been a total success, but given the circumstances, Westover did all that could have reasonably been expected. The soldiers of the expedition had justly earned the praise of General Houston, who lauded "the conduct and bravery of the officers & men who have so handsomely acquitted themselves in the affair and so deservedly won the reputation for themselves and Glory for their Country."[28]

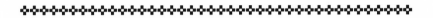

CHAPTER 4

"The Spectacle Becomes Appalling"

Siege of Béxar
November 1835

General Stephen F. Austin harbored no illusions concerning the nature of his recruits. In a November 4 dispatch to the Consultation, he complained: "This force, it is known to all, is but undisciplined militia and in some respects of very discordant materials." Moreover, many of the militiamen arrived in a drunken stupor; the following day, the general implored the Consultation: "In the name of Almighty God send no more ardent spirits to this camp — if any is on the road turn it back, or have the head [of the barrel] knocked out." This figure represents one of Austin's "discordant" citizen-soldiers.

This youth, perhaps the younger son of a well-to-do planter, likes having a grand frolic. Away from home for the first time, he is enjoying a respite from responsibility and respectability. Never before has this southern beau been required to forage for his breakfast, but he discovers a genuine talent for at least one aspect of military life. The trophies from his latest excursion adorn his rifle barrel. He is a vain, ill-disciplined, and slothful soldier — typical of most volunteers from the United States.

His battered planter's hat is modeled after one depicted in an 1830 portrait of Andrew Jackson. Revealing the rigors of hard campaigning, drop-front trousers are stuffed into stylish riding boots. The 1830s waistcoat achieved distinction by virtue of the materials from which it was fashioned. The fabric was normally expensive and, as is the case here, displayed intricate embroidery. Although worse for wear, the high-collared tailcoat was de rigueur *among those who would be "gentlemen." Draped over his shoulders is a* jorongo *(Mexican blanket) that has been "foraged," along with breakfast, from local* tejanos.

Unlike many Texas colonists, he is equipped with an enviable assortment of weapons. Secured in his sash is a .46 caliber flintlock pistol made in New Orleans by A. Whiting between 1820 and 1830. His showy .45 caliber rifle has a striped maple stock with rich silver inlay. He protects this prized firearm against the elements by wrapping the lock and plugging the bore. Measuring a full 52 3/4 inches, this long arm more than warrants that designation. Both the pistol and the rifle are drawn from specimens in the Winchester Gun Museum collection. For additional protection, the lad has slipped an "Arkansas Toothpick" in his boot top.

Not even a torrential downpour can dampen the humor of this roisterous swain. Having downed the contents of his earthenware jug, he is full of "ardent spirits." While lacking food, clothing, and ammunition, the rebel army never seemed to run short of corn liquor.

"The Spectacle Becomes Appalling"

FOR THE ARMY OF THE PEOPLE, November 1835 would prove to be a month of confusion, disorder, and indecision. As long as a Mexican army remained in Béxar, Texian victories elsewhere meant nothing. If, however, a large centralist force relieved the San Antonio garrison and mounted an offensive against the Anglo-American colonies, all earlier defeats could be erased. Many issues remained unsettled. Aside from their hatred of Santa Anna's dictatorial regime, Texians could agree on little else. Although in a state of armed insurgence, several were still unsure of their cause. While most old settlers fought to preserve the Federal Constitution of 1824, newcomers were clamoring for complete separation from Mexico. That issue would have to be settled, but Texians were finding it easier to start a war than to rationalize one. Some kind of provisional government had to be organized, if for no other reason than to validate the armed mob outside Béxar.[1]

Austin was not the only commander facing hard choices; his adversary, General Cós, also had his full share. Béxar was a centralist island surrounded by a sea of insurgents. The clash at Concepción had taught Cós the folly of pitting his poorly armed soldiers against North American riflemen on an open battlefield. In Béxar, with his artillery protected behind breastworks, the general felt relatively secure because he knew the revolutionaries lacked siege guns. If his garrison could hold out until the arrival of a relief column, the rebellion might yet be repressed. On November 1, Austin dispatched a surrender demand to Cós. He returned the letter unopened, along with a curt reply that honor and duty would not permit him to receive correspondence from rebels. The issue remained undecided; men would have to die before it would be.[2]

Many believed that Béxar must be captured if the Texian revolt were to succeed—but how? Some Texians called for an immediate assault; others favored a continuation of the siege to starve the Mexicans into submission. After Cós refused to surrender, Austin reconnoitered the town's perimeter. On November 1, he wrote Bowie and Fannin, reporting what they already knew: "The fortifications are much stronger than has been supposed and the difficulty of storming of course greater." Something had to be done, and soon, for the rebel army was running short of supplies.[3]

The burden of command weighed heavily upon Austin. Calling a council of war on November 2, he shared his concern with the officers. After much discussion, the council elected to maintain the siege until the arrival of reinforcements and an eighteen-pound cannon. Writing Dimitt at Goliad, Austin expressed his doubts: "Whether the army can be kept together long enough to await the arrival of reinforcements, and the necessary supply of heavy battering-cannon and ammunition, I am sorry to say, is somewhat uncertain." Clearly Austin was uncomfortable as commander. Whenever a decision had to be made, to avoid making a fatal error, he put the matter up for a vote.[4]

In the midst of all this confusion, Bowie, Austin's most experienced lieutenant, relinquished his command. Since Concepción, Bowie's detachment had been stationed apart from the army, functioning virtually as an independent force. In his letter of resignation dated November 2, 1835, he reported "great dissatisfaction" among his unit and spoke of its "dissolution" unless it rejoined Austin's main body. Beyond that, the secretive Bowie refused to commit himself on paper, allowing only: "The causes which have produced this state of things will be explained when I see you, when I will also explain my motives for taking the step I have taken in reference to myself."[5]

While some Texian leaders resigned and others held elections, the siege at Béxar dragged on. Unlike their officers, the men clamored for action. The army's close proximity to the enemy made firefights inevitable. On November 3, Samuel Maverick, an American resident of Béxar, recorded a night skirmish near the mission-fort of the Alamo. It came about when a squad of Texians who were probing the defenses encountered the Mexican picket guard. The Texian patrols did well to employ the cover of darkness, for Maverick reported: "The Alamo is very strongly fortified, and the streets to the plaza here well guarded; and all the trees, grass, fences and other lurking places and barricades removed and being removed in order to see the Americans when they come up."[6]

Austin had no wish to be surprised by a Mexican relief column, so he dispatched cavalry patrols to cover the various approaches to the town. Juan Seguín's *rancheros*, excellent horsemen familiar with the terrain, were especially suited for that assignment. Austin also worried about reports that the Mexicans were sneaking out of Béxar to procure fodder for their horses and food for themselves. On November 6, therefore, he dispatched Captain Andrew Briscoe and a company of mounted riflemen to patrol the area west of town with orders to prevent cattle and all other supplies from entering Béxar. Austin also ordered Briscoe to harass "the enemy in evry [and] any way possible." Although Briscoe had been ordered to range as far as the Río Medina, he patrolled for only three days before ordering his squadron back to camp. Captain William B. Travis, however, refused to return and announced that he would continue the patrol with any of Briscoe's men who had the grit to join him. Twelve volunteers remained to carry on the scout.[7]

The persistence of Travis and his men paid off. On November 9, they crossed the trail of a large *remuda* and followed it. The next day, Travis found his prize, some three hundred head of "gentle Spanish horses" tended by fewer than a dozen enemy soldiers. Travis ordered a charge on the camp. The Mexicans, taken by surprise, surrendered without firing a shot. Although the capture of the herd boosted Texian morale, most of the captured mounts were jaded and unfit for service. They were, therefore, taken to the Seguín ranch to recuperate.[8]

Austin could have used three hundred good horses, for the siege of Béxar was increasingly becoming a cavalry operation. Additional mounted companies were needed to patrol the roads entering San Antonio and to intercept Mexican couriers. Horses were also required to ride the perimeter of the town to ensure that the besieged were kept in while food and supplies were kept out. The cavalry made feints hoping to draw the enemy out of their defenses where they would be easy targets for Texian long rifles. On one occasion, Thomas J. Rusk and forty riders took up a position within three hundred yards of the town, remaining there for over twenty minutes. But Cós, still stinging from his defeat at Concepción, could not be lured from behind the barricades.[9]

The independent and ill-disciplined frontiersmen were often more of a problem for Austin than the Mexicans were. They had volunteered to fight, not to sit around and watch their enemy starve and their officers bicker. To complicate matters, the weather was turning cold, and many returned home for warmer clothing. To halt the flow of deserters, Austin ordered that "no one pass the guard lines at any time without the written permission of the Commander in Chief." He further instituted morning and evening parades during which officers would call the company rolls.[10]

Many American volunteers proved a problem for Austin even before they reached camp, for en route to Béxar they terrorized Texian civilians. An outraged Dr. Launcelot Smither wrote Austin two letters on November 4 that recounted the abuses he had suffered. One company coming through Gonzales had "treated the wimon of this place worse than all the comanshee nation could have done and draged me out of the house and nearly beat me to death." In his second letter, Smither asserted that "the conduct of wild savages would be preferable to the Insults of such Canebols."[11]

The plight of the Texian army worsened each day. Rifleman Creed Taylor remembered the officers to have been "in daily consultation" but to no apparent end, since "the men, seeing the vacillation and uncertain state of affairs, began to leave." Austin watched in dismay as the force that once numbered some eight hundred effectives dwindled to six hundred. But he was helpless. The men were not under oath to serve. As volunteers, they "went where they pleased and came when they chose."[12]

Those who remained were even more of a problem. Many sought relief from their boredom by reaching the bottom of a brown jug. Austin complained that drunks roared through camp, shooting off rifles and wasting precious powder and ball. "In the name of almighty God," he implored the politicians, "send no more ardent spirits to this camp—if any is on the road turn it back, or have the head [of the barrel] knocked out." He also called on the officers to use their "influence and utmost exertions to preserve order and regularity and to prevent shooting without leave." By November 5, however, the officers had little influence left. Few really knew who was in charge; even worse, most seemed unsure of the cause for which they were fighting. William H. Wharton, in a rancorous missive in which he resigned as judge advocate general, expressed the feelings of many: "No good will be atchieved by this army except by the merest accident under heaven." An exasperated Austin looked toward the Consultation in San Felipe to provide a miracle.[13]

It had been a near miracle that the Consultation had even managed to meet. Soon after the fighting had begun at Gonzales, the call went out for delegates to assemble at San Felipe on October 15 for the purpose of forming a provisional government. By that date, however, many of the elected representatives were with the army and on the march to Béxar. The meeting date was delayed until November 1. Through Austin's urgings, an unofficial central executive committee formed at San Felipe in the interim as the self-styled permanent council. It reflected the uncertainty of the times that a body boldly deemed "permanent" remained in existence only three weeks.[14]

Yet during its brief tenure, the permanent council served well. It took steps to organize the defense against the Indians and reinforced and supplied the volunteers in the field. It commissioned privateers, established a postal system, authorized merchant Thomas F. McKinney's trip to the United States to borrow $100,000 for the war effort, and sent out a call for much-needed men, money, and supplies. But November 1 came and went; there were still not enough representatives in San Felipe to provide a quorum for the legislative session.[15]

By November 3, however, enough delegates had finally arrived, and the Consultation speedily got down to business. The most urgent work was the adoption of a provisional government and the organization of a regular army. After bitter debate, the members voted a seeming contradiction. They formed a provisional government as a state within the Mexican federation, largely to reassure Mexican liberals and *tejano* allies; at the same time, they elected as governor Henry Smith, a staunch member of the war party and long-standing advocate of independence. Smith at least grasped the gravity of the situation; addressing the council on November 16, he lectured: "You have to call system out of chaos; to start the wheels of government, clogged and impeded as they are by conflicting interest, and by discordant materials. Without funds, without the munitions of war; with an army in the field contending against a powerful foe. These are the auspices under which we are forced to make a beginning."[16]

Less than a week later, the council awarded the empty title of commander-in-chief of the regular army to Sam Houston, hard-drinking hero of Horseshoe Bend and former governor of Tennessee. He hardly looked the part; Anson Jones, a newcomer to Texas, thought Houston's garish Mexican blanket and greasy buckskins "anything but respectable, and very much like that of a broken-down sot and debauchee." Frank Sparks, one of the volunteers serving with Austin, later explained that many of Houston's Texas associates were "of questionable character" and that the new general's "actions at times jarred the moral and high-class emigrants who had been brought in by Austin and other empresarios." Houston's roisterous behavior certainly jarred the fastidious Jones. "The first night after my arrival," he explained, "I was kept awake nearly all night by a drunken carouse in the room over that in which I 'camped.' Dr. [Branch T.] Archer and Gen. Houston appeared to be the principal persons engaged in the orgie, to judge from the noise." Jones continued, "The whole burden of the conversation, so far as it was, at times, intelligible, appeared to be abuse and denunciation of a man for whom I had the highest respect, Gen. Stephen F. Austin, then in command before San Antonio de Béxar, for not breaking up the siege of that place, and retreating to the east of the Colorado."[17]

But Houston found his Byzantine intrigues as practical as his rustic apparel, even if polite society deemed them unrefined. More important to him was the fact that the force that he was to command did not yet exist. If he wished to head an army, he would have to raise one, or else borrow Austin's. Houston might be able to recruit an army, but the Consultation would decide how it would be organized. The need for such a force was clear. On November 3, Austin had written "earnestly and pressingly" to urge the "absolute necessity of organizing a regular army and inviting a Military man of known and tried Talents to Command it." Houston had just such a man in mind: Sam Houston.

The army was to number 1,120 enlisted men divided into two groups: regulars who enlisted for two years and "permanent volunteers" who would serve for the duration of the war. Mounted rangers, commanded by a major, augmented the force. Although Houston was bound by the orders of the governor and Council, he was allowed to choose his own staff: an adjutant general, an inspector general, a quartermaster general, a surgeon general, and four aides. As commander, Houston in theory had control of "all the forces called into public service during the war." The Consultation told him in no uncertain terms, however, that he had no authority over the volunteers already serving in Austin's command.[18]

The military committee of the Consultation proposed dividing the 1,120-man force into two regiments: one of artillery and one of infantry. Each regiment would be further divided into two battalions composed of five companies of fifty-six men. Infantry field commanders were to be a colonel, a lieutenant colonel, and a major. The artillery field commanders, on the other hand, were to consist of a colonel, two lieutenant colonels, and two majors. Two lieutenants were slated for each infantry company, while artillery companies would have three, in recognition of that arm's more specialized needs.[19]

Modeled after the finest U.S. regiments, the Texas regular army was intended to be a force of the highest caliber. Officers and men were to receive the same pay and be subject to the same discipline as set forth in U.S. army regulations. Texians, however, had more land than money, so in addition to their pay, each officer and enlisted man was to receive 640 acres as a reward for his service. Later, as an inducement to join the regular army rather than the volunteers, the land bounty was raised by an additional 160 acres and $24 in cash.[20]

The regulars, according to plan, were to be well drilled and supplied. On November 27, a Consultation ordinance approved the purchase of, among other provender: 300 *jaeger* carbines, 600 muskets, 200 braces of cavalry pistols, 100 butcher knives, and 1,000 tomahawks. To ensure knowledge of proper discipline, the council also ordered 100 copies of Scott's *Infantry Drill*, 26 of Crop's *Discipline and Regulations*, and 36 of McCombs's *School of the Soldier*. Clearly, Texian leaders envisioned a war waged not by untrained militiamen but by regulars schooled in linear tactics, hence the artillery and the emphasis on muskets over rifles. Even so, as one student of the General Council has observed, the regular army consisted of "elaborate plans, numerous officers, and empty ranks." While the delegates at San Felipe envisioned an army of well-trained and splendidly equipped regulars, the rowdy and ragged Texian volunteers outside Béxar shivered around their campfires and coped with harsh reality.[21]

With the onset of cold weather, sickness swept the Texian army, compounding existent problems. Little could be done for the afflicted. The rebels lacked even the most basic needs. A frustrated Austin lamented: "There is no medicine in camp—and so far as I am informed, none on the way—There are no surgical instruments nor bandages, nor materials for making lint, nor anything else to provide for the sick and wounded."[22]

Even Austin was ill. His two years' imprisonment in Mexico had ruined his health, and the rigors of command had weakened him to the extent that Simon, his body servant, had to assist him to mount a horse. His letters to the government in San Felipe abounded with references to his poor health. On November 8, he wrote: "I believe that my worn out constitution is not adapted to a military command, neither have I ever pretended to be a military man." Modest and deferential by nature, Austin was normally among the first to point out his shortcomings, even though such forthrightness did little to inspire confidence in his men.[23]

The continued lack of necessities vexed Austin, who attempted to prevent the men from wasting their few provisions. "The public service and the welfare of evry individual in the army requires that all our resources and especially the corn should be economized and saved as much as possible," he told them. To keep cavalry mounts fit for service required enormous amounts of fodder. Austin admonished his captains to "take special care that their men do not feed on the ground which produces great waste, but that they feed on a blanket or skin, or in a small bag hung below the horses mouth."[24]

On November 18, Austin received notification from San Felipe that he had been appointed a commissioner to the United States and was formally relieved of command of the Army of the People. An ordinary man would have rejoiced at the opportunity to leave a position that daily undermined his health. But Stephen Fuller Austin was no ordinary man. "Some prudence," he explained, "will be necessary to keep this army together should I leave at once." Personal considerations bowed to an overriding sense of duty; he would not abandon a post where he thought his presence was required.[25]

Austin had hoped to storm Béxar before he departed, and signs were encouraging. Captain Thomas H. Breece's company of New Orleans Greys had just arrived, bringing two cannon with them. Raised and equipped in Louisiana by the German-born Adolphus Sterne of Nacogdoches, the company was well armed with common rifles. Resplendent in their gray U.S. army surplus uniforms and caps, they at least looked like soldiers. Austin was further encouraged when Mexican deserters reported that the siege was taking its toll. Inside Béxar, morale was at a low ebb, and desertions were frequent. Fugitive Mexicans also reported that on November 14 Colonel Ugartechea had slipped out with some one hundred dragoons. The purpose of his mission was unclear, but he had vowed to return. The obvious conclusion was that he had gone for reinforcements. Austin knew that there would likely not be a better time to storm the town. His own army might be on the verge of disintegration, but the enemy's situation seemed worse. Writing the Consultation on November 18, he indicated that he favored an assault. "The works are stronger than they were," he admitted, "but are greatly extended, and consequently the defending force is very much scattered." He concluded that the Mexican garrison, cut off from supplies and reinforcements, was "very much discouraged" and viewed the contest as hopeless.[26]

The Texians had even acquired several pieces of artillery. Insurgent artillerymen placed the one captured at Concepción in a battery constructed west of the Alamo. Inexperienced cannoneers engaged in "lively chatter" as they placed bets on the accuracy of their fire. "A hundred neat and handy musket balls against twenty," one offered, "that I hit the old barracks between the third and fourth windows." The man fired, missed, and spent the next day casting bullets. Not to be outdone, another shouted, "My pistols—by the way, the best in the place—against the worst ones in camp." The redoubtable Erastus ("Deaf") Smith accepted the wager, and after the next shot, the pistols were his. "Look here, friend," Smith generously replied, "I will also fire the gun once. If I miss my aim, then I'll return your pistols." He carefully sighted his cannon; one witness theorized that, since Smith was hard of hearing, "the noisy bustle in the redoubt left him undisturbed." When Smith was ready, he touched off the gun, and the cannonball struck the designated spot amid a crash of falling masonry. His marksmanship was met by the unanimous applause of his comrades. The wily scout presumably kept the pistols.[27]

The artillery fire, however, accomplished "little more than the trouble and expense of making a great noise" and could not root the enemy out of Béxar. Events called for decisive leadership, and Austin was acting the part of a commanding general—but too late.

On November 21, without asking for recommendations or permission, he ordered the army to prepare "for the purpose of storming Béxar to-morrow morning." But that afternoon, he received reports from Colonel Edward Burleson and Lieutenant Colonel Philip Sublett.

Both stated that the men, who were just weeks before clamoring for a fight, were now opposed to the attack and refused to participate. The army had lost confidence in Austin; no more than a hundred soldiers would follow their commander. Crestfallen, Austin countermanded his order. The siege might have to be abandoned. The next day, in a letter to his brother-in-law James F. Perry, Austin's personal dejection was apparent but even more so was his selflessness. "I have done the best I could," he reported. "This army has always been composed of discordant materials, and is without proper organization—The volunteer sistem will not do for such a service, I have had a hard and difficult task to perform— and *am really so worn out*, that *I begin to require rest*—I could have been of more use in the convention than here—and I can be of service to Texas by going to the U.S. and I wish to go there."[28]

Time had come for a change of command; the men knew it and so did Austin. On the morning of November 24, the general paraded his army for the last time and then asked the troops how many were willing to maintain the siege. Some 405 pledged to remain under a leader of their choosing. In a vote taken that afternoon, forty-two-year-old Colonel Edward Burleson was elected. Like his predecessor, he had little formal military training, but he had earned a reputation as a ranger captain and Indian fighter.

The men also elected Francis (Frank) W. Johnson as adjutant and in-spector general and asked William T. Austin to retain his post as aide-de-camp. The following day a weary Stephen F. Austin rode out of camp north toward San Felipe and the United States.[29]

Some present suspected that Austin had been undermined by intrigue. Although Houston had been expressly denied control of Austin's army, he had often made his opinions known to certain of its members. On November 13, he had written Fannin, asking rhetorically: "Wou'd it not be best to raise a nominal siege:—fall back to Labehai [La Bahía] and Gonzales, leaving a sufficient force for protection of the frontier (which by the bye, will not be invaded) furlough the balance of the army to comfortable homes, and when the Artillery is in readiness, march to the combat with sufficient force and at once reduce San Antonio!"[30]

William T. Austin and others alleged that Judge Advocate General William H. Wharton had passed along Austin's plans to his close friend Houston, and together they had plotted to subvert them. Many other officers, including Sublett, Fannin, and Bowie, were also Houston men. This view was supported when Sublett called the men together to read Houston's letter describing the folly of an assault on Béxar, even as Austin was making preparations for the attack. About the same time, the ambitious Fannin had written to Houston, accepting his offer of a commission in the regular army. He took the opportunity to ingratiate himself with his new commander by informing him that his strategy of retiring beyond the Guadalupe River "would meet with but little oppo-sition." Fannin, clearly a young man on the make, had admitted to Houston that Béxar probably *could* be taken, but obsequiously added that he would support whatever "you think best for the common cause." Following his resignation, James Bowie had ridden to San Felipe, where he spent much of his time "dead drunk." While at the Consultation he had probably tilted a jug or two with his friend Sam Houston. Soon afterward he returned to Béxar—many believed, as Houston's agent. Perhaps Austin also thought that, because, as a final order as commander, he dispatched Bowie to supervise the strengthening of the fortifications at La Bahía. Major General Houston had no need to rush to the army encamped around Béxar; his cronies there kept him well informed.

Not surprisingly, William T. Austin was certain that the mutiny of November 23 had been spawned by "designing persons from motives of ambition and jealousy." Nor was he alone in that assessment. On October 28, Houston arrived in Gonzales, where, according to Austin colonists George Huff and Spencer H. Jack, "his conduct . . . evidenced the most discontented & envious of spirits mixed with the most unmeasured vanity." Huff and Jack apprised the Council that Houston had "in the course of two or three hours stay in this Town done more to convince every reflecting mind, that he is a vain, ambitious, envious, disappointed, discontented man, who desires the defeat of our army [outside Béxar]— that he may be appointed to the command of the next. We make this statement not to create division in your councils," the pair pledged, "but to warn the friends of the country against the insidious attempts of designing and ambitious men who have an eye to their own ambitious projects rather than to the good of the country—We have mentioned but one name—ther[e] are others who may truly be styled traitors in the ranks—but these are the mere hangers on of the above named individual."[31]

Although Texian leadership had changed, conditions had not. On November 26, Wharton wrote, "The army is much in want of coffee, sugar, flour, tobacco, clothing, etc., and if not furnished as soon as possible, great and just dissatisfaction will ensue." Public support for the revolt, like the men's morale, also seemed to be waning. Complaining of the general apathy, one disgusted patriot reported, "People seams very indiferent respecting the situation of the country, they feell no dispostion to assist in conveying the things to the army, and it is discouraging to be with them." Burleson began to believe that Houston's strategy of withdrawal and consolidation might be best after all. Before that move could be made, however, the Mexicans altered the course of events.[32]

On the morning of November 26, Texian scout "Deaf" Smith dashed into camp to report that he had just sighted an enemy column advancing northward on the old Presidio Road. As that news filtered among the men, the cry "Ugartechea!" resounded through the camp. This was, of course, a reference to Colonel Domingo Ugartechea and his hundred dragoons who were said to have gone for reinforcements on November 14, twelve days earlier. Ever since Mexican deserters had informed the Texians of that party's departure, Smith and the other scouts had been on the lookout for its return. Smith reported that he had counted more than a hundred men and as many pack animals.[33]

The monotonous siege had made the Texians especially susceptible to wild talk. A rumor quickly circulated that the mule train carried a fortune in silver intended to pay the Béxar garrison. According to Creed Taylor, "all was excitement and activity" as the thoughts of the rebels were filled with "visions of suddenly acquired wealth." Such behavior was understandable, for, as Taylor explained, the volunteers were fighting without pay and "ready to take any chance in attacking and appropriating the Mexican army chest."[34]

Burleson urged caution. If this were Ugartechea with a relief column, the pack train would not be with the vanguard unless it was a ruse to lure Texians into an ambuscade. With some effort, Burleson managed to keep the entire army from storming out of camp. Burleson dispatched James Bowie, who had yet to obey Austin's instructions to go to La Bahía; he was to take a hundred mounted men to reconnoiter the Mexican column but not to attack unless he deemed it wise.[35]

Given Bowie's combative nature, the men had little doubt that he would deem it wise. He had, after all, called on "Deaf" Smith for twelve of his best marksmen and boldest riders. Then he recruited Henry Karnes, the sharp-eyed sentry of Concepción, and Bowie's detachment galloped hell-for-leather out of camp. Those left behind were suddenly struck by the fear that they were about to be beaten out of their fair share of the booty. That thought was like a torch applied to a loaded cannon. "Without orders or leave," most of the volunteers grabbed their weapons and followed in Bowie's dusty wake.[36]

The mounted company intercepted the "treasure train" about a mile south of Béxar along Alazán Creek; true to character, Bowie charged. At first the odds were fairly even, since on horseback the Texians could not bring their cumbersome long rifles to bear. Sweeping down on the Mexican outriders, they hacked and slashed, cut and ran—Texian pistol and Bowie knife against Mexican saber and lance. At length, the Mexican dragoons fell back to a dry creekbed where they assumed a defensive posture. General Cós, observing the skirmish from the town, could see that they were in trouble and ordered infantry to the aid of his dragoons.[37]

Upon the arrival of the Mexican infantrymen, Bowie's contingent found themselves outnumbered and outgunned. Hard pressed, he ordered his men to take cover in another arroyo. The Mexicans charged three times but were repulsed by accurate rifle fire.[38]

At that juncture, the rest of the Texian army arrived on the field. The rebel infantrymen, under William H. Jack, advanced "in tolerably good order" in a double file when they were "saluted" by a discharge of enemy muskets. The Mexicans were, rifleman Robert Hancock Hunter reported, "backed down in the hollow, which was a bout 10 or 12 feet deep." The two forces were no more than fifteen feet apart, but the Mexicans were completely hidden by dense mesquite brush. Three volleys were exchanged while Bowie and Jack prepared to attack.[39]

According to their plan, the Texians then moved forward in a double envelopment. Sweeping around both enemy flanks, they soon cleared the hollow of all Mexicans "except their dead and wounded." The combined force of Bowie and Jack pursued the retreating enemy within three hundred yards of the town, where they encountered yet a second column of Mexican reinforcements from Béxar, this time armed with two field cannon.[40]

The initiative shifted to the Mexicans, who opened fire with their artillery at a range of about 140 yards. The insurgents again dove for cover in a dry gulch and continued to maintain their ground.[41]

Cós and his men dared not assault. They knew that it would be costly to match their inaccurate muskets against rebel rifles. Abandoning the pack train, the Mexican artillerymen loosed a final salvo at the Texians. Under cover of this fire, the remaining infantry withdrew to the protection of the town's barricades, leaving the Texians in "quiet possession of the field."[42]

Eager volunteers rushed to examine the captured "treasure train," but they were sorely disappointed. Ransacking the packs, they found no silver, only freshly cut grass. Texians, with much self-derision, labeled the ludicrous affair the Grass Fight. The train had not been Ugartechea's vanguard, but only a party sent out that morning to cut fodder for the garrison's starving cavalry mounts.[43]

Most volunteers were chagrined, but the more thoughtful realized the import of their discovery. The siege was working. If Cós had been forced to risk sending out a party to acquire feed for his animals, he must be desperate. The loss of the fodder was more damaging to the Mexican garrison than if it had been silver; hungry horses could not eat *pesos*.

The significance of the foraging party was clear, but it was more difficult to assess the outcome of the confused melee. Casualty figures varied wildly from one report to the next. In a dispatch to the provisional government, Burleson reported one man missing and four slightly wounded. Bowie claimed that as many as sixty Mexicans had been killed. Texas historian Henderson Yoakum placed the count at two Texians wounded and some fifty Mexicans killed. Alwyn Barr, a modern student of the campaign fixes the number of Mexican dead at three. Participant Creed Taylor admitted that he did not know the exact number of enemy casualties, and neither, he suggested, did anyone else. "We were more intent upon securing the treasure than in capturing the frightened 'greasers' and so let them escape with their dead and wounded comrades."[44]

As all of their injuries were minor, the Texian wounded became the butt of raucous jests. A spent musket ball had bounced off the forehead of one of the volunteers, leaving him with a powerful headache. "Hello, pard. What are you doing," one of his buddies inquired, "Catching your brains in your hands?"[45]

In his absence, the one missing man also provided much humorous speculation. He supposedly became "so frightened or excited during the melee that he actually ran on foot at breakneck speed, and never halted until he reached the settlements."[46]

Although the Texians seemed to enjoy the Grass Fight, it in no way improved their logistical situation. In a dispatch to the provisional government, James B. Patrick and William Pettus reported "much dissatisfaction and inquietude pervading the army." Corn was so scarce that many volunteers sent their horses home. Despite the lack of almost everything required to continue the siege, more than 450 men vowed to stay until they took San Antonio. Patrick and Pettus concluded that, if the volunteers were supplied, "no fears can be entertained of their abandoning the siege of Baxar." But the makeshift government in San Felipe lacked the wherewithal to procure the needed supplies. Even if it could secure the crucial provender, it probably could not get them to the soldiers in time.[47]

The provisional government had no choice but to continue depending on volunteers, for, despite its grand plans and lofty expectations, few

Texians could be induced to join the regular army. Houston was able to commission several officers but found few men willing to serve in ranks. Texian settlers had not yet faced up to their perilous situation; they had family responsibilities and did not want to be away from home for extended periods. Most carefree volunteers from the United States shunned the discipline of regular army life. In a November 29 letter to Houston, Major Robert C. Morris of the New Orleans Greys reported that "there are now here 225 men, nearly all from the U.S. who on no consideration will enter into any service connected with the Regular Army, the name of which is a perfect Bugbear to them."[48]

He also revealed another potential source of trouble for the Texians. Many U.S. volunteers had come in search of high adventure and quick wealth but had found neither around Béxar. Some were already casting about for a more profitable campaign. Scottish-born James Grant had been calling for volunteers for an expedition to Matamoros. Morris, after declining a commission in the regular army, informed Houston that he intended to lead his men on the proposed journey to Matamoros on November 30. He reported that the Greys expected to be joined by about 100 to 150 American recruits then on the road to San Antonio. If Burleson did not take Béxar soon, he might not have enough soldiers to do so later.[49]

The Matamoros venture was delayed, however, when Burleson hinted that a fight was in the offing. Prospects for a successful attack on Béxar improved on December 1, when the Mexicans released Samuel Maverick and two other U.S. citizens who had been held inside the town. The next day, they reported that the Mexican garrison was much weakened and urged an immediate assault. Burleson announced that operations would begin at four o'clock the following morning.[50]

But as the moment of decision approached, several officers informed General Burleson that "a majority of the officers & men comprising their divisions were opposed, and unwilling to attempt an attack on the fortifications of San Antonio." Burleson, the old ranger captain, favored a fight, but following much discussion those in attendance voted to postpone the attack for an indefinite period. Against his combative nature, the general "acquiesed." Burleson canceled the attack only after his officers overruled him by a nearly unanimous vote. He then ordered a parade for ten o'clock the morning of December 3.[51]

As word of the postponement filtered through the camp, men who had spent the day mentally preparing for battle collapsed into a state of near mutiny. Entire companies failed to turn out for the morning parade. Rifleman Frank Sparks recalled how the men of his company "had no notion of retreating, many openly informing the officers that they had come to whip the Mexicans, and if they could not fight, they would go home, as they did not propose to remain in an army that ran away every time it saw a Mexican." Between 250 and 300 volunteers departed for home; others berated their officers; and more than a few got blind drunk. Maverick's diary tells the sad tale: "All day we get more and more dejected. The Gen'l mustered the remaining men and begged them to not all go; but some stay and retreat with the cannon to La Bahia. A retreat seems our only recourse. The spectacle becomes appalling."[52]

The siege of Béxar, at last so close to success, was in danger of being abandoned. Texian volunteers had been encamped around the town for about seven weeks, during which time they had defeated the Mexicans in every engagement, switched commanders, and consumed inordinate amounts of corn liquor. But for all of that, Cós and his men were still secure behind their defenses. Burleson could control the frontier rowdies no better than Austin, and with "Matamoros fever" infecting the army, he was forced to admit that Houston was correct when he argued that the siege should be called off. Possibly the army should retire to winter camp either at Gonzales or Goliad and wait for spring, when it could resume the war with trained men, larger cannon, better weather, and fuller bellies.[53]

On December 4, with his army melting around him, Burleson announced his decision to abandon the siege and go into winter quarters at Goliad. He offered the excuse that the army could not attack in the absence of freedman Hendrick Arnold, one of the guides. He added that the Mexican garrison had learned of the impending assault. This then was to be the conclusion of seven weeks of boredom—to turn tail with the enemy on the verge of surrender.[54]

For the first time since the fighting began at Gonzales, Texians had to admit that they were beaten, not by the enemy, but by their own disorganization and discord. Even so, the withdrawal orders were far from being universally approved; one witness recalled that "the scene was wholly indescribable, and serious apprehensions were entertained that our camp would become the theatre of blood." A few officers attempted to maintain order but, as A. H. Jones, the cocky veteran of Nueces Crossing, reported: "All was in vain; no persuasion had any weight; a great many mounted their horses and left Camp, expecting a total defeat." The

Texians were humiliated at the thought of what seemed to many to be retreat, but given their prospects, abandoning the siege was the only practical course.[55]

At times such as these, a leader strong of will and firm of purpose has occasionally been able to capture the imaginations of men, inspire a discouraged army, and turn defeat into victory. At this crucial juncture, such a man rode into the crumbling Texian camp outside Béxar and changed the course of Texas history.

CHAPTER 5

"Crude Bumpkins, Proud and Overbearing"

❖

The Storming of Béxar
December 5–9, 1835

From about 1670 to 1850, the smooth-bore, muzzle-loading flintlock musket served as the basic infantry weapon. Few notable differences existed between the muskets employed by European armies. The main long arm of the Mexican line infantry — the .753 caliber British India Pattern Brown Bess musket — was typical of those used throughout the world during the 1830s. Indeed, the same weapons used at Waterloo in 1815 likely saw action during the siege of Béxar in 1835. Although it could not match the Kentucky long rifle's accuracy, Brown Bess was a sturdy and reliable weapon in the hands of a disciplined infantryman. Yet to instruct a recruit to maneuver and fight in linear formation was an intricate task. For a man to prime, load, and fire his musket quickly and efficiently required almost constant drill. Nineteen specific actions were required for every round fired. Moreover, the soldier had to follow the sequence in cadence with the rest of the firing line.

To discharge his musket, the veteran of the Matamoros Battalion depicted in Gary Zaboly's reconstruction: (1) Removes his musket from the shoulder and holds it laterally across his body. (2) Draws the hammer to the safety, or "half-cock," position. (3) Wipes powder residue and fouling from the pan with the right thumb; if severely fouled, he clears the pan and touchhole with a vent pick and brush. (4) Holds the musket in his left hand while he removes a cartridge from his pouch with his right. The cartridge pouch has a deep flap of leather, and single rounds were kept in a wooden block. Dropping, or even fumbling, a round could throw a man off his rhythm. (5) Raises the cartridge to his mouth. (6) Ensures that he has identified the correct end (the cartridge has a ball end and a powder end, which is folded over) and tears off the folded end of the paper tube between his teeth, a process that required recruiting sergeants to carefully check the teeth of any potential recruit. (7) Taps a small portion of the cartridge's powder into the open firing pan. (8) Closes the metal frizzen over the priming powder in the pan. (9) Grounds the butt of the musket against his left foot. (10) Pours the remaining cartridge powder down the muzzle. If a veteran noncommis-

sioned officer were not present, soldados *who objected to the "kick" of the Brown Bess would attempt to spill the greater portion of their powder during this step. Any recruit detected intentionally spilling powder might expect the sergeant's wooden staff across the back of his neck. Yet much of the Mexican powder was so defective that* soldados *would often double charge their muskets. (11) Presses the ball, still in its paper tube, into the muzzle. The paper acts as a "wad," ensuring a tight fit. (12) Draws the ramrod upward from the "pipes" (the holding slot beneath the barrel). (13) When the ramrod is clear from the pipes, the* soldado *turns it around so that the bell-shaped end is pointing down. (14) He places the bell-shaped end of the ramrod in the muzzle and jams ball and paper into a "seat," compressing the powder charge. (15) He withdraws the ramrod and reverses it again. (16) Slides the ramrod back into the pipes. (17) On command, the* soldado *lifts his musket to the firing position. (18) The hammer is drawn back from "half-cock" to the "full-cock" position. The weapon is now primed, loaded, and ready to discharge. (19) On the command, "Fuego," the* soldado *squeezes the trigger. Following "hang fire," which could last a full second or more, the priming in the pan flares in a lingering explosion; sparks travel through the touchhole to ignite the main charge. If each step has been followed exactly and if the powder is not too damp or too old, the weapon will discharge in a cloud of smoke and flame. Nevertheless, a man could perform each procedure precisely and still accomplish nothing more than a "flash in the pan."*

In the midst of battle, soldados *commonly made mistakes. The chance of misfire increased with each shot fired; expended gunpowder fouled the pan, touchhole, and barrel. After repeated vollies, men had to halt firing to clear the pan and touchhole with brush and vent pick. After twelve or so rounds, flints became chipped or shifted in the jaws of the cock, necessitating adjustment or replacement. Agitated recruits might load two, or even three, cartridges atop one another without bothering to fire. At other times, they neglected to remove their ramrods and the discharge sent them whirling across the battlefield. Without its ramrod, the musket, and consequently the soldier, was useless.*

Even when the loading procedure had been followed to the letter, wind and humidity often conspired to render a musket ineffectual. Rain and snow blew into the cartridge box, spoiling gunpowder. An eighteenth-century Prussian proverb drolly described the bane of all flintlock soldiers: "Alle Kunst ist unsonst, Wenn ein Engel in das Zundloch prunst" ("*All skill is for nought when an angel pisses down your touch-hole*"). *Men were careful to cover their locks and muzzles with oilcloth or rags when on the march or in camp. On a blustery day, powder would be blown from the pan before the frizzen could be lowered to secure it.*

Soldados *might survive the effects of Texian rifles but fall victim to their own muskets. Burning powder and wadding discharged from the guns of soldiers in the rear ranks frequently fell on the necks of the hapless elements of the front rank. Men in rear ranks, furthermore, routinely blistered those in front when they propped their hot muskets against them. On other occasions, a raw recruit misjudged the recoil of his Brown Bess, which pitched sideways, whacking the man beside him. Smoldering priming powder in the pan could produce crippling injuries; scorched cheeks and ears were occupational hazards for the black-powder soldier.*

"Crude Bumpkins, Proud and Overbearing"

BEN MILAM WAS OUTRAGED. He was not certain how it had happened, but the army had become a disorganized, leaderless mob while he had been on a scout of the area south of Béxar. Returning on December 4, he found the Texians about to break camp, abandon the siege, and go into winter quarters. Seething, Milam sought out Colonel Frank W. Johnson to find out who was responsible for this indignity.[1]

He found Johnson. Those nearby reported that their conversation was somewhat "animated." Milam convinced Johnson that the siege must be maintained. Johnson agreed that leaving was the wrong course but said that Burleson had already issued the order and that many volunteers had accordingly left. Milam found that argument unacceptable. If Burleson had issued the order, Burleson could countermand it. Soon afterward, Creed Taylor observed Milam and Johnson "walking rapidly in the direction of the commander's quarters."[2]

Determined not to throw away the results of weeks of campaigning, the two angry men burst into the general's tent and closed the flap behind them. Sensing decision in the making, soldiers halted their packing and milled around Burleson's tent. "Minutes now passed as hours," one impatient volunteer noted; behind those canvas walls, weighty matters were being discussed. Burleson informed Johnson that he also favored continuing the siege but that the last council of war had overruled him. With the majority of the Texian officers against continuing the campaign, a withdrawal to Goliad seemed prudent. Milam and Johnson argued that, given the reported weakness of the enemy, they should attempt an assault. If it failed, the men could at least leave in good conscience.[3]

At length, the Texian leaders reached a compromise. Milam could call for volunteers to storm the town. If a sufficient number responded, Burleson would hold the remainder in camp to cover a retreat in case the attack failed.[4]

Ben Milam shouldered the full responsibility and prepared to attack the following morning. Outside the tent, he confronted anxious soldiers clustered nearby awaiting the news. "Who will follow old Ben Milam into San Antonio?" he challenged. "I will, I will," the men responded. But enthusiasm was by no means universal. With many of the men already gone, several considered it rash to confront the entrenched Mexicans with "so small and unprepared a force." Of the more than five hundred Texians who remained in camp, only three hundred answered Milam's call.[5]

The others became Burleson's reserve force. Some had elaborate excuses for staying behind. One malcontent who for weeks had been advocating retreat whined, "I wouldn't mind going with you fellows, but I have no gun. My horse fell with me yesterday and broke the stock of my rifle." Colonel Johnson called his bluff. No matter, he told the man, "we'll take you along to cut bullet patchin'." Every soldier within earshot roared with laughter, and for years afterward the slacker was known as Ol' Bullet Patchin'.[6]

Milam labored under no delusions. He knew only a diversion would buy the surprise necessary for his infantry to penetrate the outer defenses. The Mexican morale might be at a low ebb, but they still had the advantage of a strong position, numbers, and artillery. J. C. Neill, a veteran artilleryman and experienced Indian fighter from Alabama, was called on to distract Cós's attention with a feint on the Alamo. Neill bore a heavy responsibility. If his diversion was in any way unconvincing, it might result in the wholesale slaughter of the Texian assault force.[7]

Before the Texians entered the town, they had to be organized into assault units. Milam had earlier toyed with the notion of three divisions, but he abandoned the plan as too cumbersome. He finally settled on two columns, with a small utility detachment as a mobile reserve. Simplicity was crucial when dealing with ill-disciplined, untrained volunteers. Milam commanded the first division, aided by Major Robert C. Morris; Colonel Frank Johnson headed the second, assisted by Aide-de-Camp William T. Austin and Dr. James Grant.[8]

Unfamiliar with the approaches into Béxar, and having to enter it in the predawn darkness, Milam enlisted the services of some of the locals as guides. One of them, Erastus ("Deaf") Smith, seemed an unlikely soldier. A native of New York, he had lived quietly with his Mexican wife and their four children in a home below Mission San José. Smith cared more about his Louisiana muley cattle than he did about politics. Even after his countrymen had surrounded the town, he sought to avoid being drawn into the conflict. But as Smith returned home one day, a squad of Mexican dragoons attempted to take him captive; one struck him in the head with a saber, knocking off his hat and wounding him slightly. That settled it. If Cós and his kind prevented an honest family man from returning to his wife and children, he would support the rebels. At first, many had wondered if Smith, at age forty-eight and hard of hearing, would be able to bear the rigors of combat, but that was before they saw him in action at Concepción and in the Grass Fight. Along with neighbor Samuel Maverick, Smith now guided Johnson's division through the darkness toward his hometown. Hendrick Arnold, a free man of color and "Deaf" Smith's son-in-law, and John W. Smith, a local carpenter, guided Milam's division. The last guide came from an unexpected quarter. Jesús Cuellar, a Mexican officer and sincere federalist, had deserted Cós to fight with the Texians. A native of Béxar, he had once been an Indian captive, hence his nickname of "Comanche."⁹

In the early morning hours of December 5, as Milam and Johnson took their respective units into position, Neill took one gun and its crew across the San Antonio River and within range of the Alamo. His was a dangerous assignment, for once on the enemy side of the river, Neill's contingent was isolated and exposed. A small number of infantrymen accompanied Neill's gun crew, but if the Mexicans counterattacked in force, the protection that they could provide would be token at best. An hour before daylight, Neill primed his cannon to fire the signal shot for Milam's and Johnson's forces to enter the town.¹⁰

While Neill's crew manhandled their gun into position, the Texian infantry huddled in the cold dark. Milam's division was composed of six companies under Captains John York, William Patton, Thomas Llewellyn, John Crane, George English, and William Landrum. They had been instructed to rush into town via Acequia Street and take possession of the Garza house. Johnson's division, consisting of the companies of Captains William Cooke, James G. Swisher, H. H. Edwards, Thomas Alley, Peter J. Duncan, J. W. Peacock, Thomas J. Breece, and Plácido Benavides, was to charge down Soledad Street to the Veramendi house. Texian officers ordered complete silence; the only sounds were the mournful howl of the north wind and the routine shouts of "*centinela alerta*" (all's well) from the Mexican sentries around the Alamo. The tension was almost unbearable for the shivering rebels impatiently listening for the sound of Neill's cannon.[11]

Finally, about five o'clock, it came. More important than the boom of the cannon itself was the reaction of the enemy. Herman Ehrenberg and the other attackers listened intently, wondering whether the Mexicans would take the bait. "The hollow roar of our cannon was followed by the brisk rattling of drums and the shrill blasts of the bugles. Summons, cries, the sudden trampling of feet, the metallic click of weapons mingled in the distance with the heavy rumblings of the artillery. Our friends had done the trick." As soon as Milam and Johnson were convinced that the Mexicans had directed their attentions toward the Alamo, they ordered their contingents to move out toward their assigned objectives.[12]

The diversion had worked to perfection, allowing both divisions to enter Béxar unopposed. As Johnson's men dashed toward the town, they noticed several Mexicans huddled around a fire in the distance. Apparently the benumbed sentries had not seen the Texians, some of whom advocated ambushing them. Cuellar, however, cautioned against it. Even if the insurgents picked off all the enemy sentinels, he argued, the rifle fire would alert other Mexicans. Convinced, the Texians bypassed the sentries and moved on. Minutes later, the two groups penetrated Béxar's defenses and cautiously made their way unopposed toward the central plaza. The men fanned out and rushed down the streets with a renewed urgency, for all knew that every yard gained inside the town increased the odds against the Mexicans being able to dislodge them. Milam and Johnson were enormously relieved; they had brought off the most difficult parts of their plan without a hitch. How much longer could such luck hold?[13]

Not long. Johnson's men had almost reached the Veramendi house when a Mexican sentinel fired on them. Taking some measure of recompense for the earlier loss of his hat, "Deaf" Smith shot him dead. When the invaders were only two hundred yards from the central plaza, the Mexicans, at last fully aware of their presence, greeted them with canister. At such close range, the Mexican artillery fire was devastating; the narrow streets increased the problem for the Texians, for they could do nothing to avoid the flying metal but press their bodies flat against the building walls. Staying in the open was certain death, so the rebels broke down doors and took refuge inside the homes of startled Béxar citizens. Frank Sparks described how "men, women and children began to run out, in their night clothes and unarmed." The easy part of the assault was over. Subsequently, the fighting would be street to street, house to house, and in some cases, room to room.[14]

This glimpse-and-snipe combat gave the Texians the advantage. The Mexicans were armed with Brown Bess muskets, which had been designed for open field volley fire, not for sniping. Even if the bullets did manage to hit their targets, Mexican gunpowder had not improved since Concepción, and on more than one occasion the shots simply bounced off the Texians. Many of the insurgents, on the other hand, were armed with Kentucky long rifles, lethal and accurate up to two hundred yards. For close combat, double-barrel shotguns loaded with "buck and ball" proved effective. Creed Taylor remembered the "constant shower of balls in our direction" and remarked thankfully that if the enemy "had been trained marksmen, armed with anything but the 'escopeta,' few of us would have escaped death." Cós's soldiers were not so lucky. "No sooner did a head appear above the wall," Taylor boasted, "than it was the target for a dozen hunting rifles, and there was always another dead Mexican." In the days to come, however, the Texians would discover that the few Mexicans armed with British Baker rifles were equally deadly marksmen.[15]

Each house served as a self-contained fort. Because of the danger of Indian forays, the buildings had been constructed of thick adobe walls, with heavy oak doors and few windows. Since the streets were abuzz with enemy lead, the Texians could do little more than attempt to hold on to those strongholds like the Veramendi house that they had already captured. They secured buildings against counterattacks by bolstering the windows and doors with pieces of timber and sandbags. The insurgents knew, however, that they could not remain long on the defensive in the captured dwellings. Sooner or later, regardless of the heavy Mexican fire, they would have to mount an offensive. An idea emerged. Most Béxar houses had parapets rising two or three feet above the roof, and the rebel riflemen thought to use them for cover. Locating a ladder, a few of the Texians climbed up to the rooftops.[16]

The plan, while good in concept, failed in execution. Once on top of the houses, the men found that many of the parapets were too low to offer sufficient cover. The Mexicans, who had already taken to the rooftops, directed their fire at the exposed Texians. "Deaf" Smith and New Orleans Greys Lieutenant John L. Hall took to the roof of the Veramendi house in search of snipers, but the enemy sharpshooters found them first.

Both Smith and Hall were wounded for their efforts. Ehrenberg recalled that his comrades were especially vulnerable to Mexican sharpshooters stationed in the bell tower of San Fernando Church. From that height, Cós's snipers commanded a clear view of their enemies on the roofs below. Nor could the Texians fire back effectively; stiff gusts of wind from the norther that had blown in that morning swept the powder out of the pans of their long rifles. Within minutes most of the rebels on the rooftops had been wounded, some severely. Since many of the injured were unable to climb down the ladders, their comrades tore a hole in the ceiling of one building and lowered them by rope to the rooms below.[17]

On other rooftops, the rebels hacked through ceilings in an attempt to get at the ensconced centralists. That tactic was especially nerveracking, for when a man dropped through a hole in the roof, he had no way of knowing how far it was to the floor or whether the room was full of enemy troops. Lacking rope, the men used their blankets to lower comrades through the openings. As one anonymous veteran related, such methods had their drawbacks:

> Down I went holding on tight, as I did not know how far it was to the bottom. It was an uncomfortable position to be in, but my friends did not leave me long to my apprehensions, for the blanket slipping through their grasp, down I went ten or twelve feet into the middle of a fire which was burning on the dirt floor, scattering embers and ashes in all directions. Jumping up, the first thing that met my gaze was a Mexican officer about to make an attack up on me, but jerking a pistol from my belt, I fired at him before my somewhat disordered faculties assured me that my foe was not an officer, but an officer's uniform hanging in such a position as to resemble one.[18]

Sundown brought a temporary lull in the fighting, but the first day ended in a stalemate. Milam and Johnson had gained toeholds in the town, but the determined Mexican resistance had checked their advance far short of their goals. The rebel riflemen believed that they had killed several Mexicans, but they themselves had not emerged unscathed. A head count that night revealed that four had been wounded in Milam's group. Johnson's division fared worse, with one man killed and six wounded. The Texians had also lost one of their fieldpieces when an enemy round dismounted a twelve-pounder. The other artillery was little used inside the town for want of proper cover. By this time, it was apparent that they could root the Mexicans out of Béxar only by hand-to-hand fighting, one house at a time.[19]

Not all in the Texas army were accustomed to fighting on foot. The federalist *tejanos* were known for their expertise as mounted lancers, not as footsloggers. Early in the siege, Austin, recognizing the value of their equestrian skill, had called upon Plácido Benavides and his *rancheros*. He had also appointed Juan Seguín a captain of cavalry, with instructions to raise a company of horse. In addition to scouting the approaches to Béxar, the *tejano* riders had burned the grass along the roads leading to the town. Half-starved horses would be of little use; by depriving the enemy cavalry of forage, Seguín had displayed a shrewd understanding of mounted warfare. The Anglo-Celtic Texians marveled at *tejano* horsemanship. One volunteer observed that "we were all I suppose pretty good horsemen, as the term is understood in the 'old States,'" but after seeing the Texas Mexicans break a herd of wild mustangs, he admitted that the "rancheros . . . are unsurpassed by any people in horsemanship." There was, however, no place for cavalry in this bitter street fighting. Such being the fortunes of war, at least sixty-seven *tejanos* tethered their mounts and shouldered muskets to join Anglo-Celtic comrades as infantry. After experiencing the dangers of the first day's fighting, many of the newly initiated infantrymen no doubt yearned to be back astride their horses.[20]

Cavalry may have been useless in the street fighting, but it served well on the outskirts of town. Throughout the siege, mounted contingents had been kept busy patrolling the perimeter around Béxar. Burleson posted "efficient mounted companies" to watch for any sign of Mexican reinforcements either from the Alamo or from the direction of the Río Grande. In addition to performing their scouting duties, Burleson's horsemen combed local ranches for food and supplies. The ranch of Erasmo Seguín supplied some $4,000 worth of grain and livestock. "In this manner," William T. Austin recorded, "our troops were furnished with an abundant supply of provisions during the engagement." Burleson was well aware that any military success that Milam's men achieved would be nullified if they lacked sufficient logistical support to enable them to hold what they had won.[21]

That night Texian leaders took stock of the situation as the men's thoughts turned to food. All day Milam and Johnson had been hampered by ignorance of each other's progress; now under cover of darkness, they opened communications between the two divisions. Burleson also ventured into town to visit Johnson and review the progress of the assault, bringing with him a supply of beef. The chow was distributed among ravenous men who ate for the first time that day. After conferring with Burleson, Johnson made his way to Milam to discuss their options. Both agreed to continue fighting. Although resistance was stronger than expected, they had managed to capture a sizable portion of the town, and the men were "not only cheerful but enthusiastic." The orders went out; they would attack again the next morning.[22]

The second day of battle dawned cold and crisp. Stubbornly clinging to the positions that they held at nightfall, both sides prepared for battle with grim determination. The Mexicans had the advantage of position, but the Texians boasted superior weaponry. Ordinarily, opposing generals weighed such tactical considerations with mathematical precision. But this was no open-field encounter where armies observed firmly established rules. This was a melee. Here adversaries grappled hand to hand, brandishing Bowie knives, bayonets, pistols, and clubbed muskets. Tactics alone would not decide this fight; the issue would be settled with fortitude, aggressiveness, and guts.[23]

With renewed resolve, the Texians made steady progress on the second day. In Milam's division, Lieutenant William McDonald led a successful assault against an enemy stronghouse and then held it in the face of repeated counterattacks. With a couple of artillery-proof stone houses under their control, the insurgents could move their cannon under cover and then direct a counterfire against Cós's forces. The going was rough: Johnson lost five men wounded, three of them severely, but miraculously none were killed. The rebel invaders of Béxar were confident. True, the fighting had been heavy, and the progress slower than expected, but their daring had proved that steady men could drive the Mexicans out of their strongholds. There could be no stopping now. The men spent that evening filling sandbags and cleaning weapons. They knew that the next day would bring more combat, and they intended to be prepared for it, but they could not anticipate the heavy price it would exact.[24]

The Mexican infantry also spent the night preparing for the third day, and morning revealed a new redoubt on the Alamo side of the San Antonio River. From this position, Cós's men menaced the Texian left flank with infantry, supported by artillery from the Alamo. The location proved untenable, however, as the Texians' accurate hunting rifles scoured the works, picking off many of the defenders and compelling the remainder to flee.[25]

The Béxar garrison had also been busy inside the town. On the night of December 6, the soldiers had fortified a house on the street leading to the fort, blocking the advance of Johnson's division. The next day, his men suffered terribly from the combined small arms and artillery fire directed from the enemy stronghold. It would require more than rifle fire to clear this position, and Johnson sent a runner to borrow a six-pounder from the first division. Milam dispatched it with his compliments. A short while later, the Texians placed the gun in a covered battery and hammered the enemy building with cannon balls. The dual effects of the artillery and rifle fire forced the Mexicans to withdraw their ordnance, and Johnson noted a slackening of the small arms fire. For all their defensive maneuvers and courageous resistance, the Mexicans could not halt the methodical rebel advance.[26]

With the loss of most of their vital stronghouses, the Mexicans fought with determination born of desperation. Informed of the increased resistance, Milam summoned his officers to reconnoiter the enemy positions and organize the final assault. He had entered the courtyard of the Veramendi house and was scanning the defenses through a field glass when Félix de la Garza, a marksman reputed to be "the best shot in the Mexican army" spotted him. Cós had posted sharpshooters in the trees along the river, where they had a clear view of the plaza and its environs. From that vantage point, de la Garza marked his target, aimed his Baker rifle, and fired. Milam dropped. De la Garza's shot took "Old Ben" neatly through the head, killing him instantly.[27]

Texians were stunned and enraged by news of Milam's death. Retaliation came swiftly. Someone had seen a puff of smoke from the trees just after the fatal shot, and now all eyes turned toward the river. The rebel riflemen saw the outline of a man in the branches, and several aimed and fired at once. De la Garza's corpse pitched from the tree, struck the beveled bank, and tumbled into the river. Other Mexican marksmen remained active, but Texian marksmen employed their rifles to advantage and soon cleared the treeline of snipers.[28]

But not even skillful marksmen could sweep aside covered Mexican artillery; Henry Karnes understood that. During the afternoon of December 7, the twenty-three-year-old Tennessean crouched with the rest of his company, trying to evade the relentless Mexican cannon fire. The defenders had brought up two heavy guns that now "poured an incessant storm of shot" upon the invaders and "knocked to pieces the few jacales and adobe wall" that sheltered them. Karnes, a veteran of Concepción and the Grass Fight, was no stranger to enemy fire, but he had never seen it so heavy. A large stone house stood just a few yards opposite the Texians, but the sight of an occasional shako and the large numbers of muskets protruding from the windows and atop the roof clearly revealed its occupants to be Mexican *soldados*. Another barrage buffeted the rebel position—Karnes would stand no more. "Boys, load your guns and be ready. I am going to break open that door, and I want you to pour a steady hot fire into those fellows on the roof and hold their attention until I can reach the door, and when I break it in I want you boys to make a clean dash for that house."

The men in his company thought Karnes had gone mad. "That building is full of Mexicans; don't you see the muzzles of their escopetas in the windows?" one replied. Unlike most of the coarse frontiersmen, Karnes seldom swore. This occasion, however, called for strong invective: "Damn the Mexicans and their escopetas. It's that house or retreat. You men do as I tell you." Before the startled onlookers could reply, Karnes, armed with a crowbar in one hand and a rifle in the other, sprang over the barricades and raced toward the stone building.

The bickering Texas politicians in San Felipe had not instituted medals for valor, but if they had, the actions of Henry Karnes would have earned him one that day. Observers later said that they never knew how he had survived the welter of fire directed against him. In a few seconds, Karnes reached the door of the stone building and began frantically trying to pry it open. The Mexicans on the roof could not fire directly down upon him without exposing themselves to Texian rifles. At length, the door gave way, and Karnes forced his way into the house. But he was no longer alone. Spurred by his example, many of his company charged across the street and into the building. The Mexican occupants had no wish to confront such reckless fighting men. "As we entered," one of the rebels proudly recalled, "it was amusing to see the Mexicans tear out through a partition door. Several were made prisoners, but were paroled at once, as we had no men to spare for guard duty." There would be no decoration for Karnes, but he had won the admiration and respect of his fellow soldiers.[29]

Much of the day's bloodiest fighting took place indoors. Once, some Texians occupied one part of a house while the Mexicans held the rest. With their crowbars, the insurgents tore a hole through the wall in an effort to get at their adversaries. When a small breach was opened, men quickly thrust the muzzles of their rifles through it and unleashed a rapid, indiscriminate fire. Such tactics had to be performed with dispatch lest the waiting enemy fire back through the same aperture. Rifleman Taylor explained some of the pitfalls of this room-to-room combat: "At one time, . . . while both sides were pounding away on an adobe wall, the entire partition fell in on the Mexican side. There were eighteen soldiers and a lieutenant in the room," as Taylor remembered it, "and several were borne down in the crash and some badly bruised, others were almost suffocated in the dust and rubbish. All we made prisoners and paroled in the usual manner."[30]

While the invaders filled sandbags and prepared their weapons for the following day, General Cós detailed four troops of cavalry into the open country around Béxar in the hope of finding Ugartechea's long overdue relief column. The expedition, numbering somewhere between 200 and 250 troopers, failed not only to find Ugartechea but also to return to the beleaguered town; the entire command deserted en masse and headed toward the Río Grande. News of this abandonment came as a bitter blow to the valiant Mexicans manning the barricades in Béxar.[31]

The fourth day dawned rainy and cold, dampening powder and reducing the volume of gunfire on both sides. Despite the reduced utility of their rifles, however, the insurgents pressed on relentlessly. Now within yards of Military Plaza, the last bulwark of Cós's defense, the Texians launched another attack.[32]

Although the rebels were within sight of their objective, Mexican resistance had never been stronger. Following much hard fighting, the Texians occupied the Navarro house. That afternoon, Johnson, who was elected tactical commander after Milam's death, organized a foray into an adjacent block of buildings known as Zambrano Row. Johnson admitted that its defenders doggedly disputed "every inch of ground," but finally, after suffering severe losses in officers and men, the outgunned Mexicans evacuated Zambrano Row and fell back to fortified positions in and near the square. With the Texians in such close proximity, Cós transferred his headquarters to the Alamo.[33]

Running out of places to retreat, Cós implemented a daring plan to reduce the pressure on his crumbling defenses inside Béxar. With so many rebels committed to the assault, the Texian camp must be vulnerable. If a sortie from the town could take the rebel logistical base, Johnson's men would have no alternative but to abandon the town. The plan was a gamble, but the Mexicans had few alternatives.[34]

On the afternoon of December 8, the Mexicans sallied out of Béxar

with one column of cavalry and another of infantry. Burleson was prepared for such an attempt. The enemy horsemen approached from the
west side of the river, the infantrymen, from the east. Apparently, they
planned to engulf the federalist camp in a pincer movement. With bugles
blaring and pennants flying, the Mexicans provided Burleson's men with
a rare spectacle. One of the Texians, Henry B. Dance, was deeply impressed: "It apeared we were to be swept of[f] by a general charge by the
Cavilry, infantry, and lancers, playing more music than I ever heard.
They were in a great stir, Sallying and charging."[35]

Awaiting them were J. C. Neill and his gun crews, their ordnance
packed with canister shot. As soon as the combined force approached
"within good cannon shot distance," the Texians unleashed a hailstorm
of flying metal. "The enimy being surprised to find our encampment
strong and protected by a park of artillery," reported William T. Austin,
"declined making the intended attack & suddenly drew off & retired
within his walls." Cós's only hope now rested in Ugartechea.[36]

Nor was that hope forlorn, for during the late afternoon of December 8, Ugartechea arrived with desperately needed reinforcements.
Burleson had detailed mounted companies to watch for the relief force,
but the able Ugartechea somehow managed to slip into the Alamo. Ac-
companying Ugartechea was a career officer, Lieutenant Colonel José
Juan Sánchez-Navarro of the engineers, but most of the recruits were
unwilling convicts. Sánchez-Navarro was appalled by the sights that met
him inside the Alamo. Lacking fodder, the starving cavalry mounts had
taken to "eating the capes of the troops and even the trails of the
artillery."[37]

To the dismay of Cós and the other Mexican officers, conditions worsened after the convicts were unshackled. These felons had no intention
of dying in an obscure outpost for the men who had dragged them there.
At first they merely refused to obey orders; then they insulted and later
actually assaulted the officers. As Sánchez-Navarro told it, the mis-
creants even pummeled General Cós. Indeed, the rumor spread among
the Mexican defenders in town that these worthless reprobates had mur-
dered the general. Ugartechea's purpose was to reinforce his beleaguered
comrades; instead, his rescue attempt greatly aggravated their troubles.[38]

For the Mexicans inside Béxar, the already bad situation had pro-
gressively worsened as the battle continued into the evening of December 8. Johnson and his men could now see Military Plaza; only one
remaining obstacle stood between them and it, a fortified stone building

that the locals called the Priest's house. Johnson remembered it as a "strong position on the north side, and near the northeast angle, of the civil square." The Mexicans brought up three cannon and concentrated their remaining infantry. Sánchez-Navarro bitterly complained that Ugartechea's convicts "did not even know how to load [and] they did nothing more than add to the confusion." Toward eleven o'clock, the Texians rushed the Priest's house. Johnson praised the courage and resolve of his troops who charged in so close to the enemy's artillery and musket fire that "many of the men had their whiskers and their hair burned by the blaze of the guns, but they advanced steadily and soon carried the position, which gave us command of both squares." By midnight the Priest's house belonged to the singed frontiersmen, but the fighting continued into the early morning hours.[39]

Cós considered his dwindling list of options. He could abandon the town and withdraw his remaining forces behind the walls of the Alamo, but to what purpose? His supplies were already dangerously low, and the arrival of Ugartechea's convicts constituted an increased demand on his limited resources. It would only be a matter of days, therefore, before he would have to surrender the Alamo as well. The numerous desertions, perhaps as many as three hundred, had lowered morale. Sánchez-Navarro overheard troops who for days had offered staunch resistance now asking, "What shall we do?" and muttering, "We are lost." The engineer officer, after a perfunctory inspection of the town's remaining defenses, reported that "it was impossible to defend such an extended position with so few troops as were in the square and much less with troops in such poor state as arrived with me. Besides there were no provisions nor hopes that any help might come."[40]

During the early morning hours of December 9, Cós summoned his officers to discuss the possibility of surrender. He asked Sánchez-Navarro whether the rebels had occupied the plaza. The engineer assured him that it was still defended by about seventy stalwarts under the resourceful regular Colonel Nicolas Condelle. Cós considered his alternatives and then declared: "Sanchez, by reason of cowardice and perfidy of many of our companions all is lost. . . . Go save those brave men. I authorize you to approach the enemy and obtain the best terms possible. Save the dignity of our Government, the honor of its arms and honor, life and property of chiefs, officials and troops that still remain even though I myself perish."[41]

Peering through the smoke and early morning haze a few hours later,

Texians could see that the flag flying over the plaza was not emblazoned with the Mexican eagle and serpent but was instead solid white. Sánchez-Navarro soon set out under a flag of truce to discuss terms with the rebel commander, but on the way he had difficulty getting past his own men. Colonel Condelle and some of the regulars of the Morelos Battalion were determined to fight on. Upon discovering Sánchez-Navarro's destination, they refused to let him pass through their lines. "You will not go," they asserted, "for the Morelos Battalion has never surrendered." Only after Sánchez-Navarro convinced these proud regulars that he was obeying Cós's directives did they gloomily allow him to proceed.[42]

On December 9, Burleson, upon the arrival of Sánchez-Navarro, agreed to an immediate cease fire. Burleson and the Mexicans then negotiated the surrender terms until two o'clock the next morning. Sánchez-Navarro, following his instructions to the letter, preserved the dignity of his government and its military. The fastidious colonel and other members of the Mexican negotiating team felt somewhat threatened by the ragged, battle-weary frontiersmen hulking around the conference table. "We were surrounded with crude bumpkins, proud and overbearing," he recalled. "Whoever knows the character of North Americans may appreciate the position in which we found ourselves." Sánchez-Navarro may have been especially appalled by backwoods rowdies who flaunted the silver spurs, gaily colored blankets, and other assorted items of clothing stripped from the Mexicans they had killed. Burleson and Johnson were more amenable, however, finally accepting most of Cós's demands. Indeed, many complained that Cós behaved as if he were the victor. William R. Carey, one of the volunteers from the states, squawked: "We should have made a Treaty and not a child's bargain." But Burleson felt it best to accept terms; the Mexicans had proven formidable adversaries when on the defensive. He explained that the conditions were "highly favorable, considering the strong position and large force of the enemy."[43]

The terms were indeed generous. The Mexicans kept their personal arms and ten rounds of ammunition; they could recuperate in Béxar for six days; the sick and wounded were permitted to remain under the care of a surgeon; Cós was allowed to take with him a four-pound cannon and ten rounds of ammunition to ward off any possible Indian attack; and since Mexican supplies were exhausted, General Burleson agreed to furnish "such provisions as can be obtained" until the vanquished army crossed the Río Grande. General Cós, needing food more, traded Texian volunteer Frank Hardin a pair of silver candlesticks for the personal provisions he would require on the return journey. For their part, Cós and his men agreed to retire into the interior and pledged that they would not "in any way oppose the re-establishment of the Federal Constitution of 1824." No doubt urged to do so by anxious *bexareños*, Burleson specifically stipulated that General Cós "take the convicts brought in by General [*sic*] Ugartechea, beyond the Rio Grande."⁴⁴

With the departure of Cós and his army, most Texians believed the war had been brought to a successful conclusion. Reflecting this view, Johnson confidently wrote: "The period put to our present war by the fall of San Antonio de Béxar, will, I trust, be attended with all the happy results to Texas, which her warmest friend could desire." Old settlers were eager to return to their families. The storming of Béxar had not been the lark that it earlier had seemed to be. Colonel Milam, Captain Peacock, and two others were dead. As many as fourteen had been wounded, with one man losing a leg and another man his eye. Mexican casualties were more difficult to determine. Some Texians' accounts claimed as many as 300 killed, but 150 killed and wounded was probably a more realistic estimate. Temporarily at least, the rebels had lost their taste for combat, and most were all too willing to let Cós and his troops depart in peace.⁴⁵

Despite all the danger and hardship—or perhaps because of it—the Texian veterans of Béxar were enormously proud of their victory. In a letter to the army, Governor Smith and the Council at San Felipe praised the soldiers as "the brave sons of Washington and freedom" and called them "invincible." The volunteers themselves believed as much. "We considered ourselves almost invincible," Herman Ehrenberg remembered, "an opinion which later on brought us and our friends very near ruin." Already James Grant and others were pushing the idea of an expedition to take Matamoros.⁴⁶

Fired by their achievements, the insurgents were supremely confident. "We hoped that in a brief lapse of time reports would carry to the other Mexican states the news of our success against the Usurper's troops," Ehrenberg explained, "and that once more the whole nation would rise in revolt in order to overthrow Santa Anna and his administration." El Presidente, however, had other plans.⁴⁷

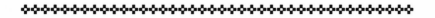

CHAPTER 6

"Scoundrels Abroad and Scoundrels at Home"

6. *SOLDADO*, ACTIVO BATALLON DE TRES VILLAS

February 1836

Standing guard in his barracks cap, the soldado *barely endures the cruel snowstorm that struck the Army of Operations in Texas in February 1836. His army blanket offers a modicum of the protection that he would have enjoyed had his government issued him a proper greatcoat.*

Men in the active militia normally received uniform items discarded from the "permanent" battalions. Two types of tailcoats saw service in Texas: the 1832 and 1833 patterns. This private wears the dark blue 1833-model tailcoat with red collar, cuffs, and turnbacks, patterned after the French surtout. His trousers are made of coarse sailcloth, which this freezing sentry has stuffed into the rags wrapped around his feet. To provide meager insulation, he has packed grass and hay inside the rags. Although well equipped by militia standards, the Batallon de Tres Villas was not issued overcoats, a blunder that created much undue suffering.

Weapons consist of the standard India Pattern Brown Bess musket, which supports a triangular socket bayonet.

The snow-laden trees "formed an amazing variety of cones and pyramids, which seemed to be made of alabaster," José de la Peña recalled. He further related that "many mules remained standing with their loads," and one of those mistreated beasts is represented here.

Recruited from the villages of Jalapa, Cordoba, and Orizaba, many of the Tres Villas soldados *were of Indian descent; this sentry's prominent features clearly bespeak his native heritage. Commanded by Colonel Agustín Alcerrica, the battalion formed part of Brigadier General Eugenio Tolsa's Second Infantry Brigade. On February 17, 1836, Colonel Don Cayatono Montoya took command of the Batallon de Tres Villas. As part of Brevet General José Urrea's Division, the battalion participated in the sweep of the Texas coastal prairies and saw action at the Battle of Coleto. Following that engagement, the* soldados *of Tres Villas stood guard over the Texian prisoners confined inside the Presidio La Bahía. On March 27, 1836, the members of the Tres Villas Batallon drew the unpleasant duty of executing Colonel Fannin and most of his command. Although they carried out Santa Anna's infamous directive, the men of Tres Villas did so much against their will. A Mexican officer who deplored the savage order recorded: "They were greatly moved upon being required to duty so alien to their rules, so degrading to brave soldiers."*

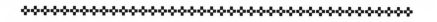

6

"Scoundrels Abroad and Scoundrels at Home"

HIS EXCELLENCY, Generalissimo Antonio López de Santa Anna Pérez de Lebrón, whose pride matched his lengthy appellation, was born into a middle-class Creole family in 1794. His rise to power was swift and steady. He had been appointed a cadet in the Fio de Cruz infantry regiment in 1810 and had served against the hostile tribes of the Provincias Internas. In 1813 he saw action in Texas under General Joaquín de Arredondo in the campaign against Anglo-American filibusters and *tejano* rebels seeking to overthrow Spanish rule and was cited for bravery at the Battle of the Medina River. After Mexican independence, Santa Anna supported Agustín de Iturbide until the emperor failed to support him in a personal quarrel with a superior officer. At that juncture, Santa Anna first displayed his talent for changing sides at the most opportune moment. He transferred his loyalties to the liberals fighting for the establishment of a republic and helped force Iturbide to abdicate.

Mexicans hailed Santa Anna as a patriot. He was appointed military governor of Yucatán but later resigned his commission to take office as the civil governor of Veracruz. In 1829 he donned his uniform again to squash Spanish attempts at reconquest near Tampico. That victory secured his reputation as the country's ablest soldier, and within three years a grateful people elected the "Hero of Tampico" president of Mexico.

Once in power, Santa Anna continued to demonstrate his skill as a political chameleon. Although he had run for office as a liberal in 1833, the next year he overturned the Federal Constitution of 1824 to establish a centralized regime. In May 1835, he crushed a federalist revolt of Zacatecans with a ruthlessness that appalled even those inured to years of bloody revolutionary warfare. That same year he dispatched his brother-in-law, General Martín Perfecto de Cós, to put down the growing disturbances in Texas, where "land pirates" from the United States had allied with liberal Mexican troublemakers. On October 27, 1835, Santa Anna met with advisers at Tacubaya to plot a course of action concerning federalist unrest in Texas. He expected that a show of force would be sufficient to cow *norteamericanos*, but reports from Cós indicated that resistance had become general. The ungrateful foreigners had revealed their perfidy; Santa Anna had learned from Arredondo how to deal with North American filibusterers. If it was blood they wanted, they would drown in it. He had annihilated federalist opposition in Zacatecas; he would do the same in Texas. He stepped down as president to command an expedition to relieve Cós and reestablish Mexican authority. This situation offered a perfect opportunity to enhance his image as the savior on horseback. Events, however, did not unfold according to plan, for in December 1835 Cós was forced to capitulate at Béxar.[1]

Outraged by the Mexican defeat and the embarrassment to his own centralist government, Santa Anna pledged that 1836 would see the utter destruction of "those who wished to betray the territory of Texas." Although American ethnocentrism was a factor in the Texian revolt, Mexicans were equally guilty of cultural hubris. Most believed that the victorious army of Zacatecas would make short work of the Anglo-Celtic backwoodsmen in the Texian army. Local newspapers painted recent immigrants from the United States as unprincipled adventurers who would flee at the first whiff of grapeshot. Juan Nepomuceno Almonte, educated in the United States and former envoy to London, had traveled to Texas in 1834 as a secret agent of the Mexican government. His report, echoing the beliefs of a majority of his class, concluded that the customs of the Anglo-American colonists were "somewhat crude" and "not compatible with the manners practiced by persons of good breeding." Secretary of War José María Tornel expressed a similar contempt. "The superiority of the Mexican soldier over the mountaineers of Kentucky and the hunters of Missouri is well known," he opined. "Veterans seasoned by twenty years of wars can't be intimidated by the presence of an army ignorant of the art of war, incapable of discipline, and renowned for insubordination."[2]

Despite the confidence of Secretary of War Tornel, the Mexican army suffered numerous handicaps; chief among them was lack of money for an expedition against Texas. The 1835 campaign against Zacatecas had all but emptied the treasury. Santa Anna attacked this problem with his customary energy. By extracting high-interest loans from the church and private money lenders, he raised more than four hundred thousand *pesos*, which were to be repaid by increased import duties and forced loans from several of the Mexican states. But for all of his devious financial machinations, Santa Anna warned his subordinates that this was to be an austere campaign. When the borrowed money ran out, none would be forthcoming from the government.[3]

Regardless of Secretary of War Tornel's smug belief, not all Mexican soldiers were seasoned veterans. While some had abundant combat experience, most were raw recruits. On paper, a Mexican infantry battalion consisted of eight companies of eighty men each. During the 1836 campaign, however, most units were under strength; many companies had fewer than forty men actually in ranks.[4]

Each infantry battalion was manned by three categories of troops. The workhorses of the army were the regular foot soldiers attached to the six line, or center, companies. These line troops were armed with the British East Indian Pattern Brown Bess musket, which hurled a massive .753 caliber ball. Bess was four feet, eleven inches long without the bayonet attached and weighed nine pounds, eleven ounces. The battalion's best were removed from the line companies to form a single grenadier company. Also armed with the Brown Bess, these elite troops were usually held in reserve to be committed at a critical juncture. A rifle company, also made up of select troops, was attached to each battalion. Riflemen were specialists who demonstrated remarkable esprit de corps; accordingly, their units were sometimes registered as "light" or "preferred" companies. The riflemen, known as chasseurs (*cazadores*), were expected to exhibit individual initiative, operating in skirmish order and taking advantage of the terrain to pick off enemy officers and to thin enemy ranks. They were armed with the British Baker .61 caliber rifle, which the British Ninety-fifth Green Jackets had made famous during Wellington's Peninsular campaign and at Waterloo. While rather slow to load and not packing the punch of a Brown Bess, in the hands of a trained marksman the Baker was lethal at ranges up to 270 yards—as Ben Milam's death had revealed.[5]

The Mexican infantry battalions consisted of two types of troops. At its core were the *permanentes* (full-time veterans of the regular army) around whom Santa Anna hoped to build his fighting force. These professionals would be augmented by *activos* (national guard or reserve

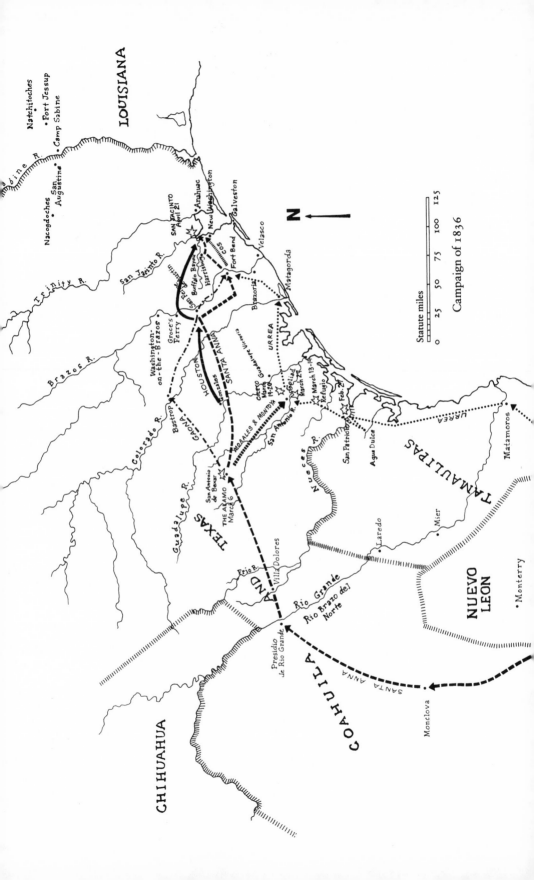

Campaign of 1836

militia). The cream of the Mexican battalions were the well-trained and highly motivated *zapadores* (engineers or sappers). José Enrique de la Peña, a professional officer and one of Santa Anna's harshest critics, complained that many of the recruits had been "snatched away from crafts and from agriculture, [including] many heads of families, who usually do not make good soldiers." To be sure, far too many men were unwilling draftees. The Army of Operations against Texas had been, in de la Peña's doleful phrase, "created by bayonets and now had to be upheld by them." [6]

The much-feared Mexican cavalry battalions were organized into four distinct cadres. Like the infantry, cavalry units were divided into *permanentes* and *activos*. These units were further supplemented by auxiliaries like *ranchero* horsemen who were recruited locally for temporary service, and the presidial cavalry, those hard-riding Indian fighters stationed in frontier outposts. Mexican cavalrymen wielded sabers, lances, and surplus British Pagent carbines. [7]

The relative inexperience of the troops was not the only drawback. The tactical organization of the army was woefully outdated and reflected the Mexican military's strong attachment to its Spanish past. The principal leaders and organizers of the Texas campaign had learned their trade in Spanish service, an education that had left an indelible stamp on their thinking. Separated by tradition and distance from the recent innovations in European weapon technology and tactical practice, Mexican officers clung to doctrines that were already dated at Waterloo in 1815. Following independence, Mexican officials changed title pages but otherwise adopted the Spanish drill manuals verbatim. A measure of modernization seemed to have been forthcoming in 1834, when army commanders at last implemented an 1824 decree that transformed certain regular and militia units into light troops. In accordance with the decree, there were now eight light companies, with one designated as sharpshooters. On the surface, these steps would seem to be progressive, but with the exception of bugle calls, the tactics remained those of 1814. By the Law of September 1, 1824, some regular regiments of horse became light cavalry. Again, these measures were apparently innovative, but in training, drill, and equipment, the Mexican light horse was shackled to outdated Spanish tactics by old manuals that had been reprinted in Mexico in 1824. [8]

The past dominated the thinking of many Mexican officers, but one figure of the recent past stood preeminent. Napoleon Bonaparte's influence on Santa Anna was paramount. Indeed, the Mexican general was wont to style himself the Napoleon of the West. A distorted reflection of the genuine article, he surrounded himself with Napoleonic bric-a-brac. Seeking to curry favor, some obsequious subordinates even entered into the charade. De la Peña noted that General Joaquín Ramírez y Sesma, Santa Anna's cavalry chief, "foolishly compared Santa Anna with Napoleon and tactlessly styled himself as his Murat." This egocentric fascination with the emperor was so complete that Italian-born General Vicente Filisola would later write that the Mexican commander-in-chief would "listen to nothing which was not in accord with [Napoleon's] ideas."[9]

Although tiny by Napoleonic standards, the various units that assembled at San Luis Potosí in December 1835 seemed, on paper, more than a match to disperse a rebel mob. The army numbered 6,019 men, not counting those in retreat with Cós. Napoleon had always preferred to mass his guns in giant batteries to pulverize enemy ranks at vital points, but the Napoleon of the West ineffectively scattered his twenty-one fieldpieces throughout the various battalions.[10]

To transport material, the army relied on the eight hundred mules it already owned and leased another thousand. But even more were needed to haul the number of four-wheeled wagons required. To supplement them, therefore, the Mexicans added two hundred two-wheeled ox carts.[11]

Late in December 1835 the Army of Operations began its long and arduous march northward. Originally, Santa Anna had hoped to rush reinforcements to Cós in time to relieve Béxar, but news of that town's surrender meant the expedition would not be one of rescue but of reconquest. Béxar was still the goal, for Santa Anna now had multiple reasons to retake the town. As the political center of Texas, it was symbolically important; as the site of the defeat of a member of his family, its submission became a point of honor. Strategically, Santa Anna wanted to utilize Béxar as his base of operations. Many officers argued in favor of transporting the army by sea to spare their men the rigors of a four-hundred-league march over inhospitable terrain. His Excellency squelched such ideas. Béxar was the linchpin of his plan. He lectured that a direct overland march to the town was necessary because it was the only one in the entire province whose inhabitants "could be relied upon to lend that cooperation which can be expected only of friends." Also, since conscripts formed the bulk of the troops, many believed that the general intended to train them on the march.[12]

Mexican logistics began to break down almost immediately. Battalions carried only one month's rations, and Santa Anna had issued strict orders to "economize with the greatest care." His orders were obeyed. Each soldier was limited to eight ounces of hardtack or toasted corn cake per day. Scarcity of water also proved a difficulty. General Ramírez Sesma's men, moving toward the Río Grande, realized that they had no water barrels. But the problem was academic. Barrels would have been useless anyway, since they lacked the mules to haul them. Ramírez finally sent a messenger to Laredo to beg for water. By the time the man returned with thirty barrels, both men and horses were almost dead from dehydration.[13]

Both mules and teamsters were in short supply. As was the custom, the government hired men to handle the supply carts. These civilian employees made it clear that they were not subject to military discipline. The high command, knowing how crucial the services of these muleteers were, told officers not to "upset" them. Indeed, after a quarrel between Acting Colonel Julián Fuente and a driver, the man complained that the officer had "wanted him to move his carts faster than they could go." Reprimanded by his commanding officer, Fuente found the dressing down so humiliating that he left the army. The high command was cautious not to offend the wagoners, but it was not as concerned about paying them. After discovering their absence from the payroll, many of the mule drivers deserted, which compounded problems of transport. Officers replaced teamsters with inexperienced soldiers, a switch not gratifying to either the troops or the mules.[14]

The army's logistics were further taxed by the large following of women and children, which was an established institution of the Mexican military. Providing comfort from the rigors of campaigning, *soldaderas* (soldiers' women) made good cooks, foragers, and nurses. Even so, the presence of so many straggling noncombatants concerned General Filisola. Santa Anna's staff shared his worry, but conventional wisdom held that if the women were sent home, half the army would follow. Conventional wisdom was probably right. Still, for all their well-intentioned contributions, *soldaderas* probably hindered more than they helped. The women and their children consumed the meager supplies, slowed the line of march, and proved a distraction to the husband-soldiers, whose primary concern was their family instead of their duty.[15]

Yet many of the men had cause to welcome the women who served as nurses when illness spread through the ranks. Hundreds fell to dysentery, overexposure, and *tele,* a fever produced by drinking stagnant water. Santa Anna had made provisions for a medical corps, but trained doctors failed to materialize. One column marched without a surgeon or even so much as a medicine kit. It finally accepted the services of a "North American practitioner who called himself a doctor." The men probably took grim satisfaction when, ironically, the quack himself became sick and died. The sad state of the medical corps could not fail to undermine the morale of men who were all too aware of their chances of survival if they fell into the hands of these assorted charlatans. "No one in the army," de la Peña reported, "is unaware that surgeons . . . are generally indifferent men of meager education, wretched, many of them ignorant, who have taken no notice of the advances in their profession that would make them proficient in carrying out their duties."[16]

Hostile Indians were even more menacing than incompetent surgeons. Santa Anna had ordered the establishment of depots along the line of march, but upon reaching them, many exhausted contingents discovered that foodstuffs and supplies had been appropriated by Comanches. At one point Comanche raids became so serious that Santa Anna released a detachment of presidial troopers and fifty dragoons for punitive operations against them. Despite all precautions, stragglers were often found scalped along the trail. The commander in chief supplied rifles and other military equipment to the political chiefs of numerous beleaguered departments. Although the borderlanders no doubt needed the weapons and supplies for their constant war against the Comanches and Apaches, these allotments were yet another drain on the army's limited resources.[17]

Of all the hardships suffered by the Mexican army, none surpassed the cruel winter of 1836, which was more severe than any on record. Blizzards blanketed the landscape with snow and ice. Filisola recalled the bitter evening of February 13, when "up to fifteen or sixteen inches of snow covered the ground."[18]

Both men and animals suffered, but the troops from Yucatán were most affected. Mostly Indians, these men, accustomed to the tropical climate of their homeland, were ill suited for winter campaigning. General José Urrea recorded that in one night, "six soldiers of the battalion of

Yucatan died from exposure to the cold." De la Peña recounted the pitiful plight of the mules and horses:

> The Tampico Regiment had left its cavalry saddled, and the mounts,
> covered to the haunches, could not be distinguished by their color.
> Many mules remained standing with their loads; others, as well as
> some horses, died, for those that fell and tried to get up inevitably
> slipped from being so numb, and cracked their heads. The snow was
> covered with the blood of the beasts, contrasting with its whiteness.[19]

Although most were not battle-hardened veterans, the men of the
Mexican Army of Operations were not lacking in courage and fortitude.
Many overconfident North American newcomers to Texas scorned their
adversaries, certain that the "spirit of the degraded Mexican" could be
"easily subdued." They drastically underestimated their foe. Regardless
of the hardships, and despite the inefficiency and indifference of the high
command, the individual Mexican soldiers stoically pressed forward.
Had their spirits been "easily subdued," they would never have survived
such an ordeal. Secretary of War Tornel justly commended their conduct:
"The army underwent great privations during its march and consequently deserves the highest praise for its constancy and resignation,
qualities characteristic of the Mexican soldier."[20]

While Santa Anna's army continued its inexorable advance, Texians
resumed their customary bickering. The preposterous proposal to mount
an offensive against Matamoros was the source of most of the dissension.
As early as December 2, 1835, Goliad Commandant Philip Dimitt had
effusively supported a drive that would "enable us to hurl the thunder
back in[to] the very atmosphere of the enemy, drag him, and with him
the war out of Texas." He was convinced that such bold action would
arouse dormant Mexican federalists: "The liberal of all classes would
immediately join us, the neutrals would gather confidence, both in themselves and us, and the parasites of centralism, in that section, would be
effectually panic-struck and paralyzed."[21]

Despite Dimitt's talk of enlisting the aid of Mexican federalists, new
passions were on the rise in Goliad that would make such assistance impossible. The volunteers, arriving daily from the United States, possessed
no loyalty to Mexico and scorned all help from its people. For these newcomers, the question was one more of race than of politics; to them, fed-

eralism versus centralism meant only American against Mexican. On December 20, 1835, the Goliad garrison issued a declaration of independence from Mexico. The document, however, reflected only the will of the headstrong Goliad volunteers; it shocked the Council at San Felipe, which had exercised great care not to alienate Mexican and *tejano* federalists. The Goliad declaration of independence was, therefore, suppressed. It did, however, indicate a reckless spirit of independence among the army's U.S. volunteers that was not then shared by many established colonists.[22]

Mexican officials had reason to distrust Anglo-Americans, especially since the ill-fated Tampico expedition of November 1835. Ardent Mexican federalist José Antonio Mexía had fled to New Orleans, where he and his fellow revolutionary, George Fisher, conspired to invade Tampico. After the city had fallen to federalist forces, they reasoned, liberals would flock to their banner and overthrow the tyrant Santa Anna. On November 6, 1835, Mexía and Fisher sailed from New Orleans aboard the schooner *Mary Jane*, at the head of a company of "efficient immigrants," most of whom believed they were bound for Texas.

From the outset, the foolhardy expedition was plagued by a series of disasters. On November 13, Tampico *federalistas* rose prematurely, and the following day the rebel schooner ran aground on a sandbar outside the city. Meanwhile, fresh troops from Tuxpan reinforced the centralist garrison. Nevertheless, on November 15, Mexía doggedly attacked Tampico. Predictably, the reinforced garrison easily repulsed the contingent of green excursionists. Mexía escaped, but he abandoned thirty-one hapless adventurers. Three died of their wounds; the rest were executed as marauders. The defeated federalist leader, fleeing aboard the U.S. schooner *Halcyon*, arrived in Texas on December 3. Once there, Mexía, ever the optimist, attempted to persuade the Council to provide men and supplies for yet another invasion of Mexico.[23]

The Council, moved by the pro-offensive arguments of Mexía, James Grant, Philip Dimitt, Frank Johnson, and the growing number of volunteers from the United States, authorized a move against the Mexican city of Matamoros. Governor Henry Smith's enthusiasm for an invasion of Mexico had cooled considerably. Against his better judgment, however, he bowed to pressure from the Council and ordered Commander in Chief Sam Houston to make a "demonstration" against Matamoros, but he warned that the vital port at Copano must be maintained at all cost. Although later a vocal critic of the Matamoros Expedition, Houston supported the venture as long as he believed he would be in command. Houston ordered James Bowie to make initial preparations for the march, but warned the impetuous knife fighter not to move without specific instructions.[24]

Back in Béxar, Dr. James Grant advocated an immediate drive against Matamoros and called for the ouster of Houston as commander in chief. He had convinced Frank Johnson of the wisdom of the operation, and now both lobbied the Council. Most of the volunteers supported Grant and his Matamoros scheme. His stories recounting the pleasures to be found south of the Río Grande were enough to spark the imaginations of young Anglo-Celtic Americans far from home. Grant, who had been wounded during the storming of Béxar, was to the volunteer's liking—an audacious man's man, disdainful of political restraints. But his motivation had little to do with patriotism; before the Mexicans had forced him out, he had owned rich estates in Coahuila. Grant realized that armed conquest was the only way that he was likely to retrieve his holdings.[25]

Houston planned to join Bowie's unit with the new companies of American volunteers gathering around Goliad and Refugio under Colonel James W. Fannin. Placing himself at the head of this combined force, Houston would then begin a march on Matamoros, thus luring away Grant's volunteers. On Christmas Day 1835, Houston retired to Washington-on-the-Brazos to make final preparations.[26]

Confusion, incompetence, and ambition stymied Houston's plans. The Council bypassed Houston and authorized Johnson and Fannin to march on Matamoros. That irresponsible body, violating the principle of unity of command, also named both men as commanders. Both Johnson and Fannin claimed the title of commander, but the troops were unsure whether either of them was actually in charge. To confuse matters even further, Governor Smith ordered Houston, who was, after all, still officially commander in chief of all Texians under arms, to go to Goliad and personally assume command of the proposed offensive. On January 3, however, Johnson informed the Council that he had ordered volunteers southward on an expedition against Matamoros, leaving Lieutenant Colonel J. C. Neill in San Antonio with a skeleton force of one hundred men. Neill realized that he could not defend the town or the Alamo fort with so few men; Cós had not been able to do so with more than ten times that number. Neill therefore chose to concentrate the Béxar garrison behind the thick adobe walls of the Alamo, but he lacked provisions and clothing for his men. In order to supply the Matamoros venture, Grant and Johnson had callously stripped the Béxar garrison of even the basic supplies.[27]

Neill complained bitterly. On January 6, he wrote Smith and the Council, deploring the heavy-handed measures of Johnson, Grant, and the newly arrived American volunteers, as well as others who had succumbed to Matamoros fever. "The clothing sent here by the aid and patriotic exertions of the honorable council was taken from men who endured all the hardships of winter and who were not even sufficiently clad for summer," Neill complained. He further charged that many of the men left to him had "but one blanket and one shirt, and what was intended for them [had been] given away to men, some of whom had not been in the army more than four days, and many not exceeding two weeks."[28]

In a January 10, 1836, proclamation, Johnson expressed little concern for the destitute Béxar garrison and even less concerning the threat of a Mexican counteroffensive. Instead, he called for "the extermination of the last vestige of despotism from the Mexican soil." Envisioning an international monarchist plot, he exhibited a frame of mind that would ultimately find expression in the phrase Manifest Destiny:

> To arms! then, Americans, to aid in sustaining the principles of 1776, in this western hemisphere. To arms! native Mexicans, in driving tyranny from your homes, intolerance from your altars, and the tyrant from your country. In this very hour the crowned despots of Europe have met in unholy conclave, to devise the means of crushing liberal principles. Louis Philippe of France, faithless to his oath, now sits side by side with the monarchs of Russia, and Austria, and Prussia, and Spain, and the minister of Santa Anna is seen among them. Before this, it is more than probable that the freedom of Mexicans has been sold to the tyrants, and that European force is to sustain the diadem on the head of the traitor Santa Anna. Not only Texas and Mexico, but the genius of liberty, demands that every man do his duty to his country, and leave the consequences to God. Our first attack will be upon Matamoros; our next, if Heaven decrees, wherever tyranny shall raise its malignant form.[29]

Smith, who had been outraged by Neill's report, was even more incensed by Johnson's jingoistic pronouncements. The army had been lucky to defeat Cós's meager force at Béxar; now, only a month later, Johnson was ranting about attacking Santa Anna inside Mexico. Smith loudly denounced the Matamoros Expedition as idiocy and anyone who supported it as either a fool or a traitor. He then castigated the unruly Council. In an address dripping with vehemence and vituperation, Smith excoriated the patrons of the Matamoros Expedition as men who had "acted in bad faith" and who were determined "to destroy the very institutions which you are pledged and sworn to support."

That was but a prelude. Smith thundered that he had grown "tired of watching scoundrels abroad and scoundrels at home." But who were these ne'er-do-wells, and how might they be identified? Smith bitterly answered his own question:

> Look around upon your flock, your discernment will easily detect the scoundrels. The complaint; contraction of the eyes; the gape of the mouth; the vacant stare; the head hung; the restless fidgety disposition; the sneaking sycophantic look; a natural meanness of countenance; an unguarded shrug of the shoulders; a sympathetic tickling and contraction of the muscles of the neck anticipating the rope; a restless uneasiness to adjourn, dreading to face the storm [they] themselves have raised.[30]

Council members were understandably offended. The rift that had for some time been developing between governor and Council widened into a complete schism. Smith proclaimed the Council dissolved. The Council responded by impeaching Smith, and it continued to meet with Lieutenant Governor James W. Robinson serving as acting governor. Neither Smith nor the Council had been granted the right to depose the other, and bewildered Texians, now finding themselves blessed with two quarreling governments, wondered whether either had legal authority. Hedging his bets, the desperate Neill wrote to both, but to his disgust neither was able or willing to render succor to his Béxar garrison.[31]

Houston arrived in Goliad on January 14, 1836, intent on reclaiming his army, only to discover that Dr. Grant had appropriated the title "acting commander in chief." Houston said nothing and bided his time. To his initial dismay, Houston found Bowie still in Goliad; the knife fighter had never received the orders to anticipate Grant with his own demonstration against Matamoros. That portion of Houston's plan had failed badly, but at least he had found one man he trusted. He could, at last, send someone to evacuate Neill from what was clearly an untenable position. On January 17, therefore, Houston dispatched Bowie and a company of volunteers to Béxar. The general later claimed that he instructed Bowie to "blow up the Alamo and abandon the place," but the order appeared to have been discretionary.

The situation had deteriorated so badly that Bowie was one of the few men in Goliad still willing to obey Houston. The independent volunteers were wary. He may have had Smith's trust, but where had Houston been at Gonzales, at Concepción, at the Grass Fight, at the storming of Béxar? They had actually seen Grant fight and bleed for the cause. To them, Houston seemed a mere poseur.[32]

Having sent Bowie off to Béxar, Houston joined Grant's army on its march to Refugio but made no effort to assert his claim as its commander. He had not trained under Andrew Jackson without acquiring the ability to win a crowd. On the road, he regaled the men with much good-natured banter. Employing all the lessons he had learned in the rough-and-tumble school of Tennessee politics, he worked to win them over. In Refugio the expedition received Johnson, who had fresh news: the Council had deposed Governor Smith, ousted Houston as commander in chief, and authorized James Fannin to lead the drive on Matamoros. Under the circumstances, there was little for Houston to do but depart, but he would first give the men something to think about. He harangued the volunteers with his considerable oratorical skills. He questioned how Matamoros, with a population of twelve thousand, could be taken by a "handful of men who have marched twenty-two days without bread-stuffs." He reminded the troops that Mexicans would justifiably regard them as mercenaries and treat them as such. "In war," Houston admonished, "when spoil is the object, friends and enemies share one common destiny." On January 28 he rode away, leaving numerous bewildered soldiers in his wake. Two days later he reported to Smith, who still claimed to be governor. On Smith's instructions, Houston then visited his old friend Chief Bowles in East Texas to arrange a treaty between the insurgent Texians and the Cherokee Nation. If the Indians were to aid the Mexican army, the Texas rebels would be caught between two foes. Houston's goal, therefore, was to persuade them to remain neutral.[33]

Before leaving Goliad, Houston had accomplished more than was immediately apparent, for he had planted the seeds of doubt. Talking among themselves, many of the volunteers decided that there might be something to what Houston had said. It was true that they were already short of food and supplies. If Fannin was in charge, why were they with Grant? Perhaps it would be better to fall back to Goliad and join the Georgia Battalion that had just arrived from the states. Grant had mentioned none of Houston's concerns. Perhaps Houston had been correct, and Dr. Grant was just using them to recover his confiscated Mexican estates. Doubt blossomed into action as many volunteers deserted to join Fannin at Goliad. Left with barely seventy men, Grant and Johnson retired to San Patricio to await developments. By mid-February, indecision, confusion, and a scarcity of supplies had all but ruled out the quixotic Matamoros Expedition. Dr. Grant would not be the first nor the last to be undone by Sam Houston's cunning; it had been a humiliating descent for the "acting commander in chief."[34]

Back in Béxar, stocks of provender were low, but morale ran surprisingly high. Neill had kept his men busy bolstering the Alamo's defenses. He felt no special attachment to the old mission, but as an artilleryman he was loath to abandon the cannon that Cós had left behind. Lacking the teams to transport them, he decided to stay with his guns. On January 19 Bowie and his contingent rode into the compound with Houston's instructions to blow up the Alamo and withdraw.[35]

Bowie, however, was impressed with Neill's improvements; the mission had begun to take on the appearance of a fort. Neill had hauled in nineteen of Cós's best cannon, including one massive eighteen-pounder. Green Jameson, the garrison's chief engineer, had installed most of the guns on the walls. Writing to Houston, Jameson boasted that if the Mexicans were imprudent enough to storm the Alamo, the defenders could "whip 10 to 1 with our artillery."[36]

Such bravado was contagious. Bowie joined the assiduous Neill in "labouring night and day, laying up provisions for a siege, encouraging our men, and calling on the Government for relief." Neill's leadership impressed Bowie. "I cannot eulogise the conduct & character of Col. Neill too highly," he wrote Smith, "no other man in the army could have kept men at this post, under the neglect they have experienced."[37]

Both men knew the value of a good defensive position. Neill had manned the "Come and Take It" cannon at Gonzales and had commanded the battery that had prevented the Texian camp from being captured during the storming of Béxar. Bowie, of course, was the tactical commander during the Battle of Concepción, where the deadly rifles of his men had repulsed a force many times their own number. Whenever

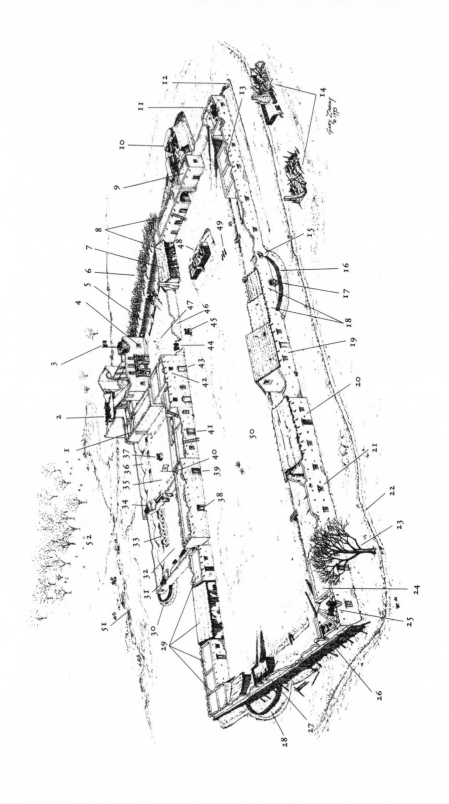

Gary Zaboly © 1975

The plan of the Alamo shown here was based on a three-dimensional model of the fort to produce a correct perspective of the relationship of the walls and buildings as viewed from the northwest. The numbers in the following key relate to those on the drawing, the latter having been positioned in a mostly clockwise order:

1. Sacristy. This was used by the Texian defenders both as officers' quarters and as a provisions storehouse. Adjoining rooms served similar purposes. During the March 6 assault Suzanna Dickenson, her infant daughter, Angelina, and several other noncombatants were sheltered here.

2. Cavalier battery of three cannon of six-, eight-, and twelve-pound calibers, situated atop a high platform built on rubble and arches pulled down by Mexican engineers in the fall of 1835. A slope of rubble extended from here almost to the door of the church, supporting a ramp and scaffolding of wood that were burned by Mexican troops evacuating the Alamo in May of 1836. This position was dubbed *Fortín de Cós* (Little Fort of Cós) by Santa Anna's besieging army.

3. Tricolor flag with two gold stars in its central white field, its position clearly indicated in José Juan Sánchez-Navarro's eyewitness "Vista" of the fort (seen from the west), as published over one hundred years later in *La Guerra de Tejas*. Further confirmation of the existence of this flag is found in the journal of Colonel Juan Nepomuceno Almonte, who noted that, on the arrival of the Mexican army on the outskirts of San Antonio de Béxar at 2 P.M. on February 23, "the enemy, as soon as the march of the division was seen, hoisted the tricolored flag with two stars, designed to represent Coahuila and Texas. The President with all his staff advanced to Campo Santo [burying ground]. The enemy lowered the flag and fled, and possession was taken of Bexar without firing a shot" (Almonte's journal, captured at San Jacinto and published in the *New York Herald*, June 23, 1836).

4. Baptistry, used as a gunpowder magazine during the siege, as was its opposing room north of the church door.

5. Short palisade, its inner firing step made of earth dug from a trench. Another trench (not seen) defended its exterior. A single cannon was placed here. During the final battle, a number of defenders attempted to escape over the palisade; most were immediately intercepted and killed by the

deployed Mexican lancers under Joaquín Ramírez y Sesma.

6. Abatis of felled trees, their cut and sharpened limbs pointing toward the enemy, serving as an outwork to defend the approaches to the palisade. This was an effective barrier against infantry; Marquis Louis Joseph de Montcalm positioned his army behind such an abatis at Ticonderoga in 1758 and successfully checked the onslaught of a vastly superior British army, inflicting severe losses on it.

7. Kitchens.

8. Rooms serving both as officers' quarters and as a hospital. Jim Bowie was killed in the room closest to the main gate.

9. Room of the Officer of the Guard.

10. Lunette and trench, with at least two cannon, defending the main gate. These guns might have had overhead protection in the manner of entrenched or fortified batteries in the eighteenth and nineteenth centuries; in Sánchez-Navarro's "Vista" drawing, this position appears to be an almost boxlike closure.

11. The iron-barreled eighteen-pounder, firing *en barbette* (over the wall).

12. Incomplete trench.

13. Artillery command post, serving also as a warehouse containing tools and lumber.

14. Two of the *jacales* burned by the Texians during the siege. Other "huts" continued in a general line from this point to *La Villita* in the south.

15. Iron twelve-pound gunade, placed on a low ramp and platform and firing through a hole cut in the adobe wall.

16. Semicircular palisade and narrow trench. Outguards might have been stationed here, or riflemen to provide enfilade fire along the otherwise bastionless west wall.

17. Blocked-up opening for a branch of the acequia dating back to the early days of the mission San Antonio de Valero.

18. Officers' quarters.

19. Headquarters of the Alamo.

20. Officers' quarters.

21. Cannon on low ramp and platform firing through a window opening.

22. Acequia, an irrigation ditch filled with water.

23. Large pecan tree.

24. Officers' quarters.

25. Platform and ramp in northwest corner, called *Fortin de Condelle* by the Mexicans, supporting two eight-pounders. This battery fired through embrasures cut in the wall. Sánchez-Navarro's two plans of the compound show three guns here, but the LaBastida map indicates only two embrasures in the wall.

26. Cribbing of horizontal logs supported by vertical braces extending the entire length of the north wall. The adobe wall itself was in a ruinous state; the Texians packed earth between the wall and the cribbing as a buttress against enemy round shot. José Enrique de la Peña, however, reported that "its excavation was hardly begun," meaning that the defenders had not finished banking earth against its exterior as an additional reinforcement (the eastern end of the wall is shown here as the entire barricade would have appeared when completed). From a careful study of the two Navarro plans, as well as of descriptions made by de la Peña and Filisola, it is manifest that this timber outwork covered not just a portion of the north wall but its entirety.

27. *Fortín de Terán*, a three-gun battery of eight pounders, firing through embrasures. Travis died on its ramp.

28. Semicircular palisade and narrow trench, serving the same purpose as no. 16.

29. Quarters for artillerymen.

30. Semicircular palisade and narrow trench, serving the same purpose as nos. 16 and 28.

31. Cannon on low ramp and platform firing north through a hole cut in wall.

32. Cattle pen.

33. Beehive ovens, which were common to missions of the Spanish borderlands. Their structure is hinted at but not explained in Navarro's "plano."

34. Cannon on low ramp and platform firing north through a hole cut in wall.

35. Horse corral, bounded on the west by the partly roofed arcade corridor of the convent. This corral was formerly the convent garden.

36. Earthen banquettes and trenches dug by the Texians.

37. Old mission well.

38. Barracks. Most of the houses surrounding the Alamo's plaza had loopholes cut in their walls, facing both inside and outside the fort. Many had within them semicircular breastworks made of two curtains of hides secured by stakes and filled with earth. Almost all the rooms had ditches dug in their floors to protect the defenders from incoming shells and balls.

39. Jail cell.

40. Conjectured location of blue silk flag of the New Orleans Greys.

41. Barracks.

42. Hospital rooms on the second floor of the old convent building.

43. Armory for small arms.

44. Gun position noted on Navarro's battle plan.
45. Well dug by the defenders during the siege.
46. Wall, probably six feet high, forming inner courtyard.
47. Remains of the old mission cemetery.
48. Two-gun redoubt covering the inner side of the main gate.

49. Three unmounted iron cannon barrels.
50. Parade ground, or Alamo plaza, with a dry acequia running through its western side.
51. Ponds supplying water to acequias.
52. Orchard.

Texians had faced the Mexicans on good defensive ground, they had emerged victorious. Bowie had been able to triumph when his men were shielded only by a riverbank and a few trees; now he had a real fort and cannon. Although he had reportedly traveled to Béxar with orders to demolish the Alamo, Bowie came to consider it and the cannon far too valuable to abandon. By February 2, he was committed. That day he wrote Smith that he and Neill had resolved to "die in these ditches" before they would surrender the post.[38]

Smith knew that Jim Bowie did not make such declarations lightly. If both Bowie and Neill believed the Alamo so important, he had better send them reinforcements. For that purpose, he directed Lieutenant Colonel William Barret Travis to raise a company and bolster the Béxar garrison, but that ambitious officer was not pleased by the prospect. The settlers had grown tired of war, and of the hundred volunteers that Smith had requested, only thirty responded, most without proper weapons. Travis pleaded with Governor Smith to reconsider: "I am willing, nay anxious, to go to the defense of Bexar, but sir, I am unwilling to risk my reputation (which is ever dear to a soldier) by going off into the enemy's country with such little means, so few men, and with them so badly equipped." Travis even threatened to resign his commission, but Smith ignored such theatrics. Against his better judgment, Travis finally obeyed orders and dutifully made his way toward the Alamo with his thirty troopers.[39]

Reinforcements began to trickle into Béxar. Travis and his contingent reached the Alamo on February 3. Like Bowie, he was reassured by improvements to the works and Neill's leadership. Travis, who had come to the fort under duress, was soon describing it as the "key to Texas." Morale enjoyed a boost on February 8, when former U.S. Congressman David Crockett arrived with a contingent of Tennessee volunteers.[40]

The forty-nine-year-old Crockett was already a frontier luminary. He had established a reputation in his native Tennessee as an Indian fighter and bear hunter (he claimed to have bagged 105 bears in a single season). In 1821 and 1823 he parlayed his popularity into a seat on the Tennessee Legislature. Crockett was elected to the U.S. Congress on three separate occasions.[41]

While in Washington, Crockett continually identified with the common folk and reflected their contempt for the professional soldier by recommending the abolishment of the United States Military Academy at West Point. It was, he asserted, a bastion for the "sons of the rich and influential," who believed they were "too nice to work." Fumed Crockett: "They are first educated there for nothing and then must have salaries to support them after they leave there."[42]

Crockett never tired of parading his humble origins and lack of education. He declared that during his tenure as a Tennessee magistrate he "relied on natural born sense, and not on law learning to guide me; for I had never read a page in a law book in all my life." He liked to remind his constituents that he had been a volunteer during the Creek War. As Crockett saw it, "The volunteer goes into the war for the love of his country," implying that the professional soldier was little more than a "hireling" who served for money or position. To enhance his appeal as a "common man," he created the impression that he had served as a lowly private. In fact, he ended his nine-month stint as a sergeant.[43]

His tall tales and personal charisma made him popular among his constituents, and while he normally wore the conventional gentleman's attire of his day—frock coat, cravat, and waistcoat—Crockett affected a hunting shirt on the stump and in campaign portraits in keeping with his growing image as the "Lion of the West." When he opposed the Jackson machine, however, Tennessee voters abandoned him. Defeated in what he considered to have been a rigged election, he informed his former constituents that they "might go to Hell" and he "would go to Texas."[44]

With wounded pride and empty purse, Crockett set out for Texas to make a new beginning. He left Memphis in November 1835 with indomitable style. Playing to the hometown crowd, he donned his hunting shirt and, probably for the first time in his life, sported a fur cap. Crockett was now living his public image, but he kept his dress clothes in his saddle bags in case a formal occasion presented itself.[45]

Once across the Red River, he was immediately taken with Texas, which he described as the "garden spot of the world." Opportunity seemed to abound, and his political aspirations soon reasserted themselves. Crockett demonstrated that his reverence for representative democracy was not mere political prattle. Stopping in Nacogdoches on his way to the fighting, he took the oath of allegiance to the "provisional Government of Texas or any future government" that might subsequently be established. He, however, steadfastly refused to affix his signature until the document had been amended to read "any future republican government." He wrote his children that he had "little doubt" of finding a place in the provisional Texas government. David Crockett was on the greatest adventure of his life: "I am rejoiced at my fate. I had rather be in my present situation than to be elected to a seat in Congress for life. I am in hopes of making a fortune yet for myself and family bad as my prospects have been. . . . Do not be uneasy about me, I am among my friends."[46]

So he was. Arriving in San Antonio, he was welcomed like a visiting dignitary; the men threw an impromptu *fandango* in his honor and requested a brief speech. Mounting a crate in front of San Fernando Church, Crockett sized up his audience and reverted to type: "I have come to aid you all that I can in your noble cause . . . and all the honour that I desire is that of defending as a high private . . . the liberties of our common country." By shunning military rank, he promoted himself as a man of the people, and the crowd loved it. In his element once more, Crockett had no need of an official title; he held these men in the palm of his hand.[47]

On February 14 the mood was dampened by the departure of Colonel Neill. He had received word that his family had been stricken by illness and that he was desperately needed at home. Although he promised to return within twenty days, the men were disappointed to see him go. They may also have been more than a little apprehensive over the transfer of command to the twenty-six-year-old Travis. Neill did not mean to snub the more experienced Bowie, but Travis held a regular commission, while Bowie was only an elected colonel of volunteers. Perhaps Neill had also taken note of Bowie's declining health and his growing dependence on the bottle. Crockett was popular, but he was new to Texas and had no wish to command. Travis emerged as the logical choice. Having made that choice, Neill left the Alamo and the opportunity of lasting fame.[48]

Posterity has been unkind to J. C. Neill. Recent studies have characterized him as "unimaginative," a "second-rater," a man "overshadowed" by "abler" leaders. Yet despite hardship and neglect by the Council, he kept the garrison at that perilous outpost and maintained its morale, a remarkable feat. He had worked tirelessly to transform the crumbling mission into a fort. By the time Travis arrived on the scene, Neill had already bolstered the fort's defenses and the men's will to resist. This is not to denigrate Travis. Once in command, he performed with courage and skill. The point is, rather, that had it not been for the equally courageous and skillful Neill there would have been no garrison for Travis to inherit, no fort, no epic battle, and no entry into Texas legend.[49]

The men did not immediately warm to Travis. Neill had been their commander since January, and many of the volunteers resented having this "regular" foisted upon them. On February 12 the men insisted on an election. With little say in the matter, Travis acquiesced. The men tended to cast their votes along party lines: the regulars voted for Travis; the volunteers, for Bowie.[50]

The election placed Travis in an "awkward situation." The night following the election, Bowie celebrated his victory in his cups, and as the *bexareños* knew only too well, Señor Jim was a bad drunk. He was especially unruly this time; abusing his authority, he interfered with private property and released convicted felons from the local jail. Travis dashed off an indignant letter to Smith, asserting that he refused to be "responsible for the drunken irregularities of any man"—not even the redoubtable Jim Bowie.[51]

The Travis-Bowie feud was, however, short-lived. Bowie awoke on February 13 suffering from both a hangover and remorse at his actions. He had made an ass of himself, and he knew it. As soon as he was sufficiently sober, he made his way to Travis with a proposition. Bowie would command the volunteers, Travis the regulars; all orders and correspondence would be signed by both until Neill's return. It was an obvious peace gesture on Bowie's part, and Travis accepted the magnanimous offer in the same spirit.[52]

There was no more time for personality differences. Juan Seguín's scouts reported Santa Anna's vanguard across the Río Grande. Texian leaders had heard so many rumors of the enemy's approaching that they refused to take any of them seriously, especially when they came from *tejanos*, many of whom were known to be *centralistas*. These reports were, nevertheless, correct; Santa Anna *had* crossed the Río Grande.[53]

The unfortunate General Cós and his battered Béxar garrison had arrived in Monclova on January 20, where Cós informed his illustrious brother-in-law of his surrender terms. Santa Anna patiently assured him that one's word of honor given to rebels meant nothing. He then ordered Cós and his paroled men to enjoy a period of recuperation, after which they would join the Army of Operations. They would return to San Antonio de Béxar, this time as conquerors.[54]

Santa Anna intended to crush the rebellious Texians in a strategic pincer movement. On February 16, he crossed the Río Grande at Paso de Francia. He correctly surmised that the Texians were expecting him to advance from the south via the Laredo Road. By driving up the Camino Real, he would actually approach Béxar from the west. On February 17, General José Urrea forded the Río Grande at Matamoros with a force of some 550 men. His part in the strategic plan involved a sweep of the coastal prairies, which would culminate in the retaking of Goliad.[55]

Although Travis had received intelligence reports regarding the advance of the Mexican army, he and his subordinates concluded that the enemy could not possibly arrive before mid-March. Yet the behavior of *bexariños* suggested that there could be something to the rumors. On February 20, many of them began packing their belongings and evacuating the town. The following day as many as fifteen of the garrison's *tejano* volunteers explained to Travis that this would be a convenient time to terminate their services.[56]

On February 23 Travis placed a lookout in the bell tower of San Fernando Church. Almost immediately the man signaled that enemy troops were marching along the Presidio Road. Travis had not thought the Mexicans able to reach Béxar until at least March 15; their appearance on the twenty-third convinced him otherwise. The Texians quickly fell back into the fort with as much food and water as they could carry. Travis dispatched a courier to Gonzales with a hastily scribbled missive: "The enemy in large force is in sight. We want men and provisions. Send them to us. We have 150 men and are determined to defend the Alamo to the last."[57]

For all his determination, Travis well understood that without reinforcements the Alamo could not long stand. The issue now rested in the hands of the Council in San Felipe, with Fannin at Goliad, and with any other Texian volunteers who might harken to his impassioned pleas.

❖❖❖

CHAPTER 7

"Determined Valor and Desperate Courage"

❖❖❖

Gary Zaboly
© 1993

The Alamo
March 6, 1836

Having abandoned the perimeter, Alamo defenders have fallen back into the long barracks. The Mexicans turn the fort's cannon on the barricaded entrances, blast openings, and push through. The fighting is bitter and hand to hand. The remaining Texians find themselves cornered. They know attempting to surrender would be fruitless: foreign rebels can expect no quarter.

Although the Greys were among the best equipped of the uniformed volunteer units from the United States, they have been in the field since October, and this fellow's ragamuffin appearance reveals the rigors of much hard campaigning. In January, Alamo commander J. C. Neill had fired off an angry dispatch to General Sam Houston: "The men all under my command have been in the field for the last four months. They are almost naked." Now, nearly two months later, clothing has deteriorated almost beyond the point of pudency. He wears the model 1825 forage cap, and his U.S. surplus canteen and knapsack hang on the wall. Additional gear, such as the ornate powder canister, is also U.S. army surplus.

This Grey makes his last stand in the corner of a blackened room, his back, quite literally, against the wall. As uniformed shapes charge through the door, he discharges both his model 1816 U.S. musket and his .54 caliber model 1819 pistol, manufactured by the firm of Simeon North. He pulls a civilian pattern Bowie knife; this one drawn after a specimen at the Star of the Republic Museum. Yet as six shako-clad figures close on him, he knows full well that his huge knife will provide scant defense against advancing bayonets.

7

"Determined Valor and Desperate Courage"

ALAMO DEFENDERS WATCHED their adversaries pour into Béxar in what seemed an unending stream. So that the rebels would not misunderstand their intent, Mexicans hoisted the red flag of no quarter atop San Fernando Church. Then in accordance with established procedures of siege warfare, they offered the garrison an opportunity to surrender and made their requirements known: "The Mexican army cannot come to terms under any conditions with rebellious foreigners to whom there is no other recourse left, if they wish to save their lives, than to place themselves immediately at the disposal of the Supreme Government from whom alone they may expect clemency after some considerations are taken up." Travis informed the enemy courier that a response would be forthcoming. And it was—a single shot hurled from the eighteen-pounder. There could be no mistaking the meaning of such a succinct reply.[1]

With the formalities out of the way, the Mexican cannoneers set about reducing the adobe walls. Once they had knocked down the walls, the garrison would have to surrender in the face of overwhelming odds. Although Jameson had once referred to the works as "Fortress Alamo," he had clearly done so in jest. "The Alamo never was built by a military people for a fortress," he had explained to Houston, "tho' it is strong, there is not a redoubt that will command the whole line of the fort, all is in the plain wall and intended to take advantage with a few pieces of artillery."[2]

Jameson had detected a major drawback; all was, indeed, "in the plain wall." Unfortunately, the advent of heavy cannon had rendered the curtain wall obsolete four centuries earlier, necessitating a complete transformation of defensive positions and siege craft. The most important developments in both were the work of French engineer Marquis Sébastien Le Prestre de Vauban. By the nineteenth century, it was accepted that one would storm a fortress only if no other option were available. Rather, a careful siege with sufficiently powerful artillery placed in prepared trenches would eventually breach a wall, whereupon the garrison would surrender, defeat being a foregone conclusion.[3]

By the standards of its day, the Alamo was certainly no fortress. It lacked mutually supporting strong points—demilunes, bastions, hornworks, ravelines, sally ports, and the like. There were simply no strong points from which its defenders could oppose an assault. Nor was it logistically self-sustaining; the defenders could not hope to outlast the besiegers. Although the fort contained a good water well, the food supply might have lasted four weeks at most. It did not even command a significant terrain feature, such as a vital pass or port. A perceptive Texian, Dr. J. H. Barnard, identified the chief disadvantage of both La Bahía and the Alamo: "Situated in an open prairie country, they controlled no passes, nor obstructed any route that could check or impede the march of an enemy army. They simply defended what ground they stood upon, and what their guns could reach, and no more, and were from fifty to seventy miles distant from any settlers upon which they could rely for supplies and succor."[4]

Of course, the Spanish priests and presidial troopers who had constructed Mission San Antonio de Valero in 1718 never intended it to function as a fortress. The adobe walls were more than sufficient to stop the arrows of the hostile Indians and to keep friendly neophytes from escaping. The abandoned mission had served as the barracks for the dragoons of the Flying Company of San José y Santiago del Alamo de Parras, who gave it the unit's name. For convenience, locals shortened the post's name to the Alamo. Presidial troopers rested easily behind those thick walls; the Comanches did not have artillery.[5]

But Santa Anna did. The chances are remote that any Texian inside the Alamo, including the lawyer-turned-engineer Green Jameson, was aware of Vauban's system of fortification. They were not, however, blind to the obvious. Travis and Bowie were firm in their determination to defend the Alamo, but both understood it would be only a matter of days before the enemy artillery breached the walls; they were well aware that their survival depended on the speed with which Texians rallied to their aid. They made that clear on the first day of the siege when the co-

commanders wrote Fannin in Goliad: "We have but little Provisions, but enough to serve us till you and your men arrive. We deem it unnecessary to repeat to a brave officer, who knows his duty, that we call on him for assistance." Despite all the hyperbole about preferring to "die in these ditches" and "victory or death," Bowie and Travis were not suicidal. They simply could not imagine that fellow Texians, once aware of their perilous position, would not rush to their aid.[6]

Neither could Santa Anna. He was more concerned about Texian reinforcements coming to break the siege than the meager force bottled up inside the fort. He did not intend to be caught in Béxar as Cós had been. When he heard rumors that two hundred men from Goliad were on the march to relieve the Alamo, Santa Anna ordered General Ramírez y Sesma to intercept them with his cavalry. In addition to sending Ramírez y Sesma's horsemen, he also dispatched the Jiménez infantry battalion out in search of the enemy.[7]

Mexican officers never seemed to worry about the Alamo itself; when its food was exhausted, its fall was certain. His Excellency dismissed the post as an "irregular fortification hardly worthy of the name." Never missing a chance to criticize Santa Anna, de la Peña described the Alamo as "an irregular fortification without flank fires which a wise general would have taken with insignificant losses." Filisola agreed: "By merely placing twenty artillery pieces properly, that poor wall could not have withstood one hour of cannon fire without being reduced to rubble."[8]

Perhaps, but the Mexicans did not have twenty pieces of artillery. They had brought fewer than ten light fieldpieces. Artillerymen customarily relied upon heavy siege guns to reduce enemy fortifications; such weapons were on the way but could not arrive until March 7 or 8. Lacking heavy ordnance, the gunners had to place their smaller cannon closer to the walls, but venturing within two hundred yards of the fort in daylight was an invitation to the deadly Texian riflemen. Working after dark, therefore, the Mexicans began digging a series of entrenchments that grew nearer to the old walls each night.[9]

Inside the Alamo, Bowie's health continued to decline. On the second day of the siege, he collapsed completely. The malady must have been a form of respiratory ailment, for it was variously described as "hasty consumption" and "typhoid pneumonia." (Contrary to persistent legend, Bowie did *not* fall from a gun platform.) Whatever his affliction, Bowie could no longer function as commander, so he instructed his volunteers to obey Travis.[10]

Now in full command, Travis prepared to meet the enemy. If the Mexicans made a frontal assault with infantry, the defenders could inflict heavy losses with rifles and artillery. Anglo-Celtic frontiersmen reared on stories of the victory of Jackson's riflemen over British regulars at New Orleans were naturally drawn to the thick walls around the Alamo. The high adobe ramparts would be as impenetrable as the cotton bales that had shielded their forebears a generation before. Far from being bent on self-sacrifice, Travis and the garrison remained in the fort because they were convinced that they could hold it until reinforcements arrived.[11]

Texian rifles continued to take their toll on the enemy. Atop walls that were in some places twelve feet high, defenders could easily hit unwary Mexicans at two hundred yards. The Mexicans' Brown Bess muskets, on the other hand, were ineffective at ranges of more than seventy yards. The "mountaineers" and "hunters," for whom Tornell had expressed such contempt, soon proved their worth as marksmen, dropping men at ranges the Mexicans thought impossible.[12]

Travis wisely placed Crockett and a unit of skilled riflemen at what seemed the weakest link in the fort's defensive perimeter, the low picket barricade between the chapel and the south wall. The Mexicans soon had reason to avoid the area opposite Crockett's post.[13]

Crockett and his riflemen could kill at long range, but in the event of an enemy assault, the defenders greatest assets would be their cannon. Neill had scrounged some twenty-one pieces of ordnance, but Jameson had not mounted all of them by the time the siege began. Sutherland recalled that "not more than about twenty were put to use during the siege." That figure was confirmed by a number of Mexican reports. In a diagram of the fort, Sánchez-Navarro depicted tubes lying on the ground, supporting Sutherland's testimony that the defenders had not mounted all their artillery.[14]

Best estimates are that Jameson had judiciously mounted nineteen pieces at various points. He placed the eighteen-pounder on the southwest corner to cover the town. Travis commanded a battery of nine-pounders on the north wall. In the chapel, three twelve-pounders covered the area east of the fort. One of the guns was a gunade, a stubby, short-range naval gun of the period. No one has ever determined why a ship's gunade had been taken to a post 150 miles from the nearest coast, but Jameson did not stop to question Providence and reportedly mounted the seagoing ordnance on the west wall.[15]

Despite its fortunate supply of artillery, the garrison nevertheless faced some serious disadvantages. The fort was much too large for so few men to defend. The main plaza contained almost three acres, making the defensive perimeter almost a quarter of a mile long. The small number of Texians could not possibly defend a perimeter that large; it was a case of too much space and too few riflemen. It was also a matter of too few cannoneers for all the cannon. Prevailing doctrine allotted a six-man crew to each piece of ordnance. Travis began the siege with about 150 men; if he had followed that rule and manned all available cannon, 114 of his men would have been assigned as gunners. Travis, of course, did no such thing. Fewer men could fire a cannon if necessary, just not so quickly. In fact, it is unlikely that more than three gunners manned any piece of Alamo artillery. Even at that, rifles along the 440-yard perimeter were spread pitifully thin.[16]

Both riflemen and gunners were vulnerable to enemy counterfire. The Alamo, built as a mission, did not have firing ports. Jameson seemed to have constructed makeshift catwalks, but when the Mexicans approached within the seventy-yard range of their muskets, the defender's upper bodies were exposed. Those men who fired from atop the small rooms along the west wall were even more exposed. Most of the cannon were positioned to fire not through the breastworks but over them. The men had constructed gun emplacements by piling dirt against the inside of the walls, but this arrangement left artillery and artillerymen silhouetted against the sky. Colonel Juan Almonte recorded that on the second day of the siege, Mexican artillery fire dismounted two pieces of Alamo ordnance, including the prized eighteen-pounder. Texians soon had the guns back in operation, but the incident revealed their precarious position.[17]

Once the Mexicans had their artillery in place, they maintained an almost constant fire upon the Alamo. On February 24, in his famous letter addressed to the "People of Texas & all Americans in the world," Travis reported, "I have sustained a continual Bombardment & cannonade for 24 hours & have not lost a man." Although the Texians were lucky not to have suffered any casualties, that happy consequence likely stemmed from the fact that the enemy was directing most of its fire against the wall. Almonte recorded that during the night of February 25 the Mexicans erected two more batteries. Prudence demanded they work at night; that day "in random firing the [Texians] wounded 4 of the Cazadores de Matamoros battalion, and 2 of the battalion of Jimenes, and killed one corporal and a soldier of the battalion of Matamoros."[18]

At first Travis had matched the enemy shot for shot, but by day four he realized how much powder and ball that policy was consuming. The defenders needed to conserve ammunition in the event of an assault. Crockett's men were the exception. Their long rifles wasted less powder with better results. The deadly rifles rarely missed their marks. The remainder of the garrison, frustrated by a growing feeling of impotence, could only sit and endure.[19]

Exhausted defenders grew steadily weaker. Travis did not have enough men to rotate sentries, so each of them slept at his post. Conditions worsened as a blue norther swept through, dropping the temperature to thirty-nine degrees. A party of defenders sallied out of the fort to forage for firewood but were repulsed by Mexican skirmishers equipped with the Baker rifle that could kill at 170 yards. Texians accorded these enemy riflemen more respect than they did the line infantry with smoothbore muskets and so scurried back to the safety of the fort.[20]

Both Suzanna Dickenson, wife of Artillery Captain Almeron Dickenson, and Colonel Travis noted Crockett's efforts to bolster the flagging morale of the garrison. Mrs. Dickenson recalled that he often cheered the troops with his fiddle. Travis reported in a letter to Houston that "the Hon. David Crockett was seen at all points, animating the men to their duty." Even the stricken Bowie had his cot brought out in the open, where he attempted to encourage the men from his sickbed. Despite all efforts, the strain began to tell. Arkansas artilleryman Henry Warnell bitterly expressed their anxieties: "I'd much rather be out on that open prairie.... I don't like to be penned up like this." But in more thoughtful moments, others realized that without cover they could not last an hour against vastly superior Mexican numbers. By the seventh day, the men could see through the desperate attempts to boost their spirits. Only reinforcements could do that.[21]

At least a few were on their way. On February 24 Travis had dispatched Captain Albert Martin to the settlements with his "Victory or Death" letter. The courier rode all night and most of the next day to reach his hometown of Gonzales, some seventy miles away. To his commander's plea for assistance, he added one of his own: "Since the above was written I heard a very heavy Canonade during the whole day [and] think there must have been an attack made upon the alamo[.] We were short of Ammunition when I left[.] Hurry on all the men you can in haste[.]" Alamo messengers John W. Smith and Dr. John Sutherland had reached the town earlier, and Martin's arrival heightened the sense of urgency. The proud men of Gonzales had been the first to shoulder their rifles against centralist oppression; how could they refuse now when fellow Texians needed their help?[22]

The Gonzales Ranging Company of Mounted Volunteers boasted a grandiose title but only twenty-two effectives. With news of the fighting, a few others joined up. The company was a frontier potpourri: New York hatter George Kimball; nineteen-year-old newlywed Johnnie Kellogg; and Béxar carpenter John W. Smith, eager to rejoin his Alamo comrades. The oldest, at forty-one, was Isaac Millsaps; the youngest, William P. King, was only sixteen. By the time of their departure on February 27, their ranks had increased to twenty-five, and another eight joined on the march. Travis had made it clear that a "thousand or more" Mexicans surrounded the fort; fully aware of the disparity of numbers these thirty-two men gamely rode on. Numbers did not always decide a fight; in October, eighteen Gonzales men had held off a hundred Mexican dragoons until their neighbors arrived. Now the fighting men of Gonzales were riding to repay their debt.[23]

The Gonzales volunteers reached the outskirts of Béxar on the night of February 29. They had been fortunate; Santa Anna was expecting Fannin's relief force to come from La Bahía and had therefore detailed Ramírez y Sesma to patrol the Béxar-Goliad road to the southeast. Approaching from the northeast, the Gonzales contingent encountered little opposition. They could see the clusters of Mexican campfires and hear the calls of the sentries. Stealthily making their way through the brush, the men felt their way toward the walls looming ahead in the darkness. Just before three o'clock, they were nearing the fort when a skittish Alamo sentry fired, wounding one of the Gonzales men in the foot. The rest called out to stop shooting. The defenders eagerly swung open the gates to welcome the long-awaited reinforcements. Their spirits must have fallen when they saw how few there were.[24]

March 1 was, nevertheless, a day of celebration inside the Alamo. Travis, of course, had hoped for many more than thirty-two men, but the Gonzales contingent had at least shown that a determined force could make it through the Mexican cordon, and surely more were on the way. The irrepressible Crockett played his fiddle, and Scotsman John

McGregor joined in on the bagpipes. In honor of the new arrivals, Travis even allowed the gunners two precious shots to let Santa Anna know that they had not forgotten him. Knowing ammunition was in short supply, the men sighted carefully. The first ball crashed into the town's Military Plaza; the next tore through the roof of an adjoining house. The gunners had no way of knowing it, but the building served as Santa Anna's head-quarters. That shot might have produced propitious results had His Excellency been there to receive it.[25]

March 2 saw a return to siege routine. The Mexicans continued their cannonading, and the defenders observed that the enemy artillery edged even closer to the walls. Travis could not imagine why Fannin and his four hundred men had not arrived. It had been nine days since he and Bowie had summoned him, plenty of time for the ninety-five-mile journey.[26]

The next day, Travis poured out his feelings in a letter to the Independence Convention meeting at Washington-on-the-Brazos:

> Col. Fannin is said to be on the march to this place with reinforce-
> ments, but I fear it is not true, as I have repeatedly sent to him for aid
> without receiving any. . . . I look to the colonies alone for aid; unless it
> arrives soon, I shall have to fight the enemy on his own terms. I will,
> however, do the best I can under the circumstances; and I feel confident
> that the determined valor and desperate courage, heretofore exhibited
> by my men, will not fail them in the last struggle; and although they
> may be sacrificed to the vengeance of a Gothic enemy, the victory will
> cost the enemy dear, that it will be worse for him than defeat.[27]

Travis had begun to accept the fall of the Alamo as a distinct likeli-hood, but he was not a man with a death wish. He never stopped calling on Texians to rally to his aid. "I hope your honorable body will hasten on reinforcements, ammunition, and provisions to our aid as soon as possible. We have provisions for twenty days for the men we have. Our supply of ammunition is limited." In his letters to the Convention, Travis continued to stress the vital importance of Béxar, which he described as the "great and decisive ground." Better to fight Santa Anna on the fron-tier, he argued, than "to suffer a war of devastation to rage in our settlements."[28]

Travis also wrote his close friend Jesse Grimes, revealing more of his true feelings. Now as always, he asserted, the men of the Alamo were staunch supporters of Texas Independence:

> Let the Convention go on and make a declaration of independence, and we will then understand, and the world will understand, what we are fighting for. If independence is not declared, I shall lay down my arms, and so will the men under my command. But under the flag of independence, we are ready to peril our lives a hundred times a day, and to drive away the monster who is fighting under a blood-red flag, threatening to murder all prisoners and make Texas a waste desert. . . . If my countrymen do not rally to my relief, I am determined to perish in the defense of this place, and my bones shall reproach my country for her neglect.[29]

Travis's fiery words were in vain. On March 3, courier James Butler Bonham arrived from Goliad with the grim news that Fannin would not be coming. He had received the messages from Travis and Bowie calling for his assistance and on February 28 had actually begun the march to Béxar. But Fannin had never been personally committed to the relief of the Alamo, and when an ox cart broke down less than a mile from Goliad, his resolve evaporated. Accepting the advice of a council of his officers, he called off the expedition and led his men back to La Bahía.[30]

That same evening, Fannin explained his decision in a letter to Acting Governor James W. Robinson. Some have criticized Fannin's failure to relieve the Alamo, but from a strategic standpoint his reasons were valid: "It is now obvious that the Enemy have entered Texas at two points, for the purpose of attacking Béxar & this place—The first has been attacked and we may expect the enemy here momentarily—Both places are importent—and at this time particularly so."[31]

He added that his supplies were running short: "We have not in the garrison supplies of Bread Stuff for a single day and as yet but little Beef and should our Supplies be cut off our situation will be, to say the least—disagreeable." He expressed sympathy for the valiant "volunteers now shut in Béxar" but concluded that permitting his command to be cut off with them would ill-serve the interests of Texas. Abandoning Goliad would leave the eastern door open to Urrea's advance. Travis and his men would have to manage without Fannin's help.[32]

By day eleven of the siege, the constant battering by Mexican artillery had weakened the walls. Santa Anna had established a battery within "musket shot" of the north wall. At that range, he did not need siege guns; each round shot hammered the crumbling adobe until a portion of the wall collapsed. Jameson directed work parties throughout the night, buttressing the wall with odd pieces of timber. The chief engineer realized that these were only stop-gap measures. In the event of a determined attack, the north wall could not hold.[33]

On March 5, day twelve of the siege, Santa Anna called a meeting of his officers to discuss the possibility of an assault. Most of the officers present were amazed that the question was even being considered. The walls were already crumbling, and in two or three days the siege guns would arrive. Many argued that, surrounded by such a superior force, the defenders were no real threat. No Texian relief column had been sighted, so there was no reason for haste. They needed only to wait until the garrison's provisions ran out, when Travis would have no choice but to yield. Lieutenant Colonel de la Peña recorded that the majority of officers "were of the opinion that victory over a handful of men concentrated in the Alamo did not call for a great sacrifice."[34]

Despite these reasonable objections, Santa Anna stubbornly insisted on attacking. He cited morale as a factor, claiming that "an assault would infuse our soldiers with that enthusiasm of the first triumph that would make them superior in the future to those of the enemy." General Ramírez y Sesma—no doubt still fancying himself as Murat—eagerly agreed with His Excellency. Oddly, so did Colonel Almonte, who normally demonstrated better judgment. It became obvious that Santa Anna had already decided; the meeting had merely been a matter of form. De la Peña recalled that most of the officers were horrified at Santa Anna's decision but "chose silence, knowing that he would not tolerate opposition."[35]

Inside the Alamo, Travis had also assembled his men for a conclave. According to legend, he drew a line in the dust with his saber, inviting all who were resolved to stay and die with him to cross. Evidence does not support the tale, but apparently Travis did gather the men for a conference. Mrs. Dickenson remembered that he "asked the command that if any desired to escape, now was the time to let it be known, and to step out of ranks." Shortly thereafter Frenchman Louis Rose is said to have escaped, which may mean that Travis told each man to decide for himself whether to stay or go.[36]

Reliable Mexican accounts, however, suggest a different story. According to them, a *bexareña* left the fort after the meeting. She told Santa Anna that morale was low and that defenses were crumbling. De la Peña recounted:

> Travis's resistance was on the verge of being overcome; for several days his followers had been urging him to surrender, giving the lack of food and the scarcity of munitions as reasons, but he had quieted their restlessness with hope of quick relief, something not difficult for them to believe since they had seen some reinforcements arrive. Nevertheless, they had pressed him so hard that on the 5th he promised them that if no help arrived on that day they would surrender the next day or would try to escape under the cover of darkness; these facts were given to us by a lady from Bejar, a Negro who was the only male who escaped, and several women who were inside and were rescued by Colonels Morales and Minion.[37]

General Filisola also recalled that the garrison had considered the possibility of surrender:

> On that same evening [March 5] about nightfall it was reported that Travis Barnet [William Barret Travis], commander of the enemy garrison, through the intermediary of a woman, proposed to the general in chief that they would surrender arms and fort with everybody in it with the only condition of saving his life and that of all his comrades in arms. However, the answer had come back that they should surrender unconditionally, without guarantees, not even for life itself, since there should be no guarantees for traitors. With this reply it is clear that all were determined to lose their existence, selling it as dearly as possible.[38]

The prospects of an honorable surrender seemed to have alarmed Santa Anna. De la Peña speculated that the general was determined to precipitate an assault before the garrison could yield. A capitulation would not create a favorable "sensation"; the president-general "would have regretted taking the Alamo without clamor and without bloodshed, for some believe that without these there is no glory." There was no need for concern. There would be clamor and bloodshed aplenty.[39]

The Mexican army would assault in Bonaparte's column formation. The self-proclaimed Napoleon of the West intended to hurl his troops toward the Alamo like irresistible missiles, terrify the rebels with overwhelming mass, and win a glorious victory to add to his laurels. Santa Anna organized his force into five units; four columns would attack from every point of the compass, while he personally commanded the reserves. The lancers would form a cordon around the fort "to prevent the possibility of escape." [40]

The attack orders of March 5 set the onslaught for five o'clock the next morning. The Mexican artillery fell silent later that afternoon. Officers told soldiers to get plenty of rest, for they would be called to arms at midnight to take their positions. The general hoped that weary rebels would also take advantage of the lull to get some sleep. He intended to surprise the garrison. If the Mexicans approached the fort silently, they could be over the walls before the bleary-eyed defenders reached their stations. [41]

The men of the Alamo welcomed the silence, ominous though it was. For twelve days, they had endured an almost constant bombardment. Travis posted a few men in listening posts outside the fort and dispatched sixteen-year-old Jim Allen with his last request for assistance. Then, succumbing to lack of sleep, he turned the watch over to Adjutant John Baugh and collapsed on his cot. All was quiet inside the fort as the stroke of midnight heralded the beginning of day thirteen of the siege: March 6, 1836. [42]

At that same moment, the Mexican camp came alive, contrasting sharply with the stillness of the Alamo. Sergeants tapped their sleeping men awake with the wooden staffs that were the symbols of their rank; when that failed, the toe of their boots roused groggy recruits. Sappers distributed ladders and crowbars; noncoms saw that all shako straps were firmly fastened; officers made sure that all men were wearing shoes or sandals—proper footgear would be crucial when scaling walls. And, of course, weapons were inspected. The general's order had been specific: "The arms, principally the bayonets, should be in perfect order." [43]

By 5:00 A.M. all was in readiness. The morning was chilly and many of the troops had been shivering in place for hours. Column commanders informed His Excellency that the men were becoming restless. Finally at 5:30, Santa Anna gave the word to move out. [44]

All went smoothly as the Mexicans moved silently through the early morning moonlight. A massed column provided an excellent target, but it was a necessary formation for controlling recruits who were boxed in by steadier veterans. Cós, commanding the lead column, marched toward the northwest corner. Colonel Francisco Duque, at the head of the second column, angled from the northwest toward the patched breach in the north wall. Colonel José María Romero came in behind the fort from the east. Colonel Juan Morales led his column toward the low parapet by the chapel, supposedly the fort's soft spot. Lines of light infantry skirmishers fanned out several yards in advance of the columns; armed with Baker rifles, it was their assignment to pick off any defenders who showed their heads. They caught the snoozing Texian sentinels outside the walls; an efficient bayonet thrust, a blade drawn across the throat, and they died quickly—but more critical, silently. Unopposed and undetected, the columns approached inexorably nearer to the walls.[45]

Bathed in bright moonlight that cast eerie, unearthly shadows across the landscape, the Alamo loomed ahead. The tension finally became unbearable. A soldier deep within one of the columns shouted, "Viva Santa Anna!" "Viva la Republica!" another countered. Soon hundreds of voices filled the air. Santa Anna was incensed by these "imprudent huzzas," for he knew the noise would alert the slumbering rebels.[46]

It did. John Baugh heard the clamor and then saw the columns, already within musket range of the walls. The adjutant raced across the plaza, adding his voice to the cacophony from outside. "Colonel Travis! The Mexicans are coming." Joe, Travis's slave, slept in the same room with his master, and each staggered from his cot, grabbed his weapons, and rushed to the north wall battery. Travis shouted as he ran: "Come on, boys, the Mexicans are upon us and we'll give them Hell!" He must have wondered why the sentries outside the walls had not sounded the alarm. When he reached the battery and saw how far the enemy had advanced, he knew the answer.[47]

Texian gunners had loaded their cannon. Lacking proper canister shot, they had crammed their ordnance with chopped-up horseshoes, links of chain, nails, bits of door hinges—every piece of jagged scrap metal they could scavenge. Packing that lethal load, the artillery doubled as giant shotguns. In that light and at that range, they could not miss their massed targets.[48]

A gust of metal fragments swept the columns like a "terrible shower." The close-packed bodies of the soldiers soaked up the force of the scatter shot. Rusty shards slammed home, slowed as they plowed through the ranks, and finally stopped, lodged in flesh.

Then came round shot. Nine-pound iron balls probed further into the mass, gouging great swaths of destruction. Far worse than the roar of cannon was the sickening thud of iron striking flesh. The attackers were

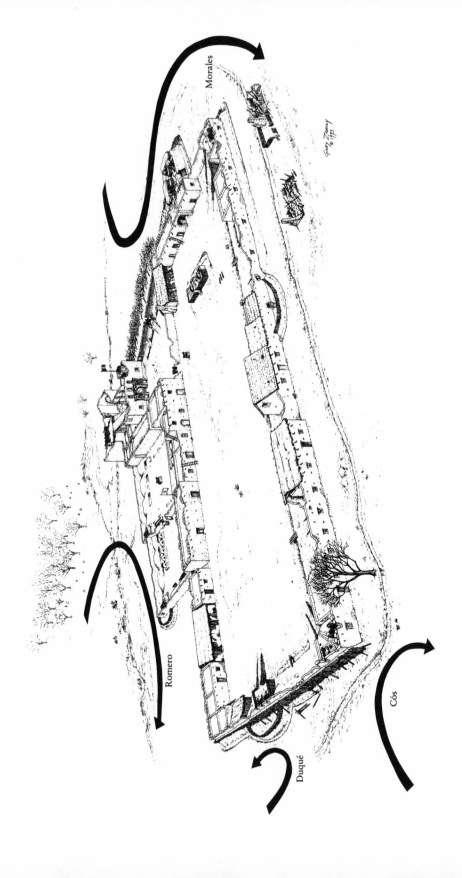

Morales

Cós

Duqué

Romero

At approximately 5 A.M. on March 6, 1836, four columns totaling about 1,100 Mexican troops move into position to begin the assault on the Alamo.

From the northwest: General Martín Perfecto de Cós with two hundred fusiliers and riflemen of the Aldama Battalion and one hundred fusiliers of the San Luis Potosí militia carrying ten ladders, two crowbars, and two axes

From the north: Colonel Francisco Duque with the Toluca Battalion (minus the grenadiers) and three fusilier companies of San Luis, about four hundred men in all, carrying ten ladders, two crowbars, and two axes

From the northeast: Colonel José María Romero with fusilier companies of the Matamoros and Jimenez battalions, about three hundred men, carrying six ladders

From the south: Colonel Juan Morales with three rifle companies of the Matamoros, Jimenez, and San Luis battalions, totaling one hundred men, carrying two ladders

Mauled by Alamo artillery and small-arms fire, the columns on the east, north, and west waver and fall back. The southern column seeks shelter behind the *jacales* at the southwest corner.

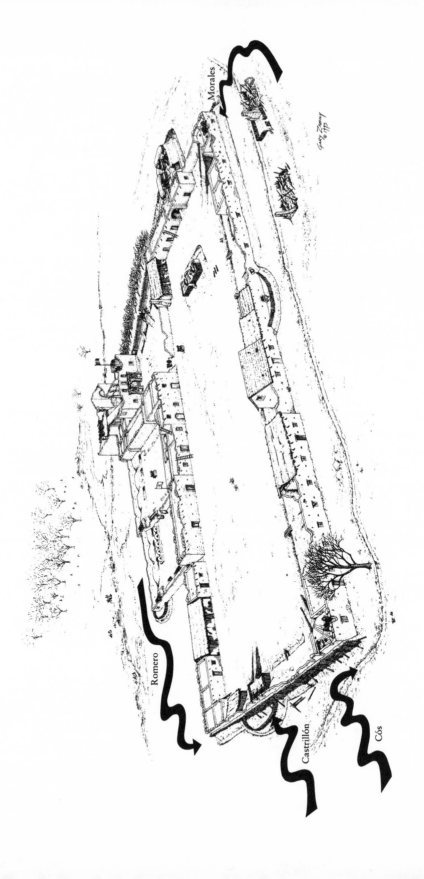

Morales

Romero

Castrillón

Cós

Second Phase — Attack and Disorder

The columns move forward again. Those on the east, north, and west converge to form an almost solid, confused mass huddling at the base of the north wall. With Colonel Duque wounded and out of action, General Manuel Fernandez Castrillón takes command of the north column. At the southwest corner, Morales's men attack bravely but have not yet entered the compound.

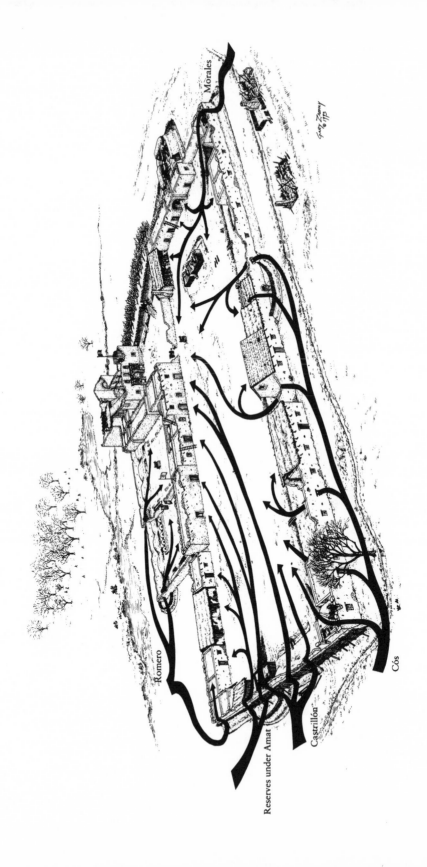

Morales

Cós

Castrillón

Reserves under Amat

Romero

His ranks shredded by cannon blasts from the *Fortin de Con-delle*, as well as by misdirected fire from the Toluca Battalion under Castrillón's command, General Cós makes an oblique movement to the right with his column and assaults a sizable portion of the west wall. Men wielding axes and crowbars break through the posterns and blocked-up windows; many more climb over the wall; and others push through the two ground-level gun ports. Colonel Romero makes a similar move to his left with most of his column and storms the two gun positions in the corrals.

Meanwhile, General Castrillón directs the assault of the north column up the wooden outerwork that covers the entire face of the north wall, but his men meet fierce resistance. Santa Anna then sends in the reserves: the Zapadores Battalion and five grenadier companies of Matamoros, Jimenez, Aldama, Toluca, and San Luis, 400 men in all.

Seeing their flanks exposed by the ingress of the columns under Cós and Romero, the Texians defending the north wall abandon it and seek shelter in the second line of defense: the long barracks and other houses within the compound.

By this time Morales's men have also entered the fort, seizing the eighteen-pounder and the main gate positions. Mexican soldiers now pour unchecked into the Alamo from almost every direction. In the barracks and the chapel, the surviving Texians ensconce themselves for their last, brutal stand.

frightfully exposed; de la Peña watched in horror as "a single cannon volley did away with half the company of chasseurs from Toluca." Huddled together as they were in tight formation, even those untouched by enemy fire were splattered with blood and bits of flesh torn from their less fortunate friends. Bashing bodies, round shot paid multiple dividends; flying bone fragments proved as lethal as grapeshot. Those trapped inside the column could see little, but they heard the bedlam— the anguished screams of mangled comrades.[49]

But Texians were also suffering losses. Rebel riflemen had to reveal themselves in order to fire on the attackers; the accurate Baker rifles swept the parapets, and at this range even Brown Bess could kill. The fort was lit from within by gunfire. Outlined against the light, the men atop the walls "could not remain for a single second without being killed." Travis was among the first to fall. He had just emptied both barrels of his shotgun into a column when a slug smacked into his forehead, sending him tumbling down the earthen ramp. With his master down and dying, Joe took refuge within one of the rooms along the west wall.[50]

The Mexicans, shattered by grape and round shot, took scant notice of Texian casualties. Facing this deadly welter of fire, some demoralized recruits faltered, but the officers and noncoms stood firm. Sergeants beat the men back into ranks with their thick staffs, the officers with the flat of their swords. The men could not retreat far, for at their rear were the lancers Santa Anna had posted to prevent the escape of his own troops as well as the Texians.[51]

The Mexican assault troops were taking heavy casualties, but ragged formations regrouped and drove forward. Viewing the debacle, Santa Anna committed the reserves, but stayed out of rifle range himself. Once more, the brave Mexican infantry charged into the maelstrom.[52]

The devastating fire savaged Mexican ranks. Ordered columns were ripped asunder, but still they came. Unit integrity broke down as the columns of Cós and Duque swirled together at the base of the north wall. Advancing from the east, Romero's formation was swept by artillery fire from atop the chapel. To avoid effects of the deadly grapeshot, the column performed a right oblique toward the north wall, where it ran into the intermingled mob of Duque and Cós. Morales's attack against the palisade faltered as well. Contrary to expectations, that portion of the perimeter was anything but weak. In the face of direct fire from a cannon and Crockett's riflemen, the column angled to the left toward the southwest corner and the eighteen-pounder.[53]

Once the surviving Mexicans reached the base of the wall, their problem became one of climbing over. They concentrated their main effort on the north wall and Jameson's makeshift repairs. Travis's nine-pounders, however, had taken a heavy toll. "The few poor ladders that we were bringing had not arrived," a Mexican officer reported, "because their bearers had either perished on the way or escaped." Yet the rough-hewn repairs to the north wall had left numerous gaps and toeholds. Realizing the time had come to conquer or die, the Mexicans began hoisting each other over the jerry-built barricade.[54]

Desperation and sheer mass finally supplanted careful planning. General Juan Amador began the difficult twelve-foot climb over the north wall, challenging his soldiers to follow. The general and his men grappled up and over the parapet and dropped into the plaza below. Amador and his men inside the Alamo located the north wall postern and swung it open. Their comrades flooded through, penetrating the Alamo's defensive perimeter. From that moment, the outcome of the assault was never in doubt.[55]

The Texians abandoned the north wall. As they fell back, Alamo gunners turned their cannon toward the wave of Mexicans rushing through the postern. Combined rifle and artillery fire ripped into the uniformed soldiers pinned against the inside of the wall. But now, when rapid fire was essential, rifles were a disadvantage; the long grooved barrels that rendered them so accurate also made them slow to load. When the fort's guns were swung northward to counter the enemy pouring through the postern, the Morales column, which had taken refuge behind some nearby stone huts, rallied and charged up and over the south wall. The cannoneers were slain before they had time to spike their gun. Seeing the enemy on the front and rear walls, outflanked Texians in the courtyard fell back to the final defensive line inside the long barracks. At the same time, Crockett's riflemen withdrew into the chapel.[56]

Jameson had prepared well. The barracks doors facing the courtyard were buttressed by semicircular parapets of dirt secured with cowhides. From windows and loopholes, the defenders shot down Mexicans in the plaza. But in their haste to fall back to the long barracks, the crews on the northwest battery had failed to spike their guns. Mexicans loaded the captured cannon, swung them around, and systematically blasted each door. Realizing the utter hopelessness of their situation, a few of the rebels tried to surrender. De la Peña remembered their pathetic attempts: "Some . . . desperately cried, 'Mercy, valiant Mexicans,' others poked the points of their bayonets through a hole or a door with a white cloth, the symbol of ceasefire, and some even used their socks." There was a brief lull as Mexicans advanced, but as they entered the quarters they were ruthlessly gunned down by other Texians who "had no thought of surrendering."[57]

Angry Mexicans charged through the shattered openings to finish the work begun by the captured cannon. In the darkened rooms of the long barracks, the adversaries grappled with Bowie knife and bayonet. Having seen their men shot down after flags of truce had been raised, the *soldados* took no prisoners, slaughtering even the wounded. A few Texians sought to escape by bounding over the east wall and running for cover, but the lancers made short work of them. The butchering was repeated in the rooms along the south wall; even the delirious Bowie, too weak to rise from his sickbed, found no mercy. But then, neither would he have asked for it.[58]

The chapel was the last to fall. The Mexicans swung the eighteen-pounder, blew down the sandbags guarding the main entrance, and pushed through by the dozens. Bonham and Dickenson fell beside their cannon on the battery at the rear of the church. Crockett and six of his men fought on until they were literally overwhelmed. This was no longer war; it was wanton slaughter; and General Manuel Fernández Castrillón ordered his soldiers to spare these helpless men.

Even after all the defenders had been killed or captured, dazed Mexicans continued to shoot at shadows. As a cat scurried among the ruins, a superstitious *soldado* shouted: "It is not a cat, but an American!" The feline was immediately killed. One can easily appreciate this wanton blood lust; these men had seen friends mangled by artillery, riddled by rifles, gutted by Bowie knives. Having survived the slaughter themselves, they were taking no chances.[59]

Upon being informed that the Alamo had fallen, Santa Anna ventured into the fort. As he was surveying the carnage, General Castrillón brought forward Crockett and the others. The chivalrous Castrillón attempted to intercede on behalf of the defenseless prisoners, but Santa Anna answered with a "gesture of indignation" and ordered their immediate execution. De la Peña reported that several officers were outraged at the murder of helpless men and refused to enforce the command. But "in order to flatter their commander," nearby staff officers who had not taken part in the assault fell upon Crockett and the others with their swords and hacked them to pieces. De la Peña recorded that "these unfortunates died without complaining and without humiliating themselves before their torturers."[60]

How true to pattern. Crockett's motto—or at least the one attributed to him—had been, "Be sure you're right, then go ahead." Once in Congress, his colleagues had urged him to support President Andrew Jackson's Indian bill. To do otherwise, they assured him, was political suicide. He replied in genuine Crockett style: "I told them I believed it was a wicked, unjust measure, and that I should go against it, let the cost to myself be what it might; . . . that I would sooner be honestly and politically d——nd, than hypocritically immortalized. . . . I voted against this Indian bill, and my conscience yet tells me that I gave a good honest vote, and one that I believe will not make me ashamed in the day of judgement."[61]

He was, of course, soundly walloped in the next election, but satisfied that he had taken the honorable course, Crockett stubbornly ignored the consequences. Most of those who had fallen alongside him readily understood that brand of righteous bullheadedness. To remain loyal to their upbringing and the legacy of their rebel forebears, resistance to Santa Anna could be their only recourse. Behind the walls of the Alamo, they cast their final vote against centralism, a system they believed "wicked" and "unjust." March 6 was judgment day for them all; like Crockett, none had reason to be ashamed.[62]

CHAPTER 8

"We Are in a Critical Situation"

❖

8. *CAZADOR*, TOLUCA BATTALION

The Alamo
March 6, 1836

José Enrique de la Peña recounted that "a single cannon volley did away with half the company of chasseurs from Toluca, which was advancing a few paces from the column." The figure depicted is one of those unfortunate chasseurs (cazadores, or light infantrymen) caught in that "terrible shower" of flying metal.

A member of Captain José Maria Herrera's cazador company, the mortally wounded private wears a dark blue coatee with red facings and turnbacks. His trousers are gray, while the battered leather shako is adorned with a red pompon.

The Baker rifle at his feet is an English import and likely a veteran weapon of several Napoleonic campaigns. Likewise, his black leather accoutrements are surplus items from the British army. Even the powder horn is English; note the powder measure attached to the powder horn. The Baker rifle's distinctive sword bayonet is affixed to the muzzle by means of a bar brazed into its brass hilt.

In the 1820s, Claudio Linati illustrated a Mexican grenadier sporting the "half-spatterdashes" (gaiters) over his shoes; it is probable that the cazadores, another "preferred" corps, employed them as well. British riflemen, the famed "Green Jackets," certainly wore gaiters, and given the Mexican penchant for English surplus items, it is likely that they also would have been purchased as part of the mix. Gaiters kept dirt and mud out of an infantryman's footwear and off his trousers. More crucial, they kept odd particles from working their way up the inside of a man's trousers — granules of dirt and dust in one's crotch produce a most disagreeable sensation.

The crippled cazador is shown after he has collapsed against the north wall's make-shift lumber reinforcement, the focus of General Perfecto de Cós's column. Santa Anna's attack order of March 5, 1836, had Cós's column equipped with "ten ladders, two crowbars, and two axes." One of the axes, its handle shattered, lies discarded at the base of the wall. According to de la Peña, the same canister round that shredded the cazador company also killed Captain Herrera and wounded a Lieutenant Vences.

153

8

"We Are in a Critical Situation"

SANTA ANNA SURVEYED THE SLAUGHTER inside the smoldering compound as daylight revealed the full extent of the horror. "The bodies," de la Peña recalled, "with their blackened and bloody faces disfigured by desperate death, their hair and uniforms burning at once, presented a dreadful and truly hellish sight." [1]

It had been a costly victory. As many as six hundred Mexican soldiers had been killed or wounded, one third of the assault force, which had been composed of Santa Anna's best battalions. José Juan Sánchez-Navarro, surveying the number of Mexican dead, ironically remarked: "With another such victory, we will all go to the devil." As Mexican officers predicted, the medical corps was inadequate to meet the needs of the wounded. Santa Anna had failed even to have a field hospital set up before the battle. Ramón Martínez Caro, Santa Anna's personal secretary, recorded that "more than a hundred of the wounded died afterward as a result of the lack of proper medical attention and medical facilities in spite of the fact that their injuries were not serious." He added bitterly that "those who lingered in pain and suffering without the proper comfort or relief" envied the men who had been instantly killed. Captain Fernando Urizza approached Santa Anna in the bloody compound and was amazed at the general's insensibility. Pointing to the charred corpses, His Excellency casually remarked: "These are the chickens. Much blood has been shed; but the battle is over. It was but a small affair." [2]

Santa Anna finally had his victory, and he knew how to make it pay political dividends. In a letter to Secretary of War María Tornel, he boasted: "The fortress at last fell into our power with its artillery, ammunition, etc., and buried among the ditches and trenches are more than

600 bodies, all of them foreigners. . . . I can assure you that there were very few who may have gone to relate the event to their companions."[3]

The number of rebel dead claimed by Santa Anna was, of course, a blatant lie. Martínez Caro, the conscientious secretary, balked at making a false report, but later confessed he wrote it "at the command of His Excellency."

Several flags had flown over the Alamo, but the azure banner of the New Orleans Greys attracted the general's special attention. He dispatched it along with his post-battle report as a trophy of war: "The bearer takes with him one of the flags of the enemy's battalions, captured today. The inspection of it will show plainly the true intentions of the treacherous colonists, and of their abettors, who came from parts of the United States of the North." The presence of the New Orleans Greys served to bolster the despot's belief that most of the problems in Texas were caused by Anglo-Americans who had entered Texas illegally.[4]

In large measure, that belief was justified. Most of those who had died defending the Alamo were fighting for a borrowed cause; the majority had only recently come from the United States to fight for Texas independence. Among them were Scots, Welsh, Danes, and English, as well as U.S. citizens. Few of the real Texians were there, for few of the old settlers had originally sought independence or war. Both were ultimately forced upon them, largely by the stream of latecomers and Santa Anna's attempt to rid Texas of its Anglo-Celtic colonists.[5]

The question arises: What might have happened if the Alamo had been abandoned as Houston claimed to have ordered, or even if the men had slipped away after the Mexican army arrived? In other words, did the Texians gain anything in exchange for the defenders' heroic stand, or was their sacrifice in vain?

Purveyors of popular culture claim that the thirteen-day siege bought the time that Texas desperately needed to prepare its defenses. Many movies and other works of fiction pretend that Sam Houston used the time to train an army, but during most of the period he was a member of the Independence Convention at Washington-on-the-Brazos and not even with the army. What "army" there was consisted of Fannin's force at Goliad and a few other contingents in the surrounding area. Being volunteers, they exercised their customary right to elect their officers; they had not taken an oath of loyalty to Texas. There is simply no evidence to support the notion that the sacrifice of the Alamo garrison allowed Houston to raise and train an army.[6]

The delay did, on the other hand, allow the creation of a revolutionary government and the drafting of a constitution. Texas needed several weeks to take these necessary steps toward independence, which even the old settlers now realized was their only recourse. The anticipated support of Mexican liberals had proven chimerical, and U.S. banks had no interest in loaning money to a Mexican state in rebellion. An independent republic, of course, was a different matter. If Santa Anna had struck the settlements immediately, he might have easily driven the Texians across the Sabine River as he intended. Even with the delay, he came closer to succeeding than is apparent.

Santa Anna helped make the defenders' loss worthwhile by chucking his best troops against the Alamo and allowing them to be decimated. If he had preserved these veteran units intact instead of wasting them, the outcome of the rebellion might have been quite different.[7]

Perhaps most important, the slaughter of the Alamo defenders finally awakened the Texians to their perilous situation. It brought home forcefully the fact that the war was far from over and that they must unite to fight or lose all. Santa Anna sent word by survivor Suzanna Dickenson that all who refused to submit would receive the same brutal treatment. The fate of the defenders and Santa Anna's threats gave Texians a will to fight that they had previously lacked. Before his death, Travis had written: "We hope our country[men] will open their eyes to the present danger, and awake from their false security." The old colonists were at last awake, and their eyes were open, but too late for the men of the Alamo. It was as Travis had predicted: "The Thunder of the Enemy's Cannon and the pollution of their wives and daughters—the cries of the Famished Children, will only arouse them." It was ironic that so heavy a sacrifice of newcomers was required to arouse the old settlers into taking up arms in their defense.[8]

In Goliad the American volunteers were outraged by the lack of local support; they had come to fight alongside the Texians in their struggle against despotism, not to shoulder the burden alone. The Texas government had no more success supplying La Bahía than it had the Alamo. John Sowers Brooks, an idealistic twenty-two-year-old volunteer from Virginia, had written his father in December swearing that he would "never disgrace the name of a soldier or that of a Virginian." In a February letter to his sister, he philosophically observed, "Death is one of the chances of the game I play and if it fall to my lot, I shall not murmur, and you should not regret." Now in March, his messages no longer reflected such youthful bravado: "We have had no bread for several days. I am nearly naked, without shoes, and without money. We suffer much, and as soon as Bexar falls we will be surrounded by 6000 infernal Mexicans.... We are in a critical situation." Writing to Acting Governor James W. Robinson on February 7, Fannin had protested:

> Out of more than four hundred men at or near this post, I doubt if twenty-five citizens of Texas can be mustered in ranks—nay, I am informed, whilst writing the above, that there is not half that number;—does this fact bespeak an indifference, and criminal apathy, [which is] truly alarming? ... Could they hear the just complaints and taunting remarks in regard to the absence of the old settlers and owners of the soil, and the total neglect in the officers of the Government, not providing them with even the necessaries of life, this our main stay would not be so confidently relied upon![9]

Fortunately for the Texians, Santa Anna was, for the moment, content to dally in Béxar. Although many of his subordinates urged him to follow up the victory with a swift drive against the American settlements, His Excellency refused to budge. He seemed to believe that once the settlers heard of the Alamo slaughter, they would trample over each other fleeing the country. He was not entirely mistaken.[10]

Santa Anna had every reason to be pleased with the progress of his campaign; the war was proceeding as planned. The able General Urrea was making great strides in his sweep through the coastal prairies. The meager remnants of the Matamoros Expedition had been caught lingering in San Patricio. Apparently ignorant of Urrea's proximity, Grant and a detachment were out rounding up wild mustangs, leaving Johnson in town with only thirty-four men. At three o'clock in the morning of February 27, Urrea launched an attack on San Patricio in the midst of a driving rain, catching the Texians completely off guard. Johnson had distributed his command into five separate parties. Two seven-man units protected the horse herds, while the remaining three were camped in and around San Patricio. The Mexicans struck with such speed and surprise that Johnson had no chance to assemble his command, which was easily defeated piecemeal. Although Urrea reported that the men behind the earthworks at Lipantitlán "defended themselves resolutely," by dawn the fort and town were his. Nine or ten Texians were killed and eighteen taken prisoner; only six, including Colonel Johnson, escaped.[11]

Meanwhile, Grant and his horse-hunting party were returning to San Patricio, unaware that Urrea had taken the town. Learning that Grant and his contingent were riding toward San Patricio, Urrea prepared an ambush along Agua Dulce Creek about twenty-six miles south of town.[12]

On March 2, Grant and his twenty-six-man company entered Urrea's trap. Grant, Plácido Benavides, and Ruben R. Brown rode about half a mile ahead of the men, who were driving several hundred head of wild horses. As the main body passed between two large mottes, more than sixty dragoons swept out of the woods. Grant looked back and saw that his command had already been cut off. The courageous Benavides wanted to return, but Grant persuaded him to rush to Fannin with word of Urrea's advance. As a native of the region with intimate knowledge of the terrain, he would have a better chance of cutting his way through to Goliad.

Benavides galloped off toward La Bahía, while Grant and Brown charged to the aid of their comrades. But as they drew near, it was clear that most of the party were already dead. A Mexican lancer killed Brown's mount, but he quickly grabbed another. At that moment, the herd stampeded, breaking through the cordon of Mexican cavalry. Seeing that they stood no chance of helping their friends, Grant and Brown attempted to escape amidst the mustangs. The Mexicans saw them and gave chase. A dragoon rushed upon Brown, who knocked the lance aside and shot his pursuer. By this time, other Mexican cavalrymen had ridden close enough to call out for the two to surrender. But the two Texians "knew better" and "continued to fly." The number of pursuers continued to increase. When Grant and Brown had galloped about seven miles, they found themselves surrounded, whereupon they dismounted, "determined to make them pay dearly for our lives." A Mexican horseman drove his lance through Brown's arm, but he did pay dearly, for Grant shot him out of the saddle. "Just as he shot the Mexican," Brown recalled, "I saw Grant fall, pierced with several lances, and a moment after I found myself fast in a lasso that had been thrown over me, and by which I was dragged on the ground."

Thus ended the ambush at Agua Dulce Creek, but the violence continued. Lashed to a horse, Brown was taken to Matamoros for interrogation. Before he left, however, he saw several Mexican officers run their swords through Grant's bloody corpse. Many of them had known Grant during the time he had lived in Mexico and, regarding him as an ungrateful opportunist, "had a bitter grudge against him." Brown recognized a Tennessee volunteer named Carpenter, who was mortally wounded. Upon discovering that the man was still alive, one of the dragoons dismounted and "while poor Carpenter was asking to have his life spared," crushed his skull with the butt of his carbine.[13]

The twin battles of San Patricio and Agua Dulce Creek confirmed the doubts of those who questioned the ability of woodlanders to fight on open ground. In October, just after the fighting had begun in Gonzales, many had predicted that if they ever ventured onto the prairies, American riflemen would be "powerless against cavalry." They needed no further proof.[14]

While the American horsemanship was proving inadequate, loyalist *rancheros* who were born to the saddle flocked to Urrea's banner. Organized under Carlos de la Garza, Manuel Sabriego, Juan Moya, and Agustín Moya, they kept Urrea well informed of rebel movements and harassed Texian outriders to the extent that Fannin had no knowledge of Urrea's position. General Urrea praised the contributions of *tejano* scouts as "truly marvelous"; their participation was critical to Mexican success.[15]

By March 1 Benavides had brought news of the defeat to Fannin at La Bahía, which the Anglo-American volunteers had renamed Fort Defiance. This news weighed heavily upon Fannin, who found himself forced to reconsider the strategic situation. Although he had completed but two years at West Point, Fannin could read a map, and the story it told was alarming. The Alamo was not the "key to Texas," as Travis had insisted. Strategically, Goliad was far more important, since it blocked the approach of the enemy force from Copano Bay. But with Béxar already under Mexican control, the Alamo cut off, and Copano Bay abandoned by the Texians, Goliad had been rendered insignificant. If Fannin remained at La Bahía, Santa Anna's army could easily sweep eastward, cutting Goliad off from the Texian settlements. The two Mexican armies could then crush Fannin's garrison between them. From a strategic perspective, whether Travis held out was academic; bottled up inside the Alamo, his small force could do nothing to halt the enemy advance. Goliad had been outflanked.[16]

No one knew that better than Fannin, but his resolve was cracking. For months he had jockeyed for high command, but now at this critical juncture he realized that he was not prepared for it. "I am a better judge of my military abilities than others," he wrote Acting Governor

Robinson, "and if I am qualified to command an Army, I have not found it out."[17]

Fannin thought it best that his garrison withdraw from Goliad, but he was loath to take responsibility for that decision. He explained his situation in a letter to Robinson:

> I learn from several sources that as soon as Bexar is retaken [the Mexicans will] march here, and thus complete their chain of communication to the interior and the Gulf. I am resolved to await your orders, let the consequence be what it may. . . . I should be pleased to have more express from Washington [on-the-Brazos], and if we are not to be sustained in a proper manner, and in good time, receive orders to fall back to the provisions and on the colonies, and *let us all go together*. I again repeat to you, that I consider myself bound to await your orders. I cannot, in a military point of view, be considered now as acting commander-in-chief, as I have never received order to that effect, nor has the army. . . . Lastly, I have orders from you *not* to make *retrograde movement*, but to await orders and reinforcements. . . . I have no doubt the enemy in Bexar . . . knowing our weakness, and want of cavalry . . . will, make a dash between us and Provisions [at Matagorda] and secure them.[18]

Fannin's strict obedience to orders was rather ironic. Heretofore the Texian war effort had been characterized by strong-willed commanders who thought they knew better than their superiors. Now the cause was undermined by a leader who lacked the ability to make the hard decisions. Fannin knew of the disunity among the Texas politicians. If the faction-ridden Council could not even agree on a basic governing policy, it certainly could not be expected to grapple with the complex problems of strategy. Fannin, as the commander on the ground and with at least some formal military training, was in a better position to make those decisions. The Texas "Hamlet," Fannin's inability to take decisive action would lead to a tragedy of Shakespearean proportions.[19]

In the meantime, the Constitutional Convention at Washington-on-the-Brazos had received Travis's letter of March 3. The delegates had finally declared independence the previous day, and most were now eager to rush to the aid of the beleaguered Alamo garrison. Sam Houston attended the Convention and signed the Texas Declaration of Independence. A masterful presence in the prime of his manhood (Houston celebrated his forty-second birthday on the day independence was declared), he always had a ready opinion to any military question. On March 4 the delegates reappointed Sam Houston commander in chief. Before accepting, however, he insisted that he be given authority over the volunteers and the militia, as well as the regular army; in other words, over all men bearing arms in the cause of Texas. The delegates accepted the general's conditions, and for the first time he was commander of all insurgent forces in Texas.[20]

On March 6 delegate Robert Potter, a North Carolina hotspur who had once castrated two men he suspected of dallying with his wife, exhibited the fiery passion for which he was infamous. In a heated speech, he moved that "the Convention do immediately adjourn, arm, and march to the relief of the Alamo." Houston condemned the plan as "madness." Now that independence had been declared, he asserted, the members of the Convention must create a government. Houston urged the delegates to remain and finish the work that they had begun; they could best serve the Republic as founding fathers, not as cannon fodder. He promised that if the Convention remained in session and "if mortal power could avail," he would personally lead a detachment to "relieve the brave men in the Alamo." Houston had no wish to lead a mob of self-important politicians, most of whom he had reason to distrust.[21]

That day he set out for Gonzales, where Colonel J. C. Neill had mustered a small group in order to rejoin his Béxar command. Houston did not look the part of a commanding general. He wore a plain Cherokee coat over a rustic buckskin waistcoat. His only symbol of rank was a cavalier's feather in his hat, which he had shaped to resemble a revolutionary war tricorne. A saber hung at his side; in his belt, which supported trousers that clashed with his coat, he had stuck a flintlock pistol. Strapped to his highheeled boots were spike-rowelled silver spurs of Mexican pattern. Most of the time, however, he wore moccasins in lieu of boots.[22]

On his way to Gonzales, Houston dispatched a courier to Goliad with orders to Fannin to join him at once. With Houston as undisputed general in chief, Fannin finally had someone to tell him what to do. He was quite willing to abandon Fort Defiance, but his men, who had worked hard to bolster its defenses, were reluctant to leave it without a fight. The indomitable Brooks had even invented a device that consisted of sixty-eight muskets rigged to fire at once.[23]

Although Houston had pledged to exert all "mortal power" to save the Alamo garrison, he did not strain his horse during his ride from Washington-on-the-Brazos to Gonzales. It took Houston five days to complete a journey that should have required, at most, two. The Alamo, of course, had already fallen, but Houston could not have been aware of that intelligence. At a time when Texians were wrought with anxiety over the fate of Travis and his men, their commander in chief dawdled. Why did Houston take so long? Texian settler W. W. Thompson, who spoke with him at Burnham's Crossing on the Colorado River, provided a possible answer. According to Thompson, Houston lingered at Burnham's "all night & all that day and all night again." When Thompson sought the general's opinion concerning the siege of the Alamo, Houston "swore that he believed it to be a damn lie, & that all those reports from Travis and Fannin were lies, for there were no Mexican forces there and that he believed that it was only electioneering schemes on [the part of] Travis & Fannin to sustain their own popularity."²⁴

When Houston finally reached Gonzales on March 11, he found the townspeople in pandemonium. Two *vaqueros* had arrived from Béxar with news that the Alamo had fallen and that the garrison had been slaughtered to a man. Houston sought to quell the panic by having the hapless *tejanos* arrested as spies, but he knew that their information was probably correct and sent "Deaf" Smith to ascertain the facts. The next day Smith returned bringing Mrs. Dickenson, her infant daughter, and Joe, Travis's slave. These were unimpeachable sources who could not be conveniently locked away. Gonzales had contributed many of its men to the Alamo contingent, and more than twenty of its women were now widows. Captain John Sharpe described the scene that night: "For hours after the receipt of the intelligence, not a sound was heard, save the wild shrieks of the women, and the heartrending screams of the fatherless children."²⁵

Santa Anna had correctly anticipated that word of the fate of Travis and his men would create panic among the settlers. News of the debacle triggered a mass exodus of Texian families known as the Runaway Scrape. The flight was an ordeal. "Uncle" Jeff Parson, a slave at the time, recalled: "People and things were all mixed, and in confusion. The children were crying, the women praying and the men cursing. I tell you it was a serious time."²⁶

As they fled, however, many Texians burned with a new resolve. One Texas matron grimly remarked while abandoning her cabin that "she was going to teach her boys never to let up on the Mexicans until they got full revenge for all this trouble." [27]

With the small force at Gonzales, Houston dared not engage the Mexican army, but once united with Fannin's four hundred volunteers, he might make a defensive stand at the Colorado River. Everything depended on Fannin retiring promptly to Victoria as ordered, but he still lingered in Goliad. He was not, however, entirely to blame, for events beyond his control had prevented his immediate withdrawal. [28]

In response to Urrea's rapid advance, Fannin had dispatched Captain Amon B. King and some twenty-eight men with most of his wagons to Refugio to evacuate American settlers. The contingent reached the town on March 12 but wasted time punishing loyalist *rancheros* in the area. While engaged in this fruitless punitive action, King and his men clashed with the vanguard of Urrea's cavalry. King sent a messenger to Fannin and took refuge in the old Mission Nuestra Señora del Rosario, where his riflemen kept the Mexican horsemen at bay. Fannin sent Colonel William Ward with the Georgia Battalion, which arrived at Refugio about three o'clock the afternoon of March 13, and quickly scattered the Mexican force around the mission. [29]

If Ward and King had immediately departed for Goliad, they might have averted disaster. Instead, still spoiling to punish local tories, they actually went in search of a fight. On the night of March 13, King split his command from Ward's and marched to a nearby ranch to attack a camp of *tejanos* thought to be spies. King's men ambushed the group, killing eight and scattering the rest. Meanwhile, General Urrea had sent Captain Rafael Pretalia's cavalry company ahead to pin down the *norte-americanos* until he could reach Refugio with infantry. [30]

At dawn, when Urrea arrived with his main force, he found Pretalia skirmishing with Ward's men. Two of Ward's companies had left during the night, but upon hearing the shooting, one had returned. Ward had taken advantage of the walls of Mission Rosario before King's party returned from its vengeance raid. Three times the Mexicans attacked Ward's men in the mission, but each time they were repulsed by the accurate rifles. King's men finally arrived about mid-afternoon, but they ran into the rear of Urrea's army. They managed to reach a grove of trees along the Mission River, and protected by natural cover, King's riflemen inflicted heavy casualties upon any of Urrea's soldiers who ventured within range. [31]

Wherever Texians could fire their long rifles from behind trees or walls, the Mexicans paid a heavy price to dislodge them. In that regard, the Battle of Refugio continued the pattern established at Concepción, Nueces Crossing, and the Alamo. At those places, however, the rebels had been expecting a fight. King and Ward had not brought sufficient ammunition for a daylong encounter, and by night both were dangerously short of powder and ball. Rather than surrender, both sought to escape under cover of darkness.[32]

For men unfamiliar with the terrain and afoot on the open plains, escape was a forlorn hope. Discovering their absence the next morning, Urrea dispatched vengeful locals, who soon tracked them down. King's contingent had crossed the Mission River during the night and found, when the loyalist *rancheros* appeared, that what little powder remained was hopelessly wet. The tories rounded up King's men and dragged them back to Refugio, where they were shot on March 16. Ward's people had been more fortunate. Urrea had expected them to retreat north toward Goliad, but instead they headed southeast along the Copano Road, thereby avoiding enemy patrols. Even so, cut off in enemy territory with little food or ammunition, they were far from safe.[33]

Fannin was in a quandary. Aware of the necessity for rapid withdrawal, he was anxious to obey Houston's orders. He could not, however, bring himself to abandon the men under King and Ward. They should have returned, but Fannin had heard nothing and feared the worst. He could send additional reinforcements to Refugio, but such action would further delay the retreat and run the risk of having his various contingents swallowed up piecemeal. King had, furthermore, taken most of the wagons and teams to transport civilians, leaving Fannin without adequate transportation.[34]

Fannin spent March 15 and 16 waiting for Ward's return; he dispatched couriers to Ward, but most were captured. Finally, at four o'clock on the evening of March 17, one got through the Mexican cordon with news of the defeat of Ward and King. But instead of marching at once, Fannin spent March 18 taking the "necessary measures for retreat in accordance with the resolution of the officers in council."[35]

Dr. Jack Shackelford, captain of the Alabama Red Rovers, believed Fannin had blundered in splitting his command. "Had he not done this," he later wrote "we should have been prepared to fall back on Victoria, as ordered, with a force sufficient to contend with every Mexican we might have encountered. Fannin's great anxiety, alone, for the fate of Ward and King, and their little band, delayed our march."[36]

By the eighteenth, the Mexican scouts were "roving about" the fort. Although Captain Albert C. Horton sallied out with his mounted contingent to engage them, the *rancheros* were far from intimidated; indeed, they seemed to enjoy toying with Horton's inexperienced cavalrymen. Volunteer Abel Morgan observed: "When our men would turn to come back the Mexicans would pursue them until they would get within gun shot of our footmen, when they would turn and our men would pursue again. They kept alternately chasing and being chased until dusk when the Mexicans left." After a day of impotent skirmishing, Horton had succeeded only in exhausting his horses. Fannin had hoped to retreat under the cover of darkness, but Horton reported the night too murky for a proper march. Departure was further postponed until morning. This delay was fatal.[37]

The volunteers should have moved as light and as fast as humanly possible. Houston had ordered that all guns be sunk in the river to facilitate rapid march. Fannin, however, insisted on hauling nine cannon and about five hundred spare muskets. Lacking a sufficient number of draft horses, the garrison depended on oxen to haul baggage and artillery. While Horton's horsemen spent the day fruitlessly chasing *rancheros*, the oxen had been held in corrals without fodder. As a result, the oxen, slow-moving even when well fed, were in no condition for the long journey. The men also carried an overabundance of personal belongings. The next day's withdrawal promised to be anything but expeditious.[38]

The dawn was gray and foggy. Fannin could have used the haze to conceal his movements, but true to character, he procrastinated. Although they had been planning to leave for days, last-minute details further delayed their departure. Fannin, determined to leave nothing useful to the Mexicans, ordered his men to burn nearby houses and everything that could not be carried. Around eight o'clock that morning, the garrison finally began the march. The pillar of smoke that rose above the fort could have only one meaning; loyalist *rancheros* raced to Urrea with word that the *gringos* had destroyed their stores and were pulling out.[39]

Fannin sent Horton's mounted men ahead as scouts and was heartened when they reported no enemy in sight. The colonel would have to savor that bit of good news, for it was the last he would receive. Morgan recalled that the hungry oxen were "wild and contrary," and before they traveled four miles, they stubbornly stopped to graze. A howitzer bogged down crossing the river, costing more valuable time. Herman Ehrenberg, the young German who had gone with Milam into Béxar, now rode along with Horton's mounted riflemen. He later remembered that "several wagons were broken up or merely abandoned and their teams hitched to the remaining carts. After crawling on a little farther, disgust at the creeping pace of our column induced us finally to abandon all our equipment." About mid-morning, the sense of disgust increased when the men discovered no one had remembered to pack food. Somehow, supplies of dried meat, wheat, and corn had inadvertently been burned in the confusion.[40]

Despite the chaos, the command seemed in remarkably good spirits. The pace might be slow, but it seemed as if they had made a clean getaway. "Contrary to our expectations," wrote Chicago physician J. H. Barnard, "we had not been worsted," and "no manifestations of attack or pursuit were apparent." Far from the somber mood one would expect from men in desperate flight, the general attitude was that of schoolboys on a spring fling. The sensitive Ehrenberg even took time to admire the landscape:

> Our road took us through natural scenery of the most pleasant kind, a succession of narrow prairies and sparsely planted oak woods without underbrush. Countless herds of cattle grazed in the abundant grass, and as our caravan pushed its way through this western solitude, huge droves of deer gazed at us with wonder. There were also many wild horses, probably descended from the noble Andalusian steeds brought into this country by Cortez when he undertook his cruel conquest of Mexico. At our approach they fled shyly away in compact bands, but long after they had vanished from our sight we could hear the thud of their galloping hoofs.[41]

The column had traveled only six miles when Fannin complacently ordered a halt. Captain Shackelford "remonstrated warmly" against stopping in the middle of a prairie, for if enemy cavalry caught them in the open they would be cut to pieces. Tree-lined Coleto Creek was but five miles away. Why not push ahead and rest where they had a defensive position, Shackelford implored. "In this matter I was overruled," he later lamented, "and from the ardent manner in which I urged the necessity of getting under the *protection of timber*, I found the *smiles of many*, indicated a belief that at least I thought it prudent to take care of number one."[42]

Fannin attempted to assuage Shackelford's concerns. He had, after all, fought the Mexicans before, and he insisted that they would not dare attack a force of this size. Dr. Barnard observed that Fannin's "former experience in fighting Mexicans had led him to entertain a great contempt for them as soldiers, and caused him to neglect such precautionary measures as were requisite from their great numerical strength and superiority." Of course, Fannin's only other combat experience had been thirty minutes at Concepción, where Bowie had made most of the tactical decisions. Often the roots of a costly defeat can be found in an easy victory, and such seemed to have been the case with Fannin. True, the Texians had also been outnumbered at Concepción, but on that occasion they had enjoyed adequate cover, and the enemy commander had not been the equal of José Urrea.[43]

About 12:45 P.M. Fannin resumed the march after an hour's rest, but before the Texians had advanced four miles, they saw a large force of Mexican cavalry emerging from the timber two miles behind. The enemy horsemen split into two groups; King's sharpshooters had taught them the hazards of allowing riflemen the protection of cover, so one force galloped between the rebels and a skirt of timber about a mile and a half away; the other blocked the route to Coleto Creek. Fannin ordered the cannon unlimbered and several rounds fired, but to no effect. At the same time, the insurgents saw Mexican infantry taking position in the same woods from which their cavalry had emerged earlier. Shackelford recalled that shelter was tantalizingly near: "In front was the timber of the Coleto, about a mile distant; in the rear, was another strip of timber, about six miles distant; whilst on our right and left, equi-distant, four or five miles from us, there were likewise, bodies of timber."[44]

Most officers advocated pushing forward until they reached cover, but Fannin ordered the command to form a hollow square with the artillery posted at the corners. Dr. Barnard spoke for many when he wrote, "We ought to have moved at all hazards and all cost until we reached the timber." He acknowledged that losses might have been heavy, but argued "we could have moved on and kept them at bay as easily as we repulsed them while stationary." Even Private Ehrenberg recognized that a "swift retreat to the woods" was "the only road to safety," but bitterly added that "this obvious maneuver did not appeal to Fannin, who chose to fight it out on the prairie, where the odds were against our small, unprotected force." Demonstrating Urrea's ability to adapt his tactics to the terrain, the Mexicans now took advantage of natural cover, while the Texians stood in the open.[45]

The Mexicans immediately prepared to attack. About one o'clock in the afternoon the dragoons dismounted and advanced on foot. At a quarter of a mile, they discharged a volley, which at that distance did no harm. As they continued to approach, Fannin shouted to his men to hold their fire until the enemy came into "point blank" range. A second volley came nearer, and Shackelford ordered his company to sit down, an action emulated by other companies. The third round of shots drew blood. Fannin, conspicuous in the front rank, had the hammer of his rifle taken off by an enemy ball, while another buried itself in the breech, but still he shouted orders "not to fire yet!" When the enemy approached within one hundred yards, Fannin finally gave the order to fire; his men opened up with muskets, rifles, and artillery.[46]

Horton's mounted contingent had been scouting ahead of the column. They rode to the sound of the guns, but by the time they could see the battlefield, it was clear that the isolated main force was hopelessly outnumbered. Instead of wasting the lives of his men in a fruitless gesture, Horton led them toward Victoria, where he hoped to locate reinforcements. "So confident were we in the beginning of the fight that Colonel Horton and his men would come back and rejoin us," Barnard recorded, "that in several of [the Mexican] charges a number of the men called out: 'Don't fire; they are our horsemen!' " It was only wishful thinking, for the only Texian horseman to rejoin Fannin was the youthful Ehrenberg. The rebel infantrymen were enraged at their abandonment. "Had they been with us . . . we would have had a means of transportation for our wounded," survivor John C. Duval angrily charged, "and could easily have made our retreat to the Coletto." Perhaps, but it is more likely that the Mexican lancers, superior in both numbers and skill, would have prevented the Texas horse from ever reaching the square.[47]

Inside Fannin's square, meanwhile, the riflemen were holding their own against repeated enemy advances. Mexican dragoons, now remounted, bore down upon their position but were driven off by the devastating rifle and cannon fire. "The effect of our artillery fire was immediate and horrible," Ehrenberg recalled. Mexican sharpshooters concentrated on rebel gunners and picked off most of them, including H. Francis Petrussewicz, a Polish veteran of the Napoleonic wars. At the same time, Mexican officers ordered their *cazadores* to bring down Fannin's oxen. General Urrea had Fannin exactly where he wanted him: without teams to transport his baggage and wounded; furthermore, there he would remain.[48]

The Mexican infantry soon took cover in the high grass surrounding the square, showing themselves only long enough to pop off a quick shot. The Texas soldiers, close-packed in the square, were vulnerable to this sniping. The formation was essential, however, as it was their only protection from being overrun by Mexican cavalry.[49]

Among the wounded was Fannin, who, despite a painful hit in his thigh, refused to leave the front ranks. Many of his men had questioned his judgment, but after seeing him in battle, none doubted his courage. Barnard, earlier one of Fannin's harshest critics, later admitted that his commander "behaved with perfect coolness and self-possession throughout and evidenced no lack of bravery."[50]

Nor did the volunteers any longer doubt the courage of Mexican soldiers. Shackelford remembered one enemy cavalry charge: "They came in full tilt, with gleaming lances, shouting like Indians. When about sixty yards distant, the whole of our rear division of our little command, together with a piece or two of artillery, loaded with double canister filled with musket-balls, opened a tremendous fire upon them, which brought them to a full halt and swept them down by scores."[51]

John C. Duval carried his own artillery in the form of a short blunderbuss "heavily charged with forty 'blue whistlers' and powder in proportion." Well aware that the powerful recoil of the weapon made it "nearly as dangerous *behind*" as in front, he intended to rely on it only when he found himself to be in a "tight place." This was it. "It was during this charge and when the Mexican cavalry on our side of the square were in a few feet of us, that I concluded that I had got into that 'tight place' and that it was time to let off the 'scopet' I carried. I did so, and immediately I went heels over head through the ranks behind me."[52]

Duval's "blue whistlers" tore into horse and rider and, along with the more conventional canister, musket, and rifle shot, halted the mounted onslaught. Urrea, now convinced that massed cavalry could not break the square, again ordered his dragoons to dismount and fight on foot.[53]

By late afternoon, the volunteers were suffering from lack of water. "Our guns had now become hot—we had no water to sponge them— many of our artillerists had been wounded, and we had to rely alone on our small arms," Shackelford remembered. Most men had long since exhausted the contents of their canteens, and the heat of battle made their thirst almost unbearable. Even so, many shared the last of their water with wounded comrades who were in danger of dehydration. Soldiers on both sides welcomed sunset and the end it brought to that day's fighting.[54]

Fannin and his officers took the opportunity to review their situation. Casualties numbered nine killed and fifty-one wounded. (They had no way of knowing that the Mexicans had suffered even greater losses: 50 killed and 140 wounded.) Food and water were almost exhausted, and ammunition was low. The oxen were dead, which meant no transport for the seriously wounded. Sporadic Mexican sniper fire throughout the night revealed that Urrea had them encircled. Ehrenberg reported that a "cool shower" relieved the feverish wounded, but it also "spoiled the few good rifles we had left." Surrounded in the middle of an open prairie with nowhere to run and no place to hide, their plight was hopeless.[55]

The able-bodied might escape under the cover of darkness, but the wounded would have to be abandoned to the mercy of the victors. Typically, Fannin left the decision to the men. Duval remembered how, "after a short consultation upon the subject, it was unanimously determined to not abandon our wounded men, but to remain with them and share their fate, whatever it might be."[56]

Determined to remain, the defenders prepared makeshift breastworks. Dr. Barnard described the rigors of that cold, wet night:

> We went to work with our spades and dug a ditch three or four feet in depth. Our carts were then drawn up and disposed upon the breastworks so as to aid in our protection, and the carcasses of two horses (all that we had along with us) and two or three oxen were piled up for bastions. Thus the night wore away, the enemy's patrol keeping up incessant music with their bugles to regale us, while the shrill and discordant scream of the *Sentinel Alerto*, which afterwards became so familiar, then first jarred upon my ear. I worked with the spade until fatigued, and then lay down for a little troubled sleep, until the chilliness of my limbs forced me to seek for warmth by using the spade again, and in such alternations the dismal night was passed and day at last dawned upon us.[57]

Dawn only delivered more bad news, for the beleaguered insurgents soon learned that during the night Urrea had brought up reinforcements and three fieldpieces. Urrea recorded that "one hundred infantry, two four-pounders, and a howitzer were added to my force." Barnard wryly noted that the Mexicans "commenced the business of the day by treating us to a few rounds of grape and canister." Then as suddenly as it began, the Mexican artillery fire ceased; General Urrea had intended only to demonstrate his superior firepower. He could now lay well beyond rifle range and pulverize Fannin's helpless command at will—something he apparently had no wish to do.[58]

The rebels knew that their position was untenable; they could save their lives only by surrendering. The men agreed they would lay down their arms only if Urrea granted them honorable terms. If he refused, they would fight to the death. Colonel Fannin limped forward under a flag of truce.[59]

When the Texian commander asked for terms, General Urrea replied: "If you gentlemen wish to surrender at discretion, the matter is ended, otherwise I shall return to my camp and renew the attack." Fannin was hardly in a position to haggle. He returned to his men, telling them that Urrea had accepted their terms and that their lives would be spared. Fannin may have deliberately misled his command regarding the surrender terms in an effort to prevent needless bloodshed, or he may have misunderstood them. Whatever the reason, his men were in no condition to continue fighting; he could only hope that Urrea would regard them as prisoners of war and not captured soldiers of fortune. The volunteers lay down their arms and marched back to Goliad under guard.[60]

General Urrea had no intention of playing jailer. On the morning of March 21 he took possession of Victoria. There, Horton's men had found little assistance and, aware they could do little against superior Mexican numbers, had evacuated the town upon Urrea's advance.[61]

In the meantime, Ward's Georgia Battalion was wandering through the prairie, attempting to avoid Mexican patrols and locate Fannin's main force. Ward knew that Fannin had planned to retreat northward to Victoria and sought to rendezvous with him there. By the time they reached the settlement on March 21, however, Urrea already held the town. A number of Ward's men were captured or killed trying to enter Victoria, and the rest scattered into the woods along the Guadalupe River. With the men exhausted and starving, command structure broke down. Many deserted, but only ten managed to escape. That night Ward attempted to lead those who remained with him to Dimitt's Landing, about twenty miles eastward on the coast. They made good time and on the following day halted only two miles from their destination to slaughter a beef and reconnoiter. Soon afterward, however, the ragged remnants of the once proud Georgia Battalion were surrounded by centralist cavalry and forced to surrender. The Mexicans marched Ward's men back to Goliad, where they were held with Fannin's command.[62]

The prisoners expected to be paroled as soon as a ship was available to take them back to New Orleans. Fannin even traveled to Copano with Lieutenant Colonel Juan Holsinger, a German in Mexican service, to book passage on a vessel thought to be there, but it had sailed. Santa Anna's orders from his government were explicit: all foreigners captured under arms were to be considered pirates. He intended to carry out these instructions to the letter. Urrea wrote that he "wished to elude these orders as far as possible without compromising my personal responsibility." He respected Fannin and his men for their courage, and as a man of honor, he had no desire to play the role of executioner. Yet as a professional soldier, he was also obliged to obey the direct orders of his superior and the official dictates of the government. Urrea described his dilemma:

> [Fannin and his men] doubtlessly surrendered confident that Mexican generosity would not make their surrender useless, for under any other circumstances they would have sold their lives dearly, fighting to the last. I had due regard for the motives that induced them to surrender, and for this reason I used my influence with the general-in-chief to save them, if possible, from being butchered, particularly Fannin. I obtained from His Excellency only a severe reply, repeating his previous order, doubtlessly dictated by cruel necessity.[63]

One of Santa Anna's aides arrived with peremptory orders. On Palm Sunday, March 27, the prisoners were separated into four groups and informed they were to be taken to Matamoros. Singing as they marched, they set out in different directions until ordered to halt. Then the Mexican infantry methodically gunned them down. Mexican lancers cut off many who avoided the repeated volleys while infantrymen finished off the wounded with bayonets and butcher knives. The dead included Ira Westover, the victor at Nueces Crossing, and the youthful John Sowers Brooks, who, true to his promise, had not disgraced "the name of a soldier or that of a Virginian." When informed that he was to be shot, Fannin requested only that his watch be sent to his family, he be shot in the breast, and his remains be given a proper Christian burial. Unable to stand because of his leg wound, Fannin calmly tied a blindfold over his eyes and faced the firing squad seated in a chair. The officer commanding the firing party pocketed the watch, Fannin was shot through the face; and his body was indiscriminately burned on a pyre with the other victims. Best estimates are that 342 men were killed; 28, including Duval and Ehrenberg, escaped the carnage and thus lived to give their accounts. Because the Mexicans desperately needed their medical expertise, they spared Doctors Shackelford and Barnard.[64]

The so-called Goliad Massacre is traditionally depicted as an example of Mexican perfidy because the volunteers had believed they would be treated as prisoners of war. It also represented, however, a lost opportunity for Santa Anna. He might have reaped important dividends if he had dumped an army of defeated and demoralized volunteers on U.S. shores. Surely few would have wished to see Texas again, and their tales of Mexican humanity and Texian neglect would have discouraged others from traveling to the war. Instead of gaining the moral high ground, the Mexican dictator was painted as a barbarian. Fannin and his men, furthermore, now joined the ranks of the Alamo defenders as martyrs whose blood called out for vengeance. The Texians, who had thus far left the responsibility to the latecomers, were determined to avenge those men who had died for the cause of Texas independence. Although Santa Anna was convinced the war was finished, Sam Houston's ragged soldiers were grimly preparing to fight.[65]

CHAPTER 9

"The Enemy Are Laughing You to Scorn"

❖

The Runaway Scrape
April 1836

Texian veterans often spoke of U.S. regulars who had joined them for the 1836 campaign. General Edmund Pendleton Gaines, who had established Fort Jessup and Camp Sabine on the east bank of the Sabine River, carefully monitored events in Texas. While General Gaines officially observed the neutral status of the United States, unofficially he appears to have been in sympathy with the insurgents. Many "deserters" who skipped across the Sabine to swell Houston's ranks probably did so with Gaines's tacit approval. "Deserters, they were called," settler Noah Smithwick supposedly recounted, "but after the battle, they all 'deserted' back to the United States army, and no court martial ensued." Yet contrary to Smithwick, not all "deserted back." In the summer of 1836, a U.S. army officer came to Texas to retrieve deserters who had failed to report for duty. He discovered some two hundred at Nacogdoches who were still brazenly wearing U.S. army uniforms. Despite his entreaties, these rogues steadfastly refused to return to the United States.

Slogging along on a muddy road during the retreat to San Jacinto, the private illustrated here has vainly attempted to conceal his identity as a U.S. serviceman. Although he retains his sky-blue kersey undress jacket, he has ripped the white tape from the collar and hastily replaced the regulation buttons with civilian ones made of bone and wood. He also refuses to part with his issue brogan shoes, which are far better than those worn by most Texians.

His cartridge box, haversack, canteen, tin cup, and baldric are all U.S. government issue. Note, however, that the stamped brass plate that would have revealed his former service has been removed from the baldric. Although U.S. regulars were issued packs, this veteran campaigner prefers to travel light and so secures his few meager belongings inside his bedroll.

Weapons consist of the .69 caliber U.S. musket, model 1816 (2d type), and the triangular socket bayonet, which is housed in its leather sheath.

Note that the safety-conscious private places a leather hammer cap over the metal frizzen to prevent the possibility of an accidental discharge.

The wayfaring volunteer retains the regulation collapsible leather forage cap but is about to abandon it in favor of a discarded planter's hat left behind during the Runaway Scrape.

9

"The Enemy Are Laughing You to Scorn"

GENERAL HOUSTON'S BEST HOPE lay in organizing a defense behind the Colorado River, but at the moment his main concern was keeping his army from falling apart. Not only the citizens of Gonzales but also many of his soldiers were rendered distraught by Mrs. Dickenson's melancholy report of the fall of the Alamo. Between March 13 and 15, twenty men slipped away, but that number seemed to be smaller than Houston expected. Writing Major James Collinsworth, he explained: "Only about twenty persons deserted the camp (from the first *sensation* produced by [Mrs. Dickenson's] intelligence) up to this time. I intend desertion shall not be frequent, and to regret to say that I am compelled to regard as deserters all who left camp without leave; to demand their apprehension; and that, whenever arrested, they be sent to me at head-quarters for trial. They have disseminated throughout the frontier such exaggerated reports, that they have [spread] dismay and consternation among the people to a most distressing extent."[1]

With both citizens and soldiers afflicted by "Runaway fever," Houston ordered Gonzales burned and began a withdrawal to the Colorado River. "It would have been Madness" to try to hold the settlement with troops who "had not been taught the first principles of drill," Houston observed. Indeed, he was determined not to hold any fixed position. "Our forces must not be shut up in forts, where they can neither be supplied with men nor provisions," he asserted. The fate of the Alamo had confirmed his suspicions regarding the disorganized government's inability to support garrisons separated by great distances.[2]

Nevertheless, the Texian soldiers were deeply distressed by the plight of the women and children of Gonzales. "There were over thirty Gonzales victims who had fallen in the Alamo," Rifleman Creed Taylor recalled, "and the screams and lamentations of the mothers, wives, children and sisters of these brave men who gave their lives for Texan liberty will ring in my ears so long as memory liveth, and the preacher tells me that Memory, being an attribute of the soul, can never die." [3]

Many protested that retreat was a spineless course. Taylor asserted that the news of the enemy's approach had "stampeded" Houston. Even years later, Taylor continued to excoriate the general for his decision to abandon Gonzales:

> Sam Houston had at Gonzales 500 men, of these at least one half of them had been at Conception and San Antonio, and he didn't have a man in his army who didn't have a blood grievance against the Mexicans and that did not *know* that he could do as we had done before— whip ten-to-one of the carrion-eating convicts under Santa Anna. Let other historians rail and prate as they may[,] but be it known to all future generations of Texas forth that if [Texas Ranger Captain] Jack Hays, John H. Moore or Old "Paint" Caldwell had been in command at Gonzales on that fatal evening when Mrs. Dickinson brought the message of the Alamo's fall, the historian would have never heard of San Jacinto. Fan[n]in and his men would have been saved—the butchery of Goliad averted and the "Napoleon of the West" would have found his Waterloo. . . . The comrades who assembled at Gonzales went there to *Fight*, not to run. [4]

On the march to the Colorado, Houston's conduct transformed an admirer into a lifelong enemy. The thirteen-year-old John Holland Jenkins had joined the command and was slogging along under the weight of his heavy rifle. Houston took pity on the lad and ordered a slave to dismount so that the exhausted youth could ride and rest for a while. Jenkins quickly accepted, thinking to himself that he would "willingly die for Houston," who seemed to the impressionable youngster a "perfect model of manliness and bravery." The general, concerned for the boy's safety, forbade him to ride ahead. Mounted on a spirited horse while others walked was a heady experience for young Jenkins, who soon became absorbed in thoughts of martial glory and allowed the mount to carry him well ahead of the column. He was "rudely aroused and shocked" by the shouts of his disgruntled general: "God damn your soul!!! Didn't I order you to ride right here?" Indignant at being dressed down in front of the entire army, Jenkins dismounted, declaring that he would "rather die than ride another step." He then stubbornly rejoined the ranks of the footsloggers. "With those few harsh words," Jenkins reflected as an adult, "General Houston completely changed the current of my feelings toward him, and my profound admiration and respect was turned into a dislike I could never conquer."[5]

The incident illustrated the fragile pride of Houston's men, an aspect of their character that the general never fully appreciated. As volunteers, Texians were in ranks by their own volition. They followed a man because they respected him, but they demanded that respect be reciprocated. They despised traditional military discipline as well as officers who found it necessary to "pull rank" to enforce their orders. This egalitarian frontier attitude was ingrained in the oldest and—as Jenkins demonstrated—the youngest of them. These men would not be told how to live or behave, not by Santa Anna and certainly not by Sam Houston. The general was, of course, a product of the same southern frontier as most of his men, but he had known the prestige of high office. A natural leader (and to many, a supreme egoist), he was accustomed to being obeyed without challenge, a trait that did not endear him to volunteers accustomed to having a say in the conduct of their campaigns.[6]

On March 17 Houston and his army reached Burnham's ferry on the Colorado River. He had brought only 374 volunteers from Gonzales, but he urged the government to send him additional troops, and his force had nearly doubled. He was convinced that Burnham's was the best place to make a stand because it "covers more of the country than any other known to me." When adequate troops were available, he planned to "detach suitable numbers to each point as I may deem best." Houston seemed confident that as soon as Fannin's four hundred arrived he could stop the Mexican advance at the Colorado: "Let [the people] entertain no fears for the present. We can raise three thousand men in Texas, and fifteen hundred can defeat all that Santa Anna can send to the Colorado. We would then fight on our own ground, and the enemy would lose confidence from our annoyance."[7]

Despite such optimistic talk, Houston soon realized that he could not hope to hold off the entire Mexican army at Burnham's Crossing. Even if he did manage to halt Santa Anna's column, which was reported to be only fifteen miles away, Urrea could cross the Colorado farther down-river and then drive into the heart of the Texian settlements. Houston destroyed Burnham's ferry and marched down the east bank until reaching Beason's Crossing on March 19.[8]

There conditions improved. Texians, who had left the fighting to new-comers, were badly shaken by news of the Alamo debacle and now flocked to Houston's banner, increasing his army to about fourteen hundred effectives. The spring rains were heavy, and while they turned roads into quagmires and dampened Texian enthusiasm, they also swelled the banks of the Colorado River, rendering it temporarily an impassable barrier for the Mexicans. Houston posted guards at the three river crossings in the area and introduced his men to the fundamentals of close-order drill. He was determined to make the most of the little time he had. He knew the enemy would soon appear, for scout Henry Karnes, hero of Concepción and Béxar, returned to camp with a Mexican prisoner. The captive informed Houston that Santa Anna had divided his army. One column under General Antonio Gaona had occupied Bastrop and had orders to follow the Old San Antonio Road all the way to Nacogdoches in the heart of the piney woods. Another under General Ramírez y Sesma, rumored to be between six hundred and eight hundred strong, was headed for Beason's Crossing. The Texian volunteers were excited at the prospects of a battle. If they could not fight all of Santa Anna's army, they might at least defeat a portion of it.[9]

On March 21 Ramírez y Sesma and his contingent arrived opposite Beason's Crossing and pitched camp on the south bank of the river; the Texians urged Houston to attack. Lieutenant Colonel Sidney Sherman, a thirty-one-year-old hotspur who had just arrived in Texas at the head of fifty-two Kentucky volunteers, was especially adamant, demanding permission to cross with four hundred men and engage the enemy. Houston wisely refused. His entire purpose in taking up a position at Beason's Crossing had been to secure good defensive ground. Now Sherman and others wanted to surrender that tactical advantage and attempt a foolhardy crossing of the flooded river under the guns of the enemy.[10]

For the next six days Houston waited and watched. Ramírez y Sesma, unable to ford the swollen Colorado, did the same. Most of the Texians eagerly anticipated a fight, and at times Houston hinted that one was impending. The numbers were about right, but there were other factors Houston had to consider. Ramírez y Sesma had two field cannon, while he had none. If the Texians attacked, they must first cross the flooded river, and that would be hazardous even for trained troops. Ramírez y Sesma had, furthermore, entrenched his camp, which, along with his ordnance, would offset the Texians' slight numerical advantage. Even so, morale was high, and the Texians were eager to fight, whatever the odds. Houston was, as ever, tight-lipped about his intentions, but at least he seemed to be preparing for an assault. Although he told no one at the time, he later wrote Secretary of War Thomas J. Rusk that he had planned to attack Ramírez y Sesma on March 26.[11]

On March 23, however, Houston received shocking news that totally upset his plans. "You know I am not easily depressed," he wrote Rusk, "but before my God, since we parted, I have found the darkest hours of my past life!" He penned those words upon learning of Fannin's defeat and capture. "If what I have learned from Fannin be true, I deplore it," he lamented, "and can only attribute the ill luck to his attempt to retreat in daylight in the face of a superior force. He is an ill-fated man." Houston added that the men with him were in high spirits, but he admitted that he did not know how the news of another military disaster would affect them.[12]

Houston realized that his small army was the last hope Texas had for survival, and he did not wish to risk it against unfavorable odds. On March 26, therefore, he ordered a retreat to San Felipe. The men met the announcement with undisguised disdain. Between two hundred and three hundred men left the army: some secured furloughs to aid their families, but many simply deserted. Angry soldiers, disgusted to be running from an enemy they scorned, whispered that the army might do better under a commander who was not afraid to fight. Soon such sentiments were being spoken aloud. Captain Robert Coleman, a veteran of Concepción and the siege of Béxar, came to be one of Houston's most bitter critics. In an anti-Houston polemic published in 1837, he exclaimed: "Thirteen hundred Americans retreating before a division of 800 Mexicans! Can Houston's strong partizans presume to excuse such dastardly cowardice under the pretence of laudable prudence?"[13]

That question requires an answer. A good general, like a good chess player, must have the ability to see well beyond the next move, to grasp the strategic situation. Houston was the first Texas commander with the ability to plan beyond the next battle. An engagement at Beason's Crossing, even if it had resulted in a Texian victory, would have been costly and would have accomplished little toward winning the war. Houston evaluated the strategic realities:

While in camp on the Colorado it was learned that Fannin's regiment had been captured and that [Ramírez y] Sesma, across the river from us, was in communication with Urrea and Gaona. Urrea could, therefore, cross the Colorado at Wharton, about 40 miles below the Texian camp, with his 1500 men and attack [our] left flank. Gaona with his force of about 750 could cross the Colorado at Bastrop, about 60 miles above the Texian camp, and attack the right flank, while Sesma could attack the front.[14]

If Houston won, and he later admitted that his force at Beason's Crossing was "respectable," it still might prove a Pyrrhic victory. Attacking Ramírez y Sesma in entrenchments would be so destructive to his small army that it would stand no chance in another battle that would surely follow. He was not even sure that his tiny untrained army had more than one fight in it. There was only one reasonable course: retreat north toward San Felipe and the Brazos River, keep the army together, and pray that Santa Anna made a mistake.[15]

Houston accepted full responsibility for the retreat. "On my arrival on the Brazos," he wrote Rusk on March 29, "had I consulted the wishes of all, I should have been like the ass between two stacks of hay. . . . I consulted none—I held no councils of war. If I err, the blame is mine." Given the circumstances, there could be only one answer to Coleman's criticism. Houston did not err. He had indeed demonstrated "laudable prudence," not "dastardly cowardice."[16]

Yet Houston was not the only general looking at the big picture; in Béxar, Santa Anna was considering the best way to terminate the campaign quickly. He did not know where Houston was, so he divided his army into smaller "hunting parties," any one of which was a match for the few rebels with Houston. The spring rains, however, deprived the Mexican army of its momentum. On March 22 General Eugenio Tolsa's force joined Ramírez y Sesma's column opposite Beason's Crossing, and there they remained, confronted by the raging Colorado. Gaona had secured Bastrop, but the high water there also prevented his advance toward Nacogdoches. General Urrea had pressed ahead after taking Victoria, but found himself checked at the mouth of the Brazos near Matagorda. Even the intrepid Urrea, who had crushed every enemy force he had encountered, was idled by the Texas weather.[17]

Urrea had, however, already given Santa Anna a strategic advantage; his rapid advance up the Texas coast had deprived the rebels of every port except Galveston. Without support from the United States, the revolt would ultimately fail. The tiny Texas navy, consisting of the *Invincible, Brutus,* and *Independence,* had already proved its worth by intercepting Mexican merchant vessels and interrupting the flow of Santa Anna's seaborne provisions. But in depriving the navy of its ports, Urrea had greatly curtailed its activity. Men and materials from the United States could still make their way via the land route across the Sabine River, but that would take much longer. Houston was acutely aware of this, for he wrote Rusk: "If matters press upon us, for God's sake let the troops land at Galveston bay, and by land reach the Brazos!" The vital importance of Galveston did not escape the notice of the revolutionary government, for all three navy ships were now being used to defend the port that served as Texas's lifeline. It also soon became the refuge of that government.[18]

Given the strategic importance of the coast, which was obvious to both sides, Santa Anna's earlier drive against Béxar was a wasteful digression. Béxar was, of course, the political center of Mexican Texas, and His Excellency no doubt wished to avenge his brother-in-law Cós, but the difficult march on Béxar and the costly Alamo assault made little sense from a strategic viewpoint. San Antonio stood on the extreme edge of the western frontier. Santa Anna could have kept his army intact and driven up the coastal prairies along the same route that Urrea took. Once Goliad had fallen, Santa Anna could have sent a column to Gonzales, which was defenseless. Such a movement would have severed the Alamo's lines of communication with the Texian settlements at little cost, thereby isolating the rebel garrison. Cut off from supplies and reinforcements, Travis would have had to abandon the fort, but he could have retreated only to the north or east where the Mexican lancers would be waiting for him. Had Santa Anna been the strategist that he envisioned himself to be, he would have seen that an assault on the Alamo was pointless. He could have easily neutralized the garrison without decimating his army.[19]

Near the end of March Santa Anna and his staff departed Béxar, the town for which his army had paid so dearly. He reached the combined forces of Tolsa and Ramírez y Sesma on April 4. By then the floodwaters had subsided, and the Mexicans spent the next day fording the Colorado. During this phase of the campaign, Santa Anna was again the dynamic leader of the old days, pushing his men to the limit and making up for lost time. Once across the river, he advanced that same day to the banks of San Bernardo Creek, some thirteen miles to the north. At two o'clock in the morning of April 7, he led a force of two hundred infantry and eighty cavalrymen in a dash to San Felipe de Austin, on the west bank of the Brazos. He found the settlement in ashes. A small rear guard held the east bank of the river, but Houston had eluded him.[20]

The rebel army reached San Felipe on March 28, but after spending only one night there, Houston ordered a retreat to Jared Groce's plantation, twenty miles to the north. The abandonment of San Felipe caused a storm of protest in the Texian ranks. It was, after all, Stephen F. Austin's original town, and it had been the hub of American settlement. Many believed it the most important place in Texas, to be held at all cost. Two companies, in fact, bluntly refused to retreat beyond the Brazos. Captain Moseley Baker demanded permission to remain with his company and guard the San Felipe Crossing. Wiley Martin was determined to take his company about twenty-five miles downriver to defend the Fort Bend Crossing. As both company commanders made it clear that they were staying anyway, Houston wisely ordered them to defend the crossings. On March 29 the army, reduced to about five hundred men, began the march to Groce's plantation.[21]

Texian morale, already at a low ebb from constant retreating, was further dampened by more spring showers. The army had to wade across Mill Creek, but they were already soaked from the cloudburst. "We foundered through mud and water, pelted by the storm," lamented Private J. H. Kuykendall. The general suffered as much as any of his men, for he wore only a threadbare black dress coat. At one time he had enjoyed a warm Indian blanket, but a soldier had stolen it. Sensing the mood of his men, Houston attempted to encourage them: "My friends, I am told that evilly disposed persons have told you I am going to march you to the Redlands [the area around Nacogdoches, so called because of its red sandy soil]. This is false. I'm going to lead you into the Brazos bottom near Groce's to a position where you can whip the enemy even if he comes ten to one, and where we can get an abundant supply of corn."[22]

Many of the soaked rebels were not convinced; they had heard Houston's assurances before. He had promised they would fight at Burnham's ferry, then at Beason's Crossing, and again on the Brazos. He later concocted sound explanations for every withdrawal, but at the time it appeared to the men that their general was at the least indecisive and at the worst, as many believed, cowardly. More than a decade later, J. W. Robinson remained bitter in his denunciation of Houston's policy of retreat: "The man that has fear in his bosom may fancy that he sees it in every eye that meets his own—if it was not fear that made the Major General tuck his tail and run from the Colorado, from half his own number and from the Brazos, it was a total want of military capacity." There was, however, nothing to do but continue the march to Groce's, where they could expect some shelter. So knee-deep in mud and water, the despondent rebels plodded northward.[23]

Meanwhile, Baker's company across from San Felipe was having troubles of its own. Santa Anna brought up two fieldpieces and shelled Baker's breastworks from across the river, while Mexican snipers killed one of the Texians. The Mexicans located a flatboat, but the fire of Baker's riflemen was so accurate they could not launch it. They had, however, captured one of Baker's pickets, who informed Santa Anna that the rebel army had retired to Groce's plantation. At last El Presidente learned Houston's position but seemed in no hurry to pursue him.[24]

On April 9 Santa Anna, who did not wish to be delayed by a rear guard, left Ramírez y Sesma with eight hundred men to deal with Baker and then led a column downriver toward Thompson's ferry above Fort Bend. Arriving at the crossing on the morning of April 12, the vanguard spied a black ferryman on the opposite shore. While Santa Anna and his staff hid in the bushes, Colonel Almonte hailed the ferryman in impeccable English. The ferryman, no doubt thinking that this was a Texian who had somehow been left behind, poled the ferry across to the west bank. Santa Anna and his staff sprang from the brush and captured the unsuspecting man and, more important, his ferry. By this ruse, the Mexicans accomplished a bloodless crossing of the Brazos. Twelve miles downriver, Martin and the men guarding Fort Bend Crossing learned that the Mexicans had crossed the river in force. Outflanked, Martin had no choice but to retreat. Also outflanked, Baker was obliged to abandon his defense of the San Felipe Crossing and fall back toward Groce's.[25]

All Baker had to show for his determined stand was one dead man and a burned town. It was unclear, however, who had ordered San Felipe burned. When Houston's army left on March 29, the town was intact; when Santa Anna arrived on April 7, it was in charred ruins. Houston always maintained that the citizens took the initiative and burned the town after the army left. Baker, however, swore that Houston had ordered the town's destruction. Regardless of who issued or carried out the order, San Felipe was gone. It actually mattered little who was responsible; if the Texians had not burned it, the Mexicans would have.[26]

At Fort Bend, Santa Anna gained intelligence that would alter the direction of his campaign. Anglo civilians told him that the revolutionary government had abandoned Washington-on-the-Brazos and was now in Harrisburg, less than thirty miles away. His Excellency had by now dismissed Houston's army as a serious threat. It had, after all, done nothing but flee him. Houston could do little harm at Groce's plantation, and now Santa Anna had a force strategically placed between the rebel army and its government. A forced march could capture the Texian politicians, and once they were hanged—especially his old enemy, Lorenzo de Zavala, who was serving as vice-president—Houston's army would have no reason to continue the struggle. Santa Anna had no desire, furthermore, to take his troops into the soggy woods along the Brazos. Houston had been correct; there, the Texian riflemen probably *could* whip ten times their number. Santa Anna reasoned, moreover, that there was nothing to be gained by pursuing Houston's minuscule contingent. When he captured Harrisburg, he would also gain control of Galveston Bay and sever the rebel lifeline to the United States. That would leave Houston with two equally unpleasant alternatives: retreating northeast across the Sabine and out of Texas or starving in the Brazos bottoms.[27]

His Excellency underestimated Texian resilience. At Groce's plantation, the Texian soldiers were finally able to rest. They needed it. The march through the "foul and turbid lagoons of the Brazos bottom" had exhausted the men. While many had deserted under the strain, more had taken their places, and Houston reached his destination with about nine hundred troops. Groce, one of the wealthiest men in Texas, fed the army from his gardens and herds. His blacksmith shop became the armory for the repair of muskets. He even contributed scarce lead pipes, which were melted down for rifle balls. Groce, furthermore, turned Bernardo, his fine plantation house, over to the army's surgeons for a hospital.[28]

There was certainly a need for a hospital. After weeks of constant exposure to the elements, many soldiers had succumbed to various illnesses. According to French Canadian surgeon Nicholas Descomps Labadie, the campsite itself contributed to the problem: "While our army lay thus encamped in the Brazos Swamp, using stagnant water from the old bed of the river, a great deal of sickness prevailed among the men, which caused serious alarm." An outbreak of measles incapacitated one man in ten. Others suffered from colds, influenza, whooping cough, pink eye, mumps, and diarrhea. To many observers, it appeared as if disease was about to do Santa Anna's work for him.[29]

Yet all was not despair. Houston used the two weeks at Groce's to drill and instruct his men in the rudiments of linear combat. Austrian-born George Erath admitted that the "delay at Groce's had a good effect in disciplining us and in giving us information on military tactics." Most of those stricken with maladies gradually improved through the heroic efforts of the Texian surgeons. The army had been on the move so much in the past few weeks, the government had not known where to dispatch supplies and reinforcements. Now firmly in place along the Brazos, the army received both. Best of all, on April 11 two cannon arrived. The men later dubbed them the Twin Sisters. Their voices would soon be heard.[30]

As the soldiers trained and regained their health, their self-confidence returned, but not their faith in Houston. The interim government at Harrisburg was also dissatisfied with its general in chief. President Davis G. Burnet sent Secretary of War Rusk to Groce's camp to deliver in person a scathing letter to Houston: "Sir: The enemy are laughing you to scorn. You must fight them. You must retreat no further. The country expects you to fight. The salvation of the country depends on your doing so."[31]

If Houston refused to attack, Rusk was authorized to assume command of the army, and a more ambitious or less wise man might have done so immediately. But Rusk listened to Houston's rationalizations, saw for himself the state of the army, and concluded that the general had acted properly. Many urged Rusk to take command, but he steadfastly supported Houston. The malcontents were disgusted that the secretary of war had apparently been won over by that "God dammed old Chero-kee blackguard." Rusk nevertheless stayed with the army, not merely to oversee its conduct, but to become a part of it.[32]

In mid-April divisiveness escalated when Mirabeau Buonaparte Lamar, a thirty-eight-year-old newcomer from Georgia, joined the army. He had landed in Texas on April 6 with $6,000 to invest for a Georgia syndicate. In Harrisburg he met with officials of the interim government, apparently adopting the anti-Houston bias of Burnet and other politicians. Although he was only a private, many of the men recognized Lamar as a natural leader, and from his first day in camp he advocated a hare-brained scheme to use the *Yellowstone*, a Brazos River steamboat that had docked at Groce's Landing, to raid Mexican positions downstream. Houston learned of the plan and posted notices that anyone who attempted to raise an unauthorized force would be shot as a mutineer. Lamar backed down, but the volunteers cited this as another example of their general's high-handedness.[33]

On April 12 Houston broke camp at Groce's. The men could stomach no more drill; the general could only hope that on the day of battle it would prove sufficient. Employing the *Yellowstone* and an old yawl, the Texians appreciated a dry crossing of the Brazos, but it still required two days to transport all the men and supplies to the opposite bank. Houston then marched the army eastward, but he gave no hint as to its destination. Many speculated that they were headed for the enemy and battle; others suspected that they were bound for the Sabine and ignoble safety. Houston said nothing and rode on.[34]

By April 15 the rear guard companies under Baker and Martin had rejoined the army on the march. Baker's opinion of the general had not changed since they had parted at San Felipe. He publicly excoriated Houston for refusing to make a stand, especially since he now had artillery. Martin, once the general's friend and supporter, now loudly proclaimed that he would no longer serve under such a gutless commander. Houston knew that if Martin remained, his rancor would undo all the progress made at Groce's plantation. He therefore relieved Martin of his command and dispatched him to organize the swelling herd of civilian refugees following the army. For his part, Martin seemed delighted to distance himself from the man he so clearly despised.[35]

Santa Anna was also on the march. On April 14 he set out from Fort Bend at the head of seven hundred troops intent on capturing the rebel cabinet at Harrisburg. The rainy weather and the muddy roads continued to hinder the Mexican advance. At one small creek, several mules carrying precious supplies drowned. To make up the time lost in fording the creek, Santa Anna continued the march until well after sundown. "The night was dark; a great many men straggled off," reported Captain Pedro Delgado, "and our piece of artillery bogged at every turn of the wheel." The contingent made better progress the next day, and by noon the expedition reached William Stafford's plantation, which the Texians had neglected to burn. The general ordered a halt so his men could rest and enjoy the abundance of corn, meal, sheep, and hogs. They feasted until mid-afternoon, at which time Santa Anna had the plantation buildings burned and then ordered a forced march to Harrisburg. The Mexican vanguard arrived at the temporary capital just before midnight on

April 15. They found the town deserted except for three printers who informed Santa Anna that Burnet and his cabinet had fled only a few hours earlier in the direction of New Washington on the coast. His Excellency, disappointed that Zavala had again avoided the noose, sent Colonel Almonte and fifty dragoons in hot pursuit.[36]

In Harrisburg Santa Anna learned that the rebel army had departed Groce's plantation, but he was confident that Houston would continue to avoid battle. He had, furthermore, already dispatched orders to Filisola at Fort Bend to send up Cós with five hundred additional infantry, so he had little fear of an attack. On April 15 he composed a communique to General Filisola that reflected his complacency: "Due to reports which I have gathered at this point, I have no doubts that the entitled General Houston who was at Groce's Crossing with a force of five to six hundred men, has moved toward Nacogdoches and should have left yesterday in that direction. However, since he is escorting families and supplies in ox-drawn wagons, his march is slow. The Trinity River, moreover, should detain him many days."[37]

On April 18, Santa Anna burned Harrisburg and then hurried to New Washington to learn whether Almonte's dragoons had succeeded in their mission. They had missed their quarry by mere yards. Burnet and his party had shoved off in a rowboat just minutes ahead of the dragoons. The boat was, in fact, still within carbine range, but the chivalrous Mexican officer in charge forbade firing, as women were aboard. Although Santa Anna's hopes of capturing the Texian officials had been dashed, he was pleased with what had been accomplished: he had driven the rebel government off the Texas mainland, severed its communications with its army, and now had only to block Houston's line of retreat. The rebellion was all but crushed.[38]

The rebel army, however, was "retreating" toward Santa Anna. Colonel Almonte's scouts had heard that Houston was headed for the Trinity River via Lynchburg on Buffalo Bayou. But from there, Houston's army might board a ship and join the insurgent government on Galveston Island. To prevent such a move, Santa Anna decided to seize the crossing at Lynchburg before Houston arrived. On the morning of April 19, His Excellency hastened a squadron of dragoons back toward Lynchburg with orders to be on the lookout for Houston's band of "land thieves." All that remained for Santa Anna was to quash this last mob of filibusterers. Then he could return to the comforts of Mexico as a military hero—his standing as the Napoleon of the West confirmed.[39]

Meanwhile, the rebel army continued its eastward march with renewed determination, which apparently was not shared by its commander. It is impossible to know with certainty what was in Houston's mind, but officers under his command maintained that as late as April 15 he advocated retreating across the Sabine to Louisiana, where he hoped to raise an army of five thousand volunteers. That day he broached the subject with Rusk and selected officers, for the next day's march would bring the army to a major crossroads, both literally and metaphorically. The north road led to Nacogdoches and safety, the other toward Harrisburg and confrontation. Consensus was unanimous for engaging the enemy. Rebel officers told Houston that if he took the north fork, he would travel alone. The general, as usual, said nothing.[40]

Tension was high the next day as the army approached the crossroads; all eyes were on Houston. A rumor spread through the column that he still stubbornly insisted on retreating. Some swore that they would fight Houston and all who stood by him if such were the case. Others loudly called for Houston's removal. Three musicians marched at the head of the column, while the general rode near the rear of the line. Dr. Labadie reported: "As General Houston was now coming up, several of us desired Mr. Roberts [the owner of the land along the road], who was standing on his gate, to point out to all—*the road to Harrisburg*. General Houston was then close by, when Roberts raised his hand, and elevating his voice, cried out: 'That right-hand road will carry you to Harrisburg just as straight as a compass.'"[41]

At that moment, the independent, mud-spattered volunteers took over. A joyous shout sounded through the ranks: "To the right boys, to the right." The "band" continued, without orders, along the Harrisburg road; the rest of the cheering men followed the music. Houston rode on in silence, as if this were the route he had planned to take all along. Revolutionary armies often have a dynamic of their own, coupled with a zeal that more than compensates for their lack of formal training. On such occasions, all a general can do is point his eager soldiers in the direction of the enemy, stand out of their way, and hope for the best. Perhaps General Houston came to that realization, but whether he did or not was irrelevant; the men had made the decision on their own. For many years afterward, the anti-Houston faction claimed that, far from being the stalwart leader his sycophants claimed, the army had actually led "old Sam" toward the enemy against his will. The full truth of the matter will never be known, but at least on this occasion Houston's critics were probably correct.[42]

"Old Sam's" pride received another blow later that same day. Mrs. Pamela Mann had loaned the army a team of oxen to haul the artillery. Houston had apparently assured her that he was taking her beloved animals to the Redlands and out of harm's way. Mrs. Mann now knew differently, and Private Robert Hunter recounted the confrontation in his own singular spelling: "She rode up [to] the general & said, general you tole me a dam lie, you said [you] was going on the Nacogdoches road. Sir, I want my oxen. Well, Mrs. Mann [Houston replied], we cant spare them. We cant git our cannon a long without them. I dont care a dam for your cannon [Mrs. Mann countered], I want my oxen."[43]

With that, Mrs. Mann, brandishing a Bowie knife, cut her oxen free from the traces and led the beasts away. The rugged frontiersmen watched the performance with stunned awe. "No body said a word," Hunter recorded. "She jumpt on her horse with whip in hand & away she went in a lope with her oxen." Conrad Rohrer, the army's wagon master, protested to Houston that he simply could not haul the artillery without the oxen and said he was going after the intransigent female to retrieve the team. Houston advised him not to; this particular female, he warned, would fight. "Damn her fighting," shouted the angry wagon master as he rode after Mrs. Mann. Rohrer sheepishly returned to camp that night with his shirt in shreds. "Where are the oxen?" the men inquired. "She would not let me have them," Rohrer meekly replied.[44]

The march continued with a new sense of urgency, but there was no letup in the rain. Without the oxen to draw the cannon, they constantly bogged down in the mire. Abandoning the ordnance would be disastrous, so the men pitched in to help; even the general dismounted to put his shoulder against a stuck cannon wheel. Hot food became a distant memory; toil and hardship weighed upon the men with every soggy step. But they grimly pressed forward, covering the fifty-five miles of boggy road in only two and a half days. Exhausted and filthy, they entered Harrisburg on the afternoon of April 18. The Republic's army would run no more.[45]

❖❖

CHAPTER 10

"Nock There Brains Out"

❖❖

10. *TEJANO* VOLUNTEER

Seguín's Company
April 21, 1836

Having survived the fighting at San Jacinto, this tejano *veteran savors a smoke while surveying the carnage. His hat, typical of those adopted by most* vaqueros, *is adorned with a rosary. Also conspicuous is the cardboard that Seguín's men placed in their hatbands to identify themselves as "good" Mexicans; our man has scribbled a defiant slogan on his distinguishing emblem. Although the buckskin jacket is most often associated with the Anglo-Celtic frontiersman, there is ample evidence that Mexican frontiersmen also wore the* cuera. *The haversack and the knife are of U.S. manufacture but would have been readily available in Béxar by the mid-1830s. The* serape *and gourd canteen are, however, characteristic of the Mexican borderlands, as are his distinctive trousers, which reveal wear from weeks of hard campaigning. His firearm is the British India Pattern Brown Bess musket, which he appropriated from an unlucky* centralista *who had no further use for it; our hard-riding* tejano *has, however, cut several inches off the barrel to render it less cumbersome while on horseback. The brogan shoes fly in the face of the popular* ranchero *image but are well documented as being in use at the time. As the Texian army passed through San Felipe, Seguín signed a voucher for twenty-two pairs of "shoes" from merchant Joseph Urban. It is almost certain, therefore, that these shoes were worn at San Jacinto. Later, Urban submitted the voucher for the shoes and received payment; the voucher can be seen in the Texas State Archives.*

❖❖❖

I O

"Nock There Brains Out"

FOR THE FIRST TIME IN WEEKS, Sam Houston had some reason for confidence. On April 18 scouts Henry Karnes and "Deaf" Smith returned with a captured Mexican courier. The express rider, who carried letters addressed to Santa Anna, was obviously a veteran of the Alamo, for the dispatches were in deerskin saddlebags marked "William Barret Travis." Major Lorenzo de Zavala, Jr., son of the vice-president and recently appointed the general's aide, translated the letters. They revealed that El Presidente was personally at the head of a small force in New Washington and, more important, that he was isolated from the rest of the army. That intelligence was vital, for Houston now realized that his rival had made the mistake for which he had been waiting.[1]

The army departed Harrisburg the next day, but about 248 men who were too ill to march were left behind with the army's baggage. Houston understood that if the war were to be won he would have to strike quickly before reinforcements could reach Santa Anna.[2]

"Old Sam" probably would have preferred to meet the enemy in the dense forest of the Redlands, but if the Mexican dictator remained cut off from the bulk of his forces, Houston was willing to risk an open battle. Before leaving Harrisburg, he had written his friend Henry Raguet that "we are in preparation to meet Santa Anna. It is the only chance of saving Texas."[3]

Until that time, Houston had said little to his men other than "follow me." Now the time had come to rely again upon his oratorical dexterity. Forming his men in a hollow square around him, he delivered his only speech of the campaign. "The army will cross [Buffalo Bayou] and we will meet the enemy!" he shouted. "Some of us may be killed and must be killed; but soldiers remember the Alamo! the Alamo! the Alamo!" For weeks the Texian army had yearned for revenge, and now the general had touched a tender nerve. The ranks took up the refrain: "Remember the Alamo! Remember Goliad!" Sensing the rancor of the men, Lieutenant Colonel Alexander Somervell of the First Regiment concluded: "After such a speech, but dammed few will be taken prisoners—that I know."[4]

Utilizing a log raft and a leaky boat, the army required most of the day to cross to the east bank of Buffalo Bayou. Houston, nevertheless, ordered a forced march along the east bank of the bayou toward Lynchburg. Having little choice, he called a halt about midnight; many of the exhausted troops had fallen by the wayside; the rest collapsed on the soggy ground and slept, too weary to wait for supper.[5]

The respite was short. Reveille sounded at daybreak. Famished men called for food, but the general said there would be time for that later; first, they must march. After slogging forward for two hours, Houston finally ordered a halt for breakfast. Three beeves were slaughtered, and the men gathered firewood. But no sooner were the steaks on the fire than Texian scouts galloped up with news that the Mexicans had burned New Washington and were advancing northwestward toward Lynch's Ferry. The entire campaign came down to a race to the ferry, with the first army to arrive winning the choice ground. Houston instructed the men to break camp immediately and march; this was a competition that the rebel army could ill afford to lose. Cursing soldiers gnawed half-cooked meat and poured freshly brewed coffee on the campfires. Such ready obedience to unpopular orders may have shown that the training and discipline at Groce's plantation had been effective. More likely, it demonstrated merely that vengeful rebels hungered more for blood than for breakfast.[6]

The Texians won the race, arriving in the vicinity of the ferry about mid-morning. They immediately occupied a thick grove of oaks that ran along the elevated bank of Buffalo Bayou, perfect cover for riflemen. That would have been reward enough for their marching, but they also captured an enemy flatboat loaded with provisions. Scouts reported that the Mexicans were still some miles away. The insurgents, therefore, enjoyed a well-deserved rest under the shade of the oaks and savored a late breakfast, courtesy of Antonio López de Santa Anna.[7]

The Texians were not the only ones to have scouts out. Before leaving New Washington at eight o'clock in the morning, Santa Anna learned that Houston's army was advancing on his rear, not scurrying toward Nacogdoches as he supposed. Colonel Delgado recounted that the news had a deleterious effect upon His Excellency. He leapt on his horse and thundered along the line of march—knocking down two soldiers in the process—all the while shouting: "The enemy are coming! The enemy are coming!" Delgado scornfully reported that the "excitement of the general-in-chief had such a terrifying effect upon the troops, that every face turned pale; order could no longer be preserved, and every man thought of flight, or finding a hiding place, and gave up all idea of fighting." Despite such trepidations, the detachment pressed forward, arriving at the junction of Buffalo Bayou and the San Jacinto River at two o'clock on the afternoon of April 20.[8]

Houston had written earlier that he needed to meet the enemy on "our own ground," since doing otherwise had proven disastrous. Both culturally and geographically, the vast prairies south of the Guadalupe River were Hispanic. On the expansive, open grasslands, the advantage was with the superior Mexican horsemen and superior Mexican numbers. An occasional grove of trees might be located, and if the Texians reached it first, as they had at Concepción and Nueces Crossing, their reliable long rifles could keep hostile infantry and cavalry at bay. When, however, they could not secure natural cover, as at Coleto, or they ran out of ammunition, as at Refugio, they were at the mercy of the Mexican cavalry and artillery. Travis had sensed this tactical dilemma in January when he argued against sending his small force "into the enemy's country." He had been correct. Béxar and Goliad were the hubs of *tejano* settlement. True, many *tejanos* supported the revolt, but most embraced the *centralistas*. Furthermore, the faithfulness of Juan Seguín's *rancheros* in no way diminished the difficulty of providing logistical and moral support to men over great distances, nor did it compensate for the absence of natural cover so critical for Texian riflemen.[9]

On the other hand, the terrain north of the Colorado River seemed ideal for Texians. The grassy coastal prairies gradually gave way to more and more trees. Because this area was not well suited to Spanish ranching, with the exception of Nacogdoches, few *tejanos* lived there. Most U.S. colonists had settled on the rich bottomland along the Brazos River in Austin's Colony or on the red soil in the piney woods of East Texas. These regions, perforce, became cultural as well as geographic extensions of the southern woodlands. The Americans had made this land their own. Colonel de la Peña sensed as much: "It was the first time our soldiers would be dealing with men of a different language and a different religion, men whose character and habits were likewise different from theirs. All was new in this war, and although it was happening on our own soil, it seemed as if it were being waged in a foreign land."

Houston was willing to trade land for time. Land was, after all, among the few commodities that the Texians had in abundance. As he fell back on the Texian settlements, the Texian lines of communication became shorter and stronger while those of Santa Anna stretched to the breaking point. Also the dense forests and the marshy bottoms hindered Mexican cavalry and provided cover for rebel riflemen.[10]

The terrain around Lynch's Ferry was well suited to the modes of U.S. frontier warfare. Thick oak groves skirted Buffalo Bayou, and the marshes along the San Jacinto River hindered Mexican cavalry. Men from the swampy coastal regions of Louisiana, Mississippi, and Alabama found the area much like home. For the Mexicans, on the other hand, the land north of the Colorado seemed remarkably alien. In Santa Anna's zeal to capture the rebel officials, he was now the one who was separated from his bases of support. Houston had indeed lured him onto ground that Texians had made their own. Even so, Santa Anna ordered his men to pitch camp. Delgado was amazed that the general would select such a vulnerable campsite. It was "in all respects against military rules. Any youngster would have done better," he observed.[11]

When he arrived on the field, Santa Anna could not see the rebels. Scouts reported the presence of two pieces of artillery near the oak grove. El Presidente knew that Houston had concealed his force in the woods, and he ordered a probe against the Texian position. With luck, he might draw the rebels out of their hiding place and onto the open field away from the soggy ground where he could employ his dragoons to advantage. At any rate, he would test the mettle of this backwoods drunkard who presumed to call himself a general.[12]

Santa Anna directed the probe from an island of timber. A line of skirmishers moved against the Texian position but were brought up short by Lieutenant Colonel J. C. Neill's artillery. In response, Colonel Delgado moved up the single fieldpiece that had caused so much trouble during the march to Harrisburg. Although they had cursed it then, the Mexicans were grateful for it as they advanced the brass twelve-pounder, named the Golden Standard, toward the enemy. Soon the Twin Sisters and the Golden Standard were blasting away at each other.

All three drew blood. Rebel fire wounded Captain Urizza, the sensitive young officer who had been appalled at his commander's callousness at the Alamo. He later complained that Santa Anna saw that he was wounded but ignored him. Urizza must have wondered whether Santa Anna now considered him just another one of the "chickens." Subsequent blasts from the Sisters also killed two mules, shattered a caisson, and scattered ammunition boxes. Delgado gamely answered with grapeshot that peppered Neill's position, painfully wounding the veteran artilleryman. But Delgado soon realized that his lone gun was no match for the Twins. Fearful of losing the only available Mexican cannon, he withdrew the piece to a protected wood. The rebels had won the first round.[13]

Houston's men, encouraged to see the hated Mexicans retreat from their fire, goaded their commander to follow up the initial success with a full-scale attack. Sidney Sherman was especially adamant. Shouting at Houston, he argued that a cavalry charge could capture the enemy artillery and might even transform the withdrawal into a rout. The general was not convinced; he did not wish to gamble his mounted riflemen against trained cavalry. At last, in a compromise intended to mollify the hot-blooded Sherman, Houston allowed him to reconnoiter with his horsemen but admonished him not to bring about a general engagement.[14]

Riding at the head of sixty-one mounted riflemen, one of whom was Secretary of War Thomas Rusk, Sherman led what was supposed to be a reconnaissance. Yet as soon as he saw the enemy, Sherman ordered a charge. "Daringly the rebels threw themselves on my cavalry," Santa Anna recalled, and even he admitted that they temporarily "succeeded in throwing us into confusion." Sherman's horsemen, after discharging their cumbersome long rifles, were obliged to dismount to reload. At that moment, with over half of the rebels on foot, the dragoons countercharged with saber and lance. Enough Texian rifles were loaded to allow them to fire a point-blank volley. The Mexicans veered off, regrouped, and bore down again. Once more Sherman's riflemen hastily reloaded. The Mexican cavalrymen, however, had no need to reload. They drew their sabers, lowered their lances, and kept coming. As they galloped among the *gringos*, a wild melee ensued. Rusk was surrounded by enemy lancers and would have been killed or captured if Private Mirabeau Lamar had not charged in astride his massive stallion. Lamar's horse literally knocked aside a smaller Mexican mount, clearing an opening through which Rusk rode to safety.[15]

Nestled in the safety of the timber, Texian infantrymen observed the skirmish. When it became apparent that his cavalry was in trouble, Sherman requested infantry support. Houston wisely refused, knowing that once the riflemen abandoned their cover they would be even more vulnerable to Mexican lancers than rebel horsemen. Several officers begged their commander to allow them to reinforce Sherman. Houston remained unyielding. At that juncture, Captain Jesse Billingsley took matters into his own hands.

The independent captain was determined to assist his beleaguered comrades. "Seeing [Sherman's horsemen] under a heavy fire and receiving no orders from Gen. Houston to go to their support," Billingsley recounted, "I determined to go voluntarily, and accordingly led out the first Company of the first Regiment." As Billingsley's company moved forward, others were spurred by its example, and it was "immediately followed by the entire Regiment, under command of its gallant leader, Col. Burleson." Yet to reach the battlefield, these recalcitrant Samaritans had to march directly past their commander in chief. Houston angrily ordered them to countermarch back to the safety of the timber. As Billingsley laughingly recalled: "This order the men treated with derision, requesting him to countermarch himself, if he desired it, and steadily held on their way to the support of Col. Sherman, and succeeded in driving the enemy behind their breastworks."[16]

Sherman called for his men to fall back to the shelter of the woods and the supporting infantry, but Lamar still had one more act of heroism to perform. Walter Lane, a nineteen-year-old Irish lad, rode his mount with "more zeal than discretion," and it carried him "headlong into the midst of the enemy." Couching his lance, a Mexican cavalryman caught Lane in the shoulder, depositing him ten feet from his horse. He was knocked unconscious by the fall, and his comrades thought him dead. They were amazed, therefore, when the youth came to, rose to his feet, and staggered toward friendly lines. The Mexicans saw him too, and several lancers bore down upon the wounded Lane. As they were about to impale the boy, Lamar blocked their path and dispatched one with his pistol. The ubiquitous Henry Karnes then galloped in, pulled Lane up behind him, and carried him to safety. The Mexican dragoons, admirers of daring horsemanship, reportedly applauded as the three Texians rode for timber. The chivalrous Lamar, always mindful of the beau geste, reined in, turned his mount toward his adversaries, and acknowledged their homage with a gracious bow.[17]

Houston was livid. The entire engagement had proved a perilous burlesque. Sherman, flagrantly violating his orders, had also acted with "more zeal than discretion." In reinforcing the cavalry, the infantry had ignored direct orders. But how could one reprimand an entire regiment? As the Texians withdrew from the field, Delgado recounted that they retired "sluggishly and in disorder." [18]

The encounter demonstrated that the Mexican cavalry was still formidable. Sherman's men had made a spirited charge, but when the smoke cleared all they had to show for their efforts were two wounded men and several dead mounts. Most of those who participated in the foolhardy venture knew they had been lucky to survive. Had it not been for the timely intercession of Lamar, Secretary of War Rusk would be lying dead on the field or, perhaps worse, a prisoner of Santa Anna. Although the Texians found a new hero in Lamar, his derring-do did not alter the fact that the Mexicans had won round two. Having Santa Anna isolated from his main force, Houston momentarily held the strategic and numerical advantage. He readily understood, however, that intemperate actions could easily blunt the edge the men had achieved by much hard marching. [19]

For his part, Santa Anna also realized the precarious nature of his own position. He had no way of knowing the number of rebels under Houston, but he rightly believed that they outnumbered his own force. Cós was on the march with reinforcements, but if Houston attacked during the night, Santa Anna's small contingent might be overwhelmed. To prevent such a disaster, His Excellency worked his men all night fortifying the camp. He had his soldiers pile up saddles, crates, brush, any material that would serve as a make-shift breastwork. Those men who were not busy constructing barricades slept beside their weapons. The number of sentries was doubled. [20]

Across the field in the Texian camp, "uproar and confusion" prevailed. Sherman, Baker, and others argued that they could have whipped the Mexicans that afternoon if Houston had allowed the requested infantry support. Once again the general's fitness to command was a matter of debate. In a vituperative letter to Houston years later, Baker, who remained a bitter political opponent of his old commander, gleefully recalled that on the night of April 20 "various members of the army were seen publicly and fearlessly going from company to company, soliciting volunteers to fight the enemy without your consent." The general remained above the bickering, keeping his thoughts to himself. He personally beat tattoo, and well after his contentious soldiers snoozed snugly in their blankets, he remained awake to plan the next day's action.[21]

For Houston's sleeping insurgents, Thursday, April 21, began at four o'clock in the morning, when a freedman known to history only as "Dick" beat reveille. Most believed that the new day was certain to produce a fight. To their disgust, however, others noted that the general had left instructions not to be disturbed and slept through Dick's brattle. A "restless and anxious spirit" pervaded the camp as the anti-Houston cabal loudly wondered if the "Big Drunk" intended to sleep all day. Houston needed his rest. He had been up most of the night, and this was the first time in days that he had been out of the saddle for more than a few hours. As their commander slept, the volunteers honed Bowie knives, cleaned rifles, and, of course, grumbled.[22]

Around nine o'clock that morning, they had just cause for complaint, for General Cós entered the Mexican camp with about 540 reinforcements. The additional troops increased Santa Anna's force to about 1,200. Houston's 910 men no longer enjoyed numerical superiority. Colonel John Austin Wharton pointed out that "the enemy have thousands that they can and will concentrate at this point within the next few days; the Texians have no reasonable expectation of a stronger force." He concluded, therefore, "The enemy must . . . be fought today, least tomorrow prove too late." Houston was undoubtedly aware that Cós was in the vicinity, since the captured dispatches stated as much. Why then did he wait for Cós to arrive? Afterward Houston glibly remarked that he wished to avoid taking "two bites out of one cherry." That may or may not have been true, but Houston well understood that he could ill afford to allow additional reinforcements to reach Santa Anna.[23]

With that object in mind, he called on the redoubtable "Deaf" Smith. Apparently Smith himself suggested that he destroy Vince's Bridge, which Cós and his men had crossed that morning to reach the Mexican camp. But Houston asked Smith first to reconnoiter the enemy position and get an accurate count of the Mexican troops. Smith picked Walter P. Lane, the young fellow who had been unhorsed in the skirmish the day before, to accompany him. Smith and Lane stealthily rode to the rear of Santa Anna's camp and halted a mere three hundred yards from it. Smith told Lane to hold his mount while he sighted his telescope and methodically began counting enemy tents. The Mexicans spied the two and sent out a company of infantry to apprehend them. Lane was acutely aware of the musket balls that "whistled over our heads," but Smith, being hard of hearing, seemed not to notice them. The Texian scouts were under constant fire for twenty minutes, but Smith remained oblivious. Only when a squad of dragoons charged on them did Smith cease his counting. Turning to his startled comrade, he observed, "Lane, I think them fellows are shooting at us; let's git." As an old man, Lane recalled that he "never obeyed an order more cheerfully."[24]

After reporting the number of enemy tents to Houston, Smith expressed his intention of destroying Vince's Bridge. As Smith was leaving, Houston cryptically remarked, "Come back like eagles, or you will be too late for the day." Smith then selected six volunteers to assist him and began the five-mile ride to the bridge. Several accounts maintain that Houston ordered the bridge burned to block Santa Anna's escape route. He could have, however, retreated due south along the coast and avoided any major obstacle. It was likely that Houston was more concerned about the possibility of General Filisola arriving from Fort Bend. There was only one road that linked Harrisburg and Lynchburg, and the destruction of Vince's Bridge would greatly hinder any body of troops traveling toward the battlefield.[25]

In the Texian camp, the troops were in a near frenzy. It was noon, and Houston had already wasted half the day. Any more delay would surely bring additional Mexican reinforcements. Some speculated that Houston was simply seeking another excuse to avoid battle.[26]

Eight disgruntled officers demanded a council of war, and Rusk, heretofore a staunch Houston supporter, took part in it. The meeting lasted from noon until two o'clock. Accounts of what occurred differ. Robert Coleman, who in 1837 wrote a vicious anti-Houston polemic, claimed that the general had ordered a withdrawal across Buffalo Bayou, but the officers told him that "he *must fight*, that a further delay would not be countenanced by either soldiers or officers." Finally, according to Coleman, Houston resentfully replied, "Fight then and be damned!"[27]

The pro-Houston forces told a different story. They swore that Houston was fully committed to an attack on April 21. Charles Edwards Lester wrote in his patently partisan biography that upon awaking that morning the general "sprang to his feet, and exclaimed, 'the sun of Austerlitz has risen again.'" Houston was, Lester claimed, "probably the only man in that camp over whose mind flitted no anxious vision." Marquis James, in his Pulitzer Prize–winning biography, *The Raven*, expressed few doubts. According to him, the general, not his officers, called the meeting to decide whether they should attack the Mexicans or await attack in the splendid defensive position provided by the oak grove. "Houston expressed no opinion," James wrote, "and when the others had wrangled themselves into a thorough disagreement he dismissed the council."[28]

Two distinct images of Houston emerge. One is of a timid man, who schemed to avoid combat until his troops literally forced him into action. The other is of a stalwart hero in the Kipling mold, a confident commander who kept his head while petty and presumptuous subordinates were losing theirs. Neither view is entirely true nor entirely false. Since Houston was careful not to reveal certain aspects of himself, there will always be an air of mystery surrounding the man. It is equally true that many of the scurrilous charges against him—such as the one that the vial of hartshorn that he periodically sniffed was in reality opium—were made by those who resented his political power or envied his fame.[29]

Whatever his motivation, between three and four o'clock on the afternoon of April 21, it was Sam Houston who called the Texians to battle. The army advanced in two parallel lines, with the two six-pounders in the middle and the mounted riflemen screened behind an oak grove on the enemy's left. The Texian horse now had a new commander. Lamar, a private the day before, had so distinguished himself in Sherman's unauthorized charge that Houston had awarded to him the cavalry command. The insubordinate Sherman was back at the head of his Kentucky infantry.[30]

A slight rise covered by high grass concealed their approach from the Mexicans. With luck, they could cover most of the five hundred yards between the Texas camp and Santa Anna's breastworks before their presence was discovered. As the rebel army began its advance, "Deaf" Smith rode down the line yelling, "Vince's Bridge is down!" The destruction of the bridge would hinder the approach of Filisola on the Texian rear, but it also cut off their primary line of retreat. It was now a case of win or die.[31]

It was no splendid army of Napoleonic proportions that grimly stalked toward the Mexican camp. The men composing the rebel line represented every frontier variant. The backwoodsman in greasy buckskins stood elbow to elbow with the townsman in frockcoat and top hat. One of General Gaines's "deserters" in partial U.S. army uniform advanced next to a southern beau in planter's hat, waistcoat, and cravat. The Kentucky Rifles, a unit recruited and outfitted by Sidney Sherman, donned trim, military-cut uniforms. They did, however, have a few traits in common: all were mudstained and unshaven; all were tired of running from an enemy they despised; all were anxious to avenge the deaths of those who had fallen at the Alamo and Goliad.[32]

Among them, Juan Seguín led a detachment of about nineteen *tejanos*. Their presence in the line of battle was all the more impressive because they had been excused from combat duty. Since the execution of Fannin and his men, animosity against Mexicans—all Mexicans—had run high. Houston was fearful that in the heat of battle his vengeful rowdies might not pause to make distinctions. Before leaving Harrisburg, therefore, the general ordered Seguín's company to stay and guard the baggage. Seguín angrily reminded Houston that not all of his men were with him. Some had fallen at the Alamo. Besides, all of his soldiers hailed from the Béxar area, and until Santa Anna and his army were driven out of Texas, they could not return home. Seguín steadfastly asserted that his men had more reason to hate *santanistas* than anyone in Texas and wanted in on the kill. "Spoken like a man!" Houston exclaimed. But he insisted on one precaution; the *tejanos* must place pieces of cardboard in their hatbands to identify them. Consequently, with the distinctive cardboard insignia in place, they advanced upon the enemy with the rest of the army.[33]

Meanwhile, all was quiet in the Mexican camp. Santa Anna had expected the rebels to attack the night before. Failing that, he was certain that they would attack on the morning of April 21. Then at nine o'clock, Cós had arrived with five hundred additional troops, not the veterans that His Excellency had requested, but recruits who were exhausted and hungry after the forced march from the Fort Bend area. Still, the arrival of Cós's reinforcements had shifted the odds in Santa Anna's favor. His force now consisted of at least 1,250 men, against Houston's band of about 910. Santa Anna reasoned that Houston had seen Cós arrive and could also detect the newly erected breastworks. He doubted that the rebels would throw themselves against barricades but ordered constant readiness. Noon passed, as did early afternoon. As the shadows of late afternoon fell across the field, Santa Anna relaxed his vigilance and ordered the troops to stand down. His own force had been awake constructing defenses, and Cós's troops had spent the night marching. The weary Mexicans welcomed the opportunity to sleep. Santa Anna also needed rest. He had passed a nervous night supervising the construction of the breastworks and awaiting the arrival of Cós. But now he could enjoy his repose; if the rebels had not attacked before Cós arrived with reinforcements, they were not likely to do so now. Thinking the situation well under control, Santa Anna retired to his camp bed.[34]

Not all of the Mexican officers were as confident as their commander that the rebels would not attack. Lamenting the pitiful defensive ground his general had selected, Colonel Delgado noted:

> We had the enemy on our right, within a wood, at long musket range. Our front, although level, was exposed to the fire of the enemy, who could keep it up with impunity from his sheltered position. Retreat was easy for him on his rear and right, while our own troops had no space for maneuvering. We had in our rear a small grove, reaching to the bay shore, which extended on our right as far as New Washington. What ground had we to retreat upon in the case of a reverse? From sad experience, I answered—None![35]

Delgado sought out General Castrillón, the gallant officer who had attempted to save the lives of Crockett and others at the Alamo, to discuss his concerns. He found him standing just outside His Excellency's tent. "What can I do, my friend?" Castrillón asked caustically. "You know nothing avails here against the caprice, arbitrary will, and ignorance of that man!" Delgado was surprised that the normally mild-mannered Castrillón expressed his contempt in such an "impassioned voice" and well within Santa Anna's hearing.[36]

The unseen insurgents marching toward the Mexican camp were about to justify Delgado's concerns. Houston described the advance:

> Our cavalry was first dispatched to the front of the enemy's left for the purpose of attracting their notice, whilst an extensive island of timber afforded us an opportunity of concealing our forces and deploying from that point agreeably to the previous design of the troops. Every evolution was performed with alacrity, the whole [army] advancing rapidly in line and through an open prairie without any protection whatsoever for our men. The artillery advanced and took station within two hundred yards of the enemy's breastworks, and commenced an effective fire of grape and canister.[37]

The battle opened around 4:30, and with the firing of the Twin Sisters, events unfolded quickly. Lamar led his horsemen in a charge on the

Mexican left flank. About the same time, a four-piece band broke into a titillating ballad, "Will You Come to the Bower?" Houston, out in front astride a huge stallion named Saracen, called for the infantrymen to hold their fire. He finally halted the line, dressed ranks, and shouted orders to fire; the entire line erupted in smoke and flame. After the first volley, Houston attempted to halt the line for reloading, but Rusk rode onto the field shouting: "If we stop, we are cut to pieces! Don't stop—go ahead—give them Hell!" The Texian line disintegrated. Men surged forward in open skirmish order; losing control of his army, Houston could only follow. Rusk was correct. At that juncture, momentum meant everything. Not bothering to reload, the rebels swept over the barricades swinging clubbed rifles, wielding flintlock pistols and Bowie knives. While few Mexican soldiers understood the language, they knew only too well the deadly message of the vengeful battlecry: "Remember the Alamo! Remember Goliad!"[38]

The surprise was complete. Some Mexican officers attempted to rally their men. "The utmost confusion prevailed," Delgado recalled. "General Castrillón shouted on one side; on another Colonel Almonte was giving orders; some cried out to commence firing; others, to lie down to avoid grape shot. Among the latter was His Excellency. . . . I saw our men flying in small groups, terrified, and sheltering themselves behind large trees. I endeavored to force some of them to fight, but all efforts were in vain—the evil was beyond remedy: they were a bewildered and panic-stricken herd."[39]

Actually, commanders on both sides lost control of their troops. Houston had envisioned a more formal battle in which ranks would advance, fire, reload, and continue. Had the Texians proceeded in such a manner, however, the Mexicans may well have had time to form behind their barricades and return effective musket fire. As Houston's line dissolved into clusters of shock troops, the Mexicans had no main body against which they could direct their volley fire. Yet in open skirmish order, the rebel riflemen *could* rely on individual aimed fire, which proved extremely accurate.[40]

Texians flooded over the barricades; most of the defenders fell back. There was one, however, who won the lasting admiration of his adversaries. General Castrillón directed the gun crew manning the Golden Standard. Rifle fire soon killed most of the Mexican artillerymen, and those who had not been cut down were "running like turkeys, whipped and discomfited." His men called out for the general to come with them,

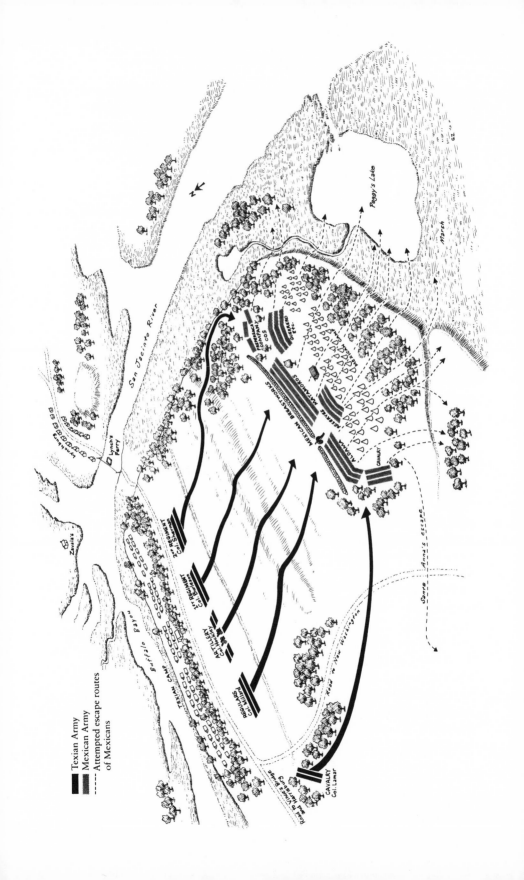

but he stubbornly refused to budge. "I have been in forty battles and never showed my back," Castrillón answered, "I am too old to do it now." With those words, he manfully turned to face the onslaught.

Viewing this remarkable demonstration of courage, Rusk sought to preserve the gallant officer's life. He rode along the line shouting, "Don't shoot him! Don't shoot him!" The secretary of war even knocked up the rifles of nearby soldiers who were aiming at Castrillón. But as the young Walter P. Lane looked on, others pushed past Rusk, drew down on the "old Castillian gentleman," and "riddled him with balls."[41]

The actual battle lasted no more than eighteen minutes, but the slaughter continued much longer. Determined to avenge the loss of those killed at the Alamo and Goliad, the bloodthirsty rebels committed atrocities at least as beastly as those the Mexicans had committed. Sergeant Moses Bryan came across a Mexican drummer boy with both legs broken. The frightened child had grabbed a Texian soldier around the legs, all the while screaming, "*Ave Maria purissima! Por Dios, salva mi vida!*" (Hail Mary, most pure! For God's sake, save my life!) Bryan begged the man to spare the youth, but the pitiless brute, in a threatening gesture, placed a hand on his belt pistol. Bryan backed away and watched in horror as the man "blew out the boy's brains."[42]

If the Mexicans expected mercy from Seguín's men, they were soon disabused of that belief. Shouting "*Recuerden el Alamo*," the *tejanos* pitched into the midst of the fight, transforming the odd bits of cardboard in their hatbands into honor badges for their unit. As the slaughter ensued, a Mexican officer recognized Antonio Menchaca as an acquaintance from Béxar and pleaded with him as a "brother Mexican" to intercede for his life. Menchaca fixed him with a cold gaze and replied, "No, damn you, I'm no Mexican—I'm an American." Then turning to his Anglo comrades, he curtly instructed: "Shoot him!" They summarily ended the pleading. For better or worse, Seguín and his *tejanos* had cast their lot with the Republic of Texas; the bitterness of San Jacinto demonstrated that for most there could be no turning back.[43]

In their haste to escape the bloodthirsty Texians, many Mexicans threw down their arms and plunged headlong into Peggy Lake. For the riflemen on the bank, it was quite literally like shooting fish in a barrel. Colonel Delgado caught a glimpse of Colonel Almonte swimming with his left arm while holding his right above the surface, still grasping his sword. The waters of Peggy Lake turned red: "It was there that the greatest carnage took place," Delgado reported. Dr. Labadie found a helpless

Mexican officer who had become bogged to his knees and could not move. "Oh, I know him," one of Seguín's *rancheros* remarked, "he is Colonel Batres of San Antonio de Béxar." The doctor had just extended his hand to help Batres when he observed the approach of several menacing Texians. "Don't shoot, don't shoot," Labadie cried, "I have taken him prisoner." Despite the surgeon's pleas, a man fired at point-blank range. The ball shattered Batres's forehead. The doctor recoiled in horror as the helpless Mexican's brains splattered his hand and clothing. This villainous deed was, however, not the worst offense Labadie beheld, for he lamented that afterward he "witnessed acts of cruelty which I forbear to recount." The imagination reels when it considers just what those acts may have been. But it is known that several of the Mexican corpses found on the battlefield had been scalped.[44]

General Houston, with a smashed ankle and mounted on his third horse of the day, rode among his soldiers trying to halt the wanton killing. Seeing the uselessness of his efforts, he admonished: "Gentlemen, I applaud your bravery, but damn your manners." The vindictive Texians were displaying bad manners indeed. Private Robert Hancock Hunter recounted the instructions of one captain upon hearing Houston's orders to take prisoners. "Boys," he told them, "you know how to take prisoners, take them with the butt of yor guns, club guns & remember the Alamo, remember Labaher, & club gun right & left, and nock there brains out!"[45]

Colonel Wharton also attempted to stop the carnage, yet one man in particular would have none of that. Jimmy Curtis had never gotten along with his son-in-law Washington Cottle while he was alive. But the young man had gone to the Alamo with the Gonzales contingent, and now Curtis swore vengeance against those who had made his daughter a widow. When Wharton rode up, Curtis had collared a Mexican officer and was terrorizing him. Brandishing a Bowie knife in the man's face, he screamed, "You killed Wash Cottle. Now I'm going to kill you and make a razor strap from your hide!" Colonel Wharton intervened and pulled the captive officer up behind him on his horse. "Men, this Mexican is mine," he shouted. But Old Man Curtis would not be denied; he raised his rifle and coolly blasted the captive Mexican off Wharton's horse. The colonel exploded in a fit of rage. The old man calmly took a drink of whisky, turned his back on Wharton, and walked away. As he was leaving, someone overheard him mutter under his breath: "Remember Wash Cottle."[46]

Wharton, nevertheless, continued his efforts to stop the heedless butchery. He rode along the banks of Peggy Lake, where the Texians were still shooting the hapless Mexicans floundering in the murky waters. Although many of the defenseless men were yelling, "Me no Alamo—Me no Goliad," the Texians fired each time any of the enemy "raised their heads out of the water to get a breath." Wharton ordered his men to cease fire. And J. H. T. Dixon, one of the executioners, rejoined, "Colonel Wharton, if Jesus Christ were to come down from Heaven and order me to quit shooting Yellowbellies, I wouldn't do it, sir!" With that, Dixon cocked his rifle, daring Wharton to enforce his orders. Sergeant Moses Austin Bryan, who observed this test of wills later recorded: "Wharton, very discreetly (I always thought) turned his horse and left." The colonel might have had compassion for the defeated Mexicans, but he was unwilling to die for them.[47]

The bloodletting continued. None of the Texian officers could control their men. They killed until they were too exhausted to kill anymore. Some 650 Mexicans were slain that afternoon. About 700 escaped the battlefield, only to be rounded up later. Houston's men captured over 300 before nightfall and apprehended the rest during the following two days.[48]

Amid the general carnage, there had been moments of individual restraint. Texian rifleman S. F. Sparks told of seeing a member of his regiment threatening one of the *soldaderas*. Sparks intervened. "No," he shouted, "she is a woman and not armed." His comrade replied that he intended to kill her anyway and confirmed his statement by making a lunge at the woman with his bayonet. Sparks parried the thrust with his rifle, then stood between the man and his would-be victim. Cocking his rifle, the angry man coldly rejoined: "You can't knock off a bullet." Sparks recalled, "I threw my gun on him and told him that if he killed her I would kill him. He asked me if I was in earnest, and I replied that I was." Bewildered, the frenzied Texian stormed off in search of other Mexicans to slaughter.[49]

To Houston's chagrin, Santa Anna was not a prisoner nor could his body be found among the dead. If Santa Anna got away, the victory would be hollow. His Excellency had escaped the battlefield only to spend a miserable night in the marsh. Rebel soldiers captured him on April 22. On the field at San Jacinto, Texas had won a great victory, but only with the capture of the Mexican commander in chief did the triumph become decisive.[50]

Careless, or perhaps chauvinistic, writers have alleged that Texians defeated the Mexican army at San Jacinto; that they most assuredly did not do. The contingent that was decimated along the banks of Buffalo Bayou was but a small portion of the total Mexican army in Texas. Forces under Filisola and Urrea were still a threat, and around nightfall Houston revealed his justifiable fear of an attack. His shattered ankle was causing him much pain, and he finally dismounted. While the general was waiting for Dr. Labadie to treat his wound, Rusk and others were rounding up prisoners. Amasa Turner described his commander's behavior as he saw the herd of prisoners of war approaching the Texian camp. "Houston threw up his hands and exclaimed: 'All is lost! All is lost! My God, all is lost!' " Turner was firmly convinced that "when the general first saw Rusk and the Mexicans on the prairie he thought it was Filisola's column coming from the Brazos."[51]

On April 22 Santa Anna justified those anxieties when he came before Houston as a captive. "You have whipped me, I am your prisoner," His Excellency admitted, "but Filisola is not whipped. He will not surrender as a prisoner of war. You must whip him first. But," Santa Anna quickly suggested, "if I give him orders to leave the limits of Texas, he will do it." Most of the rebels were eager to hang the Mexican general from the nearest limb. Houston realized, however, that alive, Santa Anna was a powerful diplomatic card; dead, he would be of no more use than the other bloated corpses that littered Peggy Lake. Houston well knew that a victory against Filisola or Urrea would be harder to achieve even if his men were in a condition to fight. It was time to run a bluff.[52]

Obeying Houston's demands, Santa Anna dispatched orders for Filisola, his immediate subordinate, to retire to Béxar and await further instructions. Urrea, de la Peña, and others harshly criticized the Italian-born Filisola for submitting to orders issued under duress. Filisola always maintained that, orders or no orders, he had no recourse but to retreat. The heavy rains continued to render movement difficult; supplies were running out; and many *soldados* were stricken with dysentery. Santa Anna had taken the army so far from its logistical bases that supply lines had broken down. According to Filisola, it was not the Texians who defeated the once proud Mexican army but the "inclemency of the season in a country totally unpopulated and barren, made still more unattractive by the rigor of the climate and the character of the land." Consequently, Filisola withdrew the Mexican army, not to Béxar, but across the Río Grande.[53]

Several factors had produced rebel victory at San Jacinto. Before April 21, 1836, most observers thought the revolt crushed. Speaking for many of his ilk, Yankee newspaperman Horace Greeley concluded that the twin disasters of the Alamo and Goliad "must naturally, if not necessarily, involve the extinction of every rational hope for Texas." Many were astonished, therefore, when the same Mexican soldiers who performed so resolutely at the Alamo on March 6 were utterly routed on April 21. Many Texian veterans condemned them as cowardly, a label that the facts hardly warranted. The troops that Santa Anna brought to Buffalo Bayou were hungry, demoralized, and far from provisions. They appeared, furthermore, to have lost all confidence in their commander. Texian insurgents, of course, were not brimming with love for Sam Houston, but they did have enormous faith in themselves. Much of that faith was justified, for once committed to battle at San Jacinto, the ferocious volunteers were unstoppable. When Santa Anna, contemptuous of the rebel army, made the fatal blunder of separating his detachment for the fruitless drive on Harrisburg, the rebel army stood ready to exploit his mistake. The fact remains, however, that the mistake was his. Houston had been able to surprise the Mexicans only because Santa Anna neglected his camp security. His Excellency had, furthermore, confidently moved his army off the prairies where his superior cavalry enjoyed an advantage and had ventured into wooded marshlands where the Texian riflemen could employ the terrain to advantage. San Jacinto was not so much a battle that Houston won, but rather one that Santa Anna squandered.[54]

Six months earlier, William H. Wharton had been unhappy in his position as the insurgent army's judge advocate. In a rancorous letter of resignation to General Stephen F. Austin, he denounced the "failure to enforce general orders" and asserted, "I am compelled to believe that no good will be atchieved by this army except by the merest accident under heaven." In more ways than one, the Battle of San Jacinto had been that accident.[55]

PHOTOGRAPHS AND PORTRAITS

S. F. Austin
Dec^t 18. 1836

When fighting began in October, *empresario* Stephen F. Austin stood as the most influential figure in Texas; by the time it ended in April, he had been almost totally supplanted by Houston. As commander of the Army of the People, he found his plans stymied by Houston's cabal and "discordant materials"—the capricious and ill-disciplined volunteers. *Courtesy of the Prints and Photograph Collection, The Center for American History, University of Texas at Austin.*

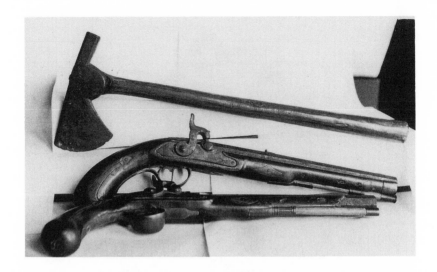

Stephen F. Austin's personal weapons. Austin almost certainly used these pistols and tomahawk during the campaign of 1835. Note that the flintlock pistols have been converted to accommodate a percussion lock. The provisional government ordered tomahawks such as this, which were employed with murderous effect at San Jacinto. *Courtesy of the Prints and Photograph Collection, The Center for American History, University of Texas at Austin.*

General Cos.

In December 1835, Martín Perfecto de Cós capitulated at Béxar and pledged never again to take up arms against the Federal Constitution of 1824—an oath that he promptly repudiated upon joining his brother-in-law's centralist force. He led a column during the Alamo assault and was captured at San Jacinto. *Courtesy of the Nettie Lee Benson Latin American Collection, University of Texas at Austin.*

Texian riflemen feared Mexican lances more than any other weapon; the sinister configuration of this example suggests why. *Courtesy of the Daughters of the Republic of Texas Library at the Alamo, San Antonio, Texas.*

Erastus ("Deaf") Smith, a peaceful family man by nature, became the rebels' ablest scout. Following the fall of the Alamo, he delivered Mrs. Dickenson to Sam Houston; prior to San Jacinto, he destroyed Vince's Bridge. *Courtesy of the Prints and Photograph Collection, The Center for American History, University of Texas at Austin.*

Sam Houston as he appeared shortly following the Texas Revolution. Although "Old Sam Jacinto" emerged as Texas's greatest hero, many veterans of the 1836 campaign took a bitter loathing of the man to their graves. *Courtesy of the Prints and Photograph Collection, The Center for American History, University of Texas at Austin.*

Indian fighter and ranger captain, Edward Burleson took charge of the Army of the People following Austin's departure and was Houston's second-in-command at San Jacinto. This 1850 daguerreotype captures something of the unpretentious determination that inspired the undying loyalty of his men. *Courtesy of the Archives Division, Texas State Library.*

Ben Milam incited the storming of Béxar through sheer force of personality, but the action cost him his life. This idealized likeness may or may not bear any resemblance to the man. Certainly, the uniform depicted here is a complete fabrication. *Courtesy of the Prints and Photograph Collection, The Center for American History, University of Texas at Austin.*

Knife fighter, gambler, and connected by marriage to one of Béxar's most influential families, James Bowie was a frontier legend long before he rode into the Alamo. This portrait captures the determined mouth and cold eyes that commanded immediate deference. *Courtesy of the Prints and Photograph Collection, The Center for American History, University of Texas at Austin.*

San Antonio's San Fernando Church as it appeared during the siege of the Alamo. Santa Anna reportedly hoisted the red flag of no quarter atop the bell tower. Extensive additions to the structure have greatly altered its modern appearance. *Courtesy of the Kevin R. Young Collection, San Antonio.*

W.B. Travis
By Wiley Martin
Dec. 1835

William Barret Travis protested orders to reinforce the Alamo. Once there, how-ever, he became convinced that the post was the "key to Texas" and vowed that he would "never surrender or retreat." His letter to "the People of Texas and all Americans in the world" is one of the most heroic in the annals of U.S. military history. Travis's friend Wiley Martin reportedly drew this likeness from life in December 1835, but the provenance is questionable. *Author's Collection.*

Jackson antagonist, bear hunter, and congressman, David Crockett was already a frontier luminary when he came to Texas. Crockett—who consistently signed his name "David" and seemingly never encouraged anyone to call him "Davy"— sometimes affected buckskins to advance his public persona as the "Lion of the West." Yet contrary to the popular culture stereotype, he preferred conventional attire. One Texian observer insisted that he was "dressed like a gentleman and not a backwoodsman." One can readily believe that when viewing this 1834 Chester Harding portrait. *Courtesy of the National Portrait Gallery, Smithsonian Institution, Washington, D.C. On loan from Katherine Bradford in honor of her mother, Dorothy W. Bradford.*

Generalissimo Antonio López de Santa Anna fluctuated between dazzling brilliance and rueful incompetence. His pointless assault on the Alamo astounded his subalterns and decimated his army; his orders to execute prisoners of war horrified the civilized world; his whimsical and amateurish actions preceding the Battle of San Jacinto lost Texas. *Courtesy of the Kevin R. Young Collection, San Antonio.*

David G. Burnet, president of Texas and certifiable curmudgeon, was almost driven to distraction by Houston's policy of withdrawal. "The enemy are laughing you to scorn," he scolded his general. "You must retreat no further. The country expects you to fight. The salvation of the country depends on your doing so." Following the war, he became one of Houston's most strident critics. *Courtesy of the Prints and Photograph Collection, The Center for American History, University of Texas at Austin.*

General José Urrea commanded the Mexican division that swept the Texas coastal prairies. Victor at San Patricio, Agua Dulce, Refugio, and Coleto, Urrea boasted an unbroken string of triumphs against the Texian rebels and emerged as the most competent general of the war. *Courtesy of the Nettie Lee Benson Latin American Collection, University of Texas at Austin.*

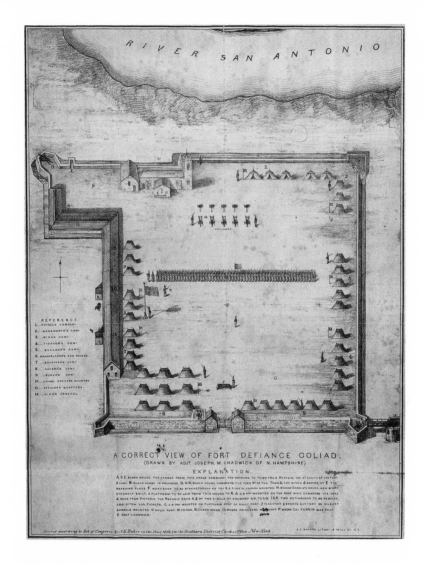

A. E. Baker's lithograph of Fort Defiance (Presidio La Bahía) after the original map drawn by Joseph M. Chadwick. For reasons known only to him, Baker changed the direction in which the chapel faces; the chapel did and does face west. Otherwise, the map is a fairly accurate depiction of the post as it appeared during the 1836 campaign. *Courtesy of the Kevin R. Young Collection, San Antonio.*

Dr. Jack Shackelford, commander of the Alabama Red Rovers. Prior to the Battle of Coleto, Shackelford begged Fannin not to halt on the open prairie, only to have his pleas ignored. The *centralistas* spared the doctor's life because they required his medical expertise, yet his son and virtually his entire company were slaughtered during the Palm Sunday massacre. *Courtesy of the Kevin R. Young Collection, San Antonio.*

Texas Mexican Juan N. Seguín fought alongside his Anglo-Celtic neighbors against Santa Anna's centralist regime. Seguín was a courier from the Alamo and commanded a *tejano* company at San Jacinto. Houston avowed that Seguín's "chivalrous and estimable conduct in the battle won for him my warmest regard and esteem." In this 1838 Jefferson Wright portrait, he wears the dress uniform of the Republic of Texas. *Author's Collection.*

A French-Canadian, Dr. Nicholas Descomps Labadie left one of the most color-ful and detailed accounts of the San Jacinto campaign. *Courtesy of the Prints and Photograph Collection, The Center for American History, University of Texas at Austin.*

Italian-born Vicente Filisola was Santa Anna's second-in-command during the 1836 Texas campaign. Urrea never forgave him for terminating the campaign following Santa Anna's capture, but the pitiful state of Mexican logistics practically compelled such a determination. Nevertheless, Filisola bore the brunt of the criticism for abandoning Texas. *Author's Collection.*

Secretary of War Thomas Jefferson Rusk carried authorization to relieve Sam
Houston but stood by the beleaguered general against his numerous critics.
Rusk participated in the skirmishing on April 20 and the Battle of San Jacinto
on April 21. *Author's Collection.*

Colonel Sidney Sherman brought a company of Kentucky volunteers to Texas and commanded the Second Regiment at San Jacinto. During the 1836 campaign, Houston and Sherman cultivated an intense dislike of each other, which only ripened as the two grew older. *Author's Collection.*

This 1840s photograph captures some of the self-willed recalcitrance that Jesse Billingsley demonstrated during the San Jacinto campaign. During the skirmishing on April 20, he led his company out in support of Sherman in deliberate disobedience of Houston's orders. *Courtesy of the Prints and Photograph Collection, The Center for American History, University of Texas at Austin.*

Poet and cavalier, Mirabeau Buonaparte Lamar joined the rebel army prior to the Battle of San Jacinto. Houston was so stirred by Lamar's courage in the April 20 skirmish that he promoted him to command of the Texian cavalry for the battle the next day. Following the war, Lamar became Houston's chief political rival; this 1840s photograph dates from his tenure as president of the Republic of Texas. *Author's Collection.*

EPILOGUE

Texians followed skeptically as the Army of Operations retreated southward. They were fully aware that the Mexicans still outnumbered them and could scarcely believe that enemy troops, the majority of whom had never known defeat in Texas, would complacently obey the orders of a captured commander.

Many Mexicans could hardly believe it either. The able General Urrea argued with Filisola that duty demanded that the campaign be continued. The victor of San Patricio, Refugio, and Coleto had smashed the rebels in every encounter. He was certain, moreover, that if he could engage Houston on the battlefield he would triumph again. But now he would never get the chance; his bungling commander in chief had denied him that opportunity. So Urrea led his men home, certain in the belief that they had done all that honor required of brave and faithful soldiers. While Santa Anna's ineptitude had cost them this campaign, they were equally sure that someday they would return to regain Mexican soil and Mexican honor.[1]

Many historians as well as Urrea were critical of Filisola's decision to retreat, but he presented compelling reasons for that course of action. The foul weather made forced marches, or indeed travel of any kind, nearly impossible. His supply lines were stretched to the breaking point, and his soldiers were on the verge of starvation. Many were ill. Given the lack of food and medicine, the large number of men in the army actually proved a disadvantage. Filisola, a trained professional, cut his losses and preserved his force. Santa Anna had presented Mexico with one military disaster; Filisola did not wish to risk another. Encouraged by Houston's victory, many American volunteers, who had previously held back upon hearing of repeated Texian defeats, poured across the Sabine. The Mexicans, however, could expect no reinforcements, no ammunition, and no food. Engaging the *norteamericanos* in East Texas might well produce another defeat that could squander the entire army and terminate any hope of regaining Texas. Filisola crossed the Río Grande with an exhausted and demoralized force, but he deserves credit for keeping the army intact and bringing it home. Both officers and men were eager to return for a second campaign that would erase the shame of the first.[2]

Yet that was not to occur. For the next decade, political turmoil and lack of funds prevented all but brief forays across the Río Grande. Even so, Mexico never formally recognized the Republic of Texas. National pride still insisted that Tejas was a province, and when conditions permitted, Mexican soldiers would reclaim that pilfered province. Annexation to the United States dashed those hopes forever. The resultant war brought another defeat that was even more disastrous than the one in Texas. Only when U.S. troops were billeted in Mexico City in 1848 did Mexicans surrender their claim on Texas by signing the Treaty of Guadalupe Hidalgo.[3]

For those U.S. citizens favoring annexation, the Texian revolt became a symbol of national greatness, a continuity of the "spirit of '76." Yet opponents saw a different kind of symbol. The paired epigraphs at the beginning of this volume indicate the divergence of perception following the revolt. To French visitor Frederic Gaillardet, the valor of the Texians compared favorably with the mythic heroes of ancient Greece. He described the conflict as a "Texian Iliad," in which all Americans could take pride. Theodore Sedgwick, an ardent foe of annexation, mistakenly emphasized the Mexicans' pathetic fighting capabilities and questioned the importance of any victory over such troops. He compared Texas "heroes" to Ben Johnson's character Captain Bobadil, a beggarly and cowardly rogue who sought to present himself as a Hector. Even Sedgwick acknowledged the "infamous" significance of the Alamo and Goliad, but in the main, he and other critics viewed the conflict as "burlesque."[4]

In truth, the conflict had provided moments that approached farce. Several examples spring quickly to mind: the first casualty (a nose broken by a rearing horse), the indignant Dr. Smithers being arrested by both the Mexicans and the Texians on the same morning, Captain Rodriguez searching for Ira Westover and his men while they were capturing his fort, the irate Mrs. Mann reclaiming her oxen. Sedgwick, however, failed to grasp the real significance of these moments.

If fighting men on occasion demonstrated behavior that approached the absurd, the reason was not lack of character, but rather that most were amateurs. Even the few trained professionals discovered that conditions in Texas were quite unlike those to which they were accustomed. Both sides came to Texas with preconceived notions of war. The Texians were products of the North American militia tradition. The Mexicans were influenced by more traditional Napoleonic tactics. Texas battlefields tested both of these tactical modes, and both were found wanting.

In the fullness of time, pro-Houston forces transformed the victorious general into "old Sam Jacinto." Immigrants who came to Texas from the United States in the wake of victory regarded Houston as the indispensable man, the single figure without whom independence could never have been achieved. Typical were the sentiments of Robert Hall, a Texas volunteer who arrived after the Battle of San Jacinto and unquestionably embraced the Houston myth:

> The Mexicans outnumbered [Houston's force] two to one, but on one side there was genius and courage, and on the other the treachery of the Alamo and the massacre of Fannin's men. Not one of those brilliant military maneuvers which originated in the brain of that master of the art of war [Napoleon Bonaparte] while he was crushing the Austrians in Italy is more worthy of the admiration of the student of history than the plan of that short campaign which drew the self-styled Napoleon of the West into a network of bayous and marshes, from which his cannon and musketry were powerless to extricate him.[5]

Yet many of the men who witnessed his actions testified that Houston exaggerated his contributions to further his political aspirations. They claimed he appropriated laurels that should have properly been bestowed upon common Texian soldiers. That old war-horse, Jesse Billingsley, expressed the convictions of many San Jacinto veterans: "The thief and the murderer I can guard against, but the *liar* I cannot. Therefore I must say that Houston is the basest of all men, as he has, by willfully lying, attempted to rob that little band of men of their well earned honors on the battle field of San Jacinto. He has assumed to himself credit that was due to others." Houston's invariable political enemy, David G. Burnet, took up the cant: "Gen. H. has long and habitually acted on the Spanish proverb, that 'a lie that can gain belief for one hour, is worth the telling.' . . . Gen. Houston knows how to appreciate and to profit by the old Spanish proverb, and he knows that his furtive laurels will wilt and wither into utter loathsomeness, under the full light of truth! He is cunning—it is his highest intellectual attribute—but his vanity often gets the mastery of his cunning, and renders his deepest tricks ridiculous."[6]

In addition to the veterans' resentment of Houston, the Texas Revolution left many military legacies. Almost every Mexican account mentions the havoc created by Texian rifles. In the future, they would be wary of the power of determined riflemen in a sound defensive position. Furthermore, they avoided the logistical nightmare of a deep drive into unfamiliar territory. Before the Mexican-American War, Mexicans engaged in numerous small-scale border probes, the most significant being General Adrian Woll's brief capture of San Antonio in 1842, but the point is that these were only forays; they could not hope to take and hold land north of the Río Grande.

Texians were well aware that they had performed poorly in what Travis referred to as "enemy country," that is to say, the Hispanic coastal prairies. Whenever they had confronted Mexican cavalry, or even the irregular *ranchero* horsemen, they were hopelessly outclassed. Many shared the view of Texian soldier B. H. Duval: "The greater portion of the Mexican troops are mounted, and of course have greatly the advantage over us." During the period of the Republic, Texian riders began to borrow heavily from their *tejano* neighbors, adopting the Spanish saddle, the *riata*, the *bandana*, and the trademark spike-roweled spurs. Slowly the equestrian skill of the Anglo-Celtic Texians improved. Moreover, they adopted a Hispanic perspective of the prairies, where the ability to ride light and strike fast meant much more than the traditional shock of heavy cavalry.[7]

This cultural borrowing transformed the Texas Rangers. To be sure, there had been hired gunmen who ranged the southern woodlands for generations. Celtic settlers seemed to have brought the word and the concept of the ranger from the Scottish borderlands. In the densely wooded southern forest, however, he could never be more than a mounted rifleman. In 1823 Stephen F. Austin mustered a company of rangers to provide protection against hostile Indians. Even during the revolt of 1835–1836, the rangers' main duty was to provide protection against the Indians while so many men were away fighting Mexicans. These men, in their linsey-woolsey hunting garb, resembled in method and outlook their counterparts in Georgia and Tennessee. The disasters of the Texas Revolution and the frequent raids of the mobile Comanches demonstrated that adaptation was necessary. That process of cultural adaptation transformed the force and rendered the Texas Ranger unique. Presently it was observed that a Texas Ranger could "shoot like a Tennessean, ride like a Mexican, and fight like the Devil!" Yet that could not have been claimed before 1835. Anglo-Americans had to be taught how to ride like Mexicans. Comrades such as Juan Seguín and Plácido Benavides proved excellent instructors.[8]

The revolt in Texas generated bitter feelings south of the Río Grande. A mere fifteen years after declaring independence from Spain, Mexicans had Texas wrested from them. Mexicans continued to have a love-hate relationship with their northern neighbors. They had admired the U.S. Constitution, and to a large degree it had provided the pattern for their own. After 1836, however, Mexicans felt betrayed by the same people they had once respected.[9]

Overwhelming sentiment inside Mexico espoused that war to regain Texas should be renewed. The next time, however, the "true enemy" would be known. Vengeance would be taken not only against the Texas colonists, who were held to be merely a "gang of thieves," but also against the citizens of the United States of the north who, while fomenting rebellion within another sovereign nation, had hidden behind an "evil mask of scandalous hypocrisy." The impotence of the Mexican military to regain Texas in no way effected consensus inside Mexico concerning the justice of that goal.[10]

One Texas authority has advanced the idea that San Jacinto was the world's sixteenth decisive battle, adding to the fifteen identified by the English military historian Sir Edward Creasy. That view is advanced by the inscription on the base of the San Jacinto Monument:

> Measured by its results, San Jacinto was one of the decisive battles of the world. The freedom of Texas from Mexico won here led to annexation and to the Mexican War, resulting in the acquisition by the United States of the states of Texas, New Mexico, Arizona, Nevada, Utah, and parts of Colorado, Wyoming, Kansas, and Oklahoma. Almost one-third of the present area of the American nation, nearly a million square miles, changed sovereignty.[11]

Such an assessment is more than a little perfervid. San Jacinto was only one link in the chain of events that led to the acquisition of the U.S.

Southwest. Truly decisive victories secure the peace as well as end conflict. San Jacinto did neither. Only a small portion of the Mexican army had been engaged, and the retreat that followed had more to do with the collapse of Mexican logistics than with the mastery of Texian arms. Although the battle provided the time needed for the new Republic of Texas to develop a genuine government, its existence was also fraught with the constant danger of Mexican invasion, a threat that did not totally cease until Mexicans surrendered their claim in the Treaty of Guadalupe Hidalgo. Winfield Scott's occupation of Mexico City in 1848 influenced that decision far more than the Battle of San Jacinto in 1836.

Even so, the Texas Revolution is significant in its own right; there is no need to embellish its gains. It left a legacy of valor that has inspired Texan soldiers on battlefields all over the world. While remembering the courage, however, one should also recall the disorganization, the pettiness, and the lust for power that required so much needless sacrifice. Moreover, it should be acknowledged that the sacrifice was not all on one side. Although unsuccessful in his attempt to stem the tide of rebellion, the Mexican *soldado* served with distinction, fought with courage, and died with honor. General Urrea emerged as the most competent general of the war.

There is another, less attractive, legacy. The bitterness and resentment that took root in the bloody Texas soil over 150 years ago still linger in the form of racial enmity. Ragged Texian soldiers won an inspiring victory on the banks of Buffalo Bayou, but so long as mistrust and anger persist, their triumph will be incomplete. The men of the Texas Revolution met the challenges of their day with Bowie knife and bayonet. Today we must arm ourselves with tolerance and understanding. The challenges of peace are perhaps less lustrous than those of war, but no less vital. The soldiers of 1836, both Texian and Mexican, accepted their tasks with fortitude and perseverance. That too is their legacy. To honor their memories, we can do no less.

NOTES

1. *"We Are All Captains and Have Our Views"*

1. For the background for the United States military experience, see Russell F. Weigley, *The American Way of War: A History of the United States Military Strategy and Policy*; for the militia tradition, see also Jim Dan Hill, *The Minute Man in Peace and War: A History of the National Guard*; for the emergence of U.S. military doctrine in the years before the Texas Revolution, see Francis Paul Prucha, *The Sword of the Republic: The United States Army on the Frontier, 1783–1834*. Also useful is Henry Putney Beers, *The Western Military Frontier, 1815–1846*. See also John Elgin, "Uncle Frank Sparks' Story," *San Antonio Express*, December 8, 1935. Sparks, a veteran of the Texas Revolution, recalled that the Texians "may have been raw recruits, undrilled, but they were not unseasoned, for most of them had had experience in Indian warfare and many of them had been with Gen. Jackson in his Indian campaigns in Florida and at New Orleans."

2. For the northern frontier in the colonial period, the best single source on the military and its policy toward the Indians is Max Moorehead, *The Presidio: Bastion of the Spanish Borderlands*. See also Sidney B. Brinckerhoff and Odie B. Faulk, *Lancers for the King: A Study of a Frontier Military System of Northern New Spain, with a Translation of the Royal Regulations of 1772*; also useful is Carlos E. Castañeda, *Our Catholic Heritage in Texas, 1519–1936*, especially good is volume V, *The Mission Era: The End of the Spanish Regime, 1780–1810*, and volume VI, *Transition Period: The Fight for Freedom, 1810–1836*.

3. For Moses and Stephen Austin, the best study remains Eugene C. Barker, *The Life of Stephen F. Austin*.

4. Henderson Yoakum, *History of Texas*, I, 361; Miles S. Bennet, "The Battle of Gonzales, the 'Lexington' of the Texas Revolution," *Quarterly of the Texas State Historical Association* 2 (April 1899): 314.

5. For the developing troubles between Mexico and the American colonists, the best single source is David J. Weber, *The Mexican Frontier, 1821–1846: The American Southwest under Mexico*. Somewhat dated, but still valuable is Eugene C. Barker, *Mexico and Texas, 1821–1835: University of Texas Research Lectures on the Causes of the Texas Revolution*. Also useful is Cecil Robinson, "Flag of Illusion: The Texas Revolution Viewed as a Conflict of Cultures," in Stephen B. Oates, ed., *The Republic of Texas*, 10–17. For the rape of Zacatecas, see Randolph B. Campbell, *Sam Houston and the American Southwest*, 48. Hereinafter, "Texian" is used rather than the more conventional "Texan." I have selected "Texian" as the more historical term. The word "Texan" did not come into general usage until after statehood. The late Professor Herbert Gambrell was of the opinion that all who came to Texas prior to 1850 were "ipso facto Texians." As he usually did, J. Frank Dobie had the last word on the subject. He strongly favored "Texian" to describe "the strongly individualized breed who made up the population of Texas during colonial days, through the era of the Texas Republic, and up to the Civil War." So do I. J. Frank Dobie to Marcelle Lively Hamer, November 23, 1939, in "Texian" Vertical File, Eugene C. Barker Texas History Center, University of Texas at Austin. This interesting file also includes other views concerning the sometimes heated Texian versus Texan debate.

6. Records of deeds issued 1838 [Minutes of the Gonzales Ayuntamiento, 1835], Julia Sinks Papers, Barker Texas History Center, University of Texas at Austin. I am indebted to Thomas Ricks Lindley for calling this document to my attention. William Kennedy, *Texas: The Rise, Progress, and Prospects of the Republic of Texas*, 467.

7. Henry Stuart Foote, *Texas and the Texans; or, Advance of the Anglo-Americans to the Southwest Including a History of Leading Events in Mexico, From the Conquest by Fernando Cortes to the Termination of the Texas Revolution*, II, 97–103; Mary Austin Holley, *Texas*, 335; Dudley G. Wooten, ed., *A Comprehensive History of Texas, 1685 to 1897*, I, 537; Noah Smithwick, *The Evolution of a State; or, Recollections of Old Texas Days*, 71.

8. See David B. Macomb's account of the Gonzales fight, in Foote, *Texas and the Texans*, II, 98–99; for the best treatment of Mexican organization, uniforms, and equipment, see Angelina Neito, Joseph Hefter, and Mrs. John Nicholas Brown, *El Soldado Mexicano, 1837–1847: Organización, Vestuario, Equipo;*

also useful is Philip Haythornthwaite, *The Alamo and the War of Texas Independence.*

9. See Charles Mason's account in Frank W. Johnson, *A History of Texas and Texans,* I, 269; Bennet, "Battle of Gonzales," 315; Andrew Jackson Houston, *Texas Independence,* 72; Edward A. Lukes, *DeWitt Colony of Texas,* 183.

10. Macomb, in Foote, *Texas and the Texans,* II, 99–100; Bennet, "Battle of Gonzales," 313.

11. Launcelot Smither to General Council, November 23, 1835, in John H. Jenkins, ed., *The Papers of the Texas Revolution, 1835–1836,* II, 491–493. This collection, compiled and edited by the late John H. Jenkins, is indispensable for anyone involved in Texas Revolution research. Professor Archie P. McDonald lauded it as "the most important publication on Texas History of its kind in years." It is to the student of the Texas Revolution what *The War of the Rebellion: A Compilation of the Official Records of the Union and Confederate Armies* is for the student of the War between the States.

12. Mason, in Johnson, *History of Texas,* I, 269. Macomb recalled 169 men under Moore's command.

13. "First Breaking Out of the Texas Revolution at Gonzales," in James M. Day, comp. and ed., *The Texas Almanac, 1857–1873: A Compendium of Texas History,* 442.

14. Smither to General Council, November 23, 1835, in Jenkins, ed., *Papers,* II, 491–493.

15. Ibid.

16. Mason, in Johnson, *History of Texas,* I, 270; "First Breaking Out at Gonzales," in Day, ed., *Texas Almanac,* 42.

17. Smithwick, *The Evolution of a State,* 71; Bennet, "Battle of Gonzales," 315; Elgin, "Uncle Frank Sparks' Story," *San Antonio Express,* December 8, 1935.

18. "First Breaking Out at Gonzales," in Day, ed., *Texas Almanac,* 442; Bennet, "Battle of Gonzales," 316.

19. Francisco Castañeda to Domingo Ugartechea, September 30, 1835, in Jenkins, ed., *Papers,* II, 5; an English translation of this document appears in Malcolm D. McLean, comp. and ed., *Papers Concerning Robertson's Colony in Texas,* XI, 514–515; Lukes, *DeWitt Colony of Texas,* 184; Kennedy, *Texas,* 470; Macomb, in Foote, *Texas and the Texans,* II, 100–101; Macomb wrote: "The Lieutenant-Colonel [Wallace] . . . formed the line of march, placing the cavalry in advance of the cannon, two companies of flankers, and two open columns on each side, with a company of infantry in the rear."

20. Castañeda to Ugartechea, October 4, 1835, in Jenkins, ed. *Papers*, II, 33–36; McLean, ed., *Robertson's Colony*, XI, 560–563; Macomb, in Foote, *Texas and the Texans*, II, 101; Mason, in Johnson, *History of Texas*, I, 270–271; Bennet, "Battle of Gonzales," 315.

21. Macomb, in Foote, *Texas and the Texans*, II, 100; Castañeda to Ugartechea, October 4, 1835, in Jenkins, ed., *Papers*, II, 33–36; McLean, *Robertson's Colony*, XI, 560–563.

22. Bennet, "Battle of Gonzales," 316; Johnson, *History of Texas*, I, 270; Smither to General Council, November 23, 1835, in Jenkins, ed., *Papers*, II, 491–493.

23. Smither to General Council, November 23, 1835, in Jenkins, ed., *Papers*, II, 491–493; Wooten, ed., *Comprehensive History of Texas*, I, 537; Lukes, *DeWitt Colony of Texas*, 186–187.

24. Smithwick, *Evolution of a State*, 72; Mamie Wynne Cox, *The Romantic Flags of Texas*, 154–157; Macomb, in Foote, *Texas and the Texans*, II, 101; Castañeda to Ugartechea, October 4, 1835, in Jenkins, ed., *Papers*, II, 33–36; McLean, ed., *Robertson's Colony*, XI, 560–563.

25. Stephen L. Hardin, "Long Rifle and Brown Bess: The Weapons and Tactics of the Texas Revolution, 1835–1836" (M.A. thesis, Southwest Texas State University, 1985); Bennet, "Battle of Gonzales," 313; Lukes, *DeWitt Colony of Texas*, 187.

26. A. J. Houston, *Texas Independence*, 73; Nieto, Brown, and Hefter, *El Soldado Mexicano*, 53–54; Macomb, in Foote, *Texas and the Texans*, II, 100; for the nature of Highland combat, see James Michael Hill, *Celtic Warfare, 1595–1763*.

27. Hubert Howe Bancroft, *History of the North Mexican States and Texas*, II, 166–167; Smithwick, *Evolution of a State*, 76, 71.

28. John Henry Brown, *History of Texas from 1685 to 1892*, I, 350.

29. Wooten, ed., *History of Texas*, I, 176, 173.

30. Hobart Huson, *Captain Phillip Dimmitt's Commandancy of Goliad, 1835–1836: An Episode of the Mexican Federalist War in Texas Usually Referred to as the Texian Revolution*, 10–11.

31. John J. Linn, *Reminiscences of Fifty Years in Texas*, 106–107.

32. Huson, *Dimmitt's Commandancy of Goliad*, 11.

33. Ibid.

34. C. A. Gulick et al., eds., *The Papers of Mirabeau Buonaparte Lamar*, I, 242.

35. Huson, *Dimmitt's Commandancy of Goliad*, 14.

36. Ibid., 16.

37. Foote, *Texas and the Texans*, II, 113–115; Lois Garver, "The Life of Benjamin Rush Milam," *Southwestern Historical Quarterly* 38 (October 1934, January 1935): 79–121, 177–202.

38. Huson, *Dimmitt's Commandancy of Goliad*, 16.

39. "Particulars of the Capture of Goliad," *New Orleans Bulletin*, n.d., 1835, in Jerry J. Gaddy, comp. and ed., *Texas in Revolt: Contemporary Newspaper Account of the Texas Revolution*, 34–36.

40. For the strategic importance of Goliad, see James W. Pohl and Stephen L. Hardin, "The Military History of the Texas Revolution: An Overview," *Southwestern Historical Quarterly*, 89 (January 1986): 288; R. R. Royal to Stephen F. Austin, October 13, 1835 (with a report on "supplies and munitions"), in Eugene C. Barker, ed., *The Austin Papers*, III, 179. The old Texians were far handier with long rifles and Bowie knives than with dictionaries and style manuals. The standard [*sic*] after every misspelling and grammatical error would have cluttered the text to little advantage. Throughout the text, therefore, quotations are presented as originally written.

41. "General Austin's Order Book for the Campaign of 1835," *Quarterly of the Texas State Historical Association* 11 (July 1907): 8.

42. N. T. Byars, "To Arms," quoted in Alex Dienst, "Contemporary Poetry of the Texas Revolution," *Southwestern Historical Quarterly* 21 (October 1917): 157–158.

43. *New York Star*, quoted in Mark E. Nackman, "The Making of the Texan Citizen Soldier, 1835–1836," *Southwestern Historical Quarterly* 78 (January 1975): 241; Macomb, in Foote, *Texas and the Texans*, II, 103.

2. *"Not Withstanding Peculiar Circumstances"*

1. "Austin's Order Book," 1–2; Johnson, *History of Texas and Texans*, I, 263–275.

2. Weber, *Mexican Frontier*, 144, 177, 244, 248; Yoakum, *History of Texas*, 361.

3. *Red River Herald*, undated, in Gaddy, *Texas in Revolt*, 26; Eli Mercer to Stephen F. Austin, October 12, 1835, in Barker, ed., *Austin Papers*, III, 176.

4. Smithwick, *Evolution of a State*, 75.

5. "Austin's Order Book," 30, 31; Austin to Committee [of Safety], October 4, 1835, in Jenkins, ed., *Papers*, II, 32.

6. Smithwick, *Evolution of a State*, 72, 75; Stephen L. Hardin, "A Vatir y Perseguir: Tejano Deployment in the War for Texas Independence, 1835–1836," in Lisa C. Davis, ed., *Essays in History: The E. C. Barksdale Student Lectures, 1985–1986*, 161.

7. William T. Austin, "Account of the Campaign of 1835 by William T. Austin, Aid[e] to Gen. Stephen F. Austin & Gen. Ed Burleson," *Texana* 4 (Winter 1966): 297.

8. Ibid., 300.

9. Ibid., 298, 302; "Austin's Order Book," 24; Hardin, "A Vatir y Perseguir," 161–162.

10. "Austin's Order Book," 28.

11. Ibid., 30, 31.

12. Johnson, *Texas and Texans*, I, 278.

13. James Bowie and James W. Fannin to Austin, October 24, 1835, in Jenkins, ed., *Papers*, II, 209.

14. The only work approaching a scholarly biography of Bowie is still Claude L. Douglas, *Jim Bowie: The Life of a Bravo*; also useful is J. Frank Dobie, "Jim Bowie, Big Dealer," *Southwestern Historical Quarterly* 60 (January 1957): 337–357. New information concerning Bowie's alleged children appears in Bill and Marjorie K. Walraven, *The Magnificent Barbarians: Little-told Tales of the Texas Revolution*, 69.

15. For Fannin's role in the fighting, see Ruby Cumby Smith, "James Walker Fannin, Jr., in the Texas Revolution," *Southwestern Historical Quarterly*, 23 (October 1919, January 1920, April 1920): 79–90, 171–203, 271–284.

16. Walter Prescott Webb, H. Bailey Carroll, and Eldon Stephen Branda, eds., *The Handbook of Texas*, I, 217; see also Adele B. Looscan, "Harris County, 1822–1845," *Southwestern Historical Quarterly* 18 (January 1915): 263–264.

17. James Bowie's Report to Austin, undated, in Foote, *Texas and the Texans*, II, 121–125.

18. "Austin's Order Book," 32–33; Moses Austin Bryan Account, in Johnson, *Texas and Texans*, I, 281; Elgin, "Uncle Frank Sparks' Story," *San Antonio Express*, December 8, 1935.

19. James T. DeShields, *Tall Men with Long Rifles: Set Down and Written Out by James T. DeShields as Told to Him by Creed Taylor, Captain during the Texas Revolution*, 42; Bowie's Report, in Foote, *Texas and the Texans*, II, 122.

20. DeShields, *Tall Men with Long Rifles*, 42; Austin to Convention, October 28, 1835, in Jenkins, ed., *Papers*, II, 242; for nineteenth-century ratios of cavalry to infantry, see Conrad H. Lanza, comp., *Napoleon and Modern War: His Military Maxims Revised and Annotated*, 117.

21. Bowie's Report, in Foote, *Texas and the Texans*, II, 122–123; DeShields, *Tall Men with Long Rifles*, 43.

22. Bowie's Report, in Foote, *Texas and the Texans*, II, 122; Smithwick, *Evolution of a State*, 77.

23. Bowie's Report, in Foote, *Texas and the Texans*, II, 123; Smithwick, *Evolution of a State*, 77.

24. DeShields, *Tall Men with Long Rifles*, 44; Smithwick, *Evolution of a State*, 80.

25. Bowie's Report, in Foote, *Texas and the Texans*, II, 124; Smithwick, *Evolution of a State*, 80.

26. *A Visit to Texas, Being the Journal of a Traveller Through Those Parts Most Interesting to American Settlers, With Descriptions of Scenery, Habits, &c. &c.*, 173–174; DeShields, *Tall Men with Long Rifles*, 47.

27. Smithwick, *Evolution of a State*, 77.

28. DeShields, *Tall Men with Long Rifles*, 46.

29. Ibid.; Smithwick, *Evolution of a State*, 80.

30. Ibid.; Nieto, Brown, and Hefter, *El Soldado Mexicano*, 53.

31. Bowie's Report, in Foote, *Texas and the Texans*, II, 124; Yoakum, *History of Texas and Texans*, 376.

32. W. T. Austin, "Campaign of 1835," 307.

33. Ibid., 311; Bryan Account, in Johnson, *Texas and Texans*, I, 280–281.

34. *Visit to Texas*, 173–174; see also M. L. Crimmins, "American Powder's Part in Winning Texas Independence," *Southwestern Historical Quarterly* 52 (July 1948): 109–111.

35. Bowie's Report, in Foote, *Texas and the Texans*, II, 124; DeShields, *Tall Men with Long Rifles*, 46. For an interesting account describing the accidental discovery of Richard Andrew's grave, see Walraven and Walraven, *Magnificent Barbarians*, 41.

36. Pohl and Hardin, "Military History of the Texas Revolution," 289–290.

37. Flavius Vegetius Renatus, *Military Institutions of the Romans*, trans. John Clark, ed. Thomas R. Phillips, 93; Antoine Henri Jomini, *Jomini and His Summary of the Art of War*, ed. J. D. Hittle, 102.

38. Austin to Convention, October 28, 1835, in Jenkins, ed. *Papers*, II, 242–243; W. T. Austin, "Campaign of 1835," 307.

39. W. T. Austin, "Campaign of 1835," 312; Pohl and Hardin, "Military History of the Texas Revolution," 287.

3. *"We Flogged Them Like Hell"*

1. Philip Dimitt to Stephen F. Austin, October 15, 1835, in Jenkins, ed., *Papers*, II, 134, 135. Note the many different spellings of Dimitt. The authoritative *Handbook of Texas* cites the commander as "Dimitt," as does Jenkins, and I have opted for that form. Hobart Huson, the man's biographer, in *Captain Phillip Dimmitt's Commandancy of Goliad, 1835–1836*, admits that "casual

research reveals that he himself subscribed his name as 'Demit,' 'Dimitt,' 'Demmit,' etc." For consistency I have used "Dimitt" throughout. Dimitt County is named for him.

2. Ibid.

3. Philip Dimitt to Stephen F. Austin, October 20, 1835, in Barker, ed., *Austin Papers*, III, 194–196.

4. Dimitt to Stephen F. Austin, October 27, 1835, in Jenkins, ed., *Papers*, II, 233–234. Presumably, "those in our power" whom Dimitt wished to clothe "with suits of iron" were Goliad *tejanos* who harbored loyalist sympathies.

5. Dimitt to Stephen F. Austin, October 30, 1835, in Barker, ed., *Austin Papers*, III, 221–223.

6. Ibid.

7. Huson, *Dimmitt's Commandancy of Goliad*, 101. Huson writes: "The expedition fared forth from Goliad at 4 o'clock on the afternoon of October 21, 1835." Obviously Huson meant to write October 31, only one of the editing slips that mars an otherwise brilliant text. The blame for the poor editing rests with his publisher. In June 1974, Huson wrote Texana dealer John Jenkins complaining that he had "nominated Von Boeckman–Jones as the publisher, not knowing that it had been taken over and gutted by a conglomerate.... I never was supplied with definitely paginated page proofs from which a proper index might be compiled." Huson's work, which writer Dan Kilgore called "basic to an understanding of events in Texas in the fall and early winter of 1835," deserves a new edition. The next time, one can only hope that the book will find a publishing firm worthy of the study that Jenkins called a "goldmine for scholars." For more on Huson and the book, see John H. Jenkins, *Basic Texas Books*, 265–266.

8. Ira Westover to Sam Houston, November 15, 1835, in Jenkins, ed., *Papers*, II, 431–432; Huson, *Dimmitt's Commandancy of Goliad*, 101. Huson interprets the approach from Refugio as a strategic masterstroke. He explains: "It is likely that the expedition was routed by way of Refugio, rather than the Refugio contingent joining at Goliad for the purpose of misleading the Centralists as to its true objective. It would be reckoned that Captain Sabriego would be promptly informed of the departure from Goliad. The movement in the direction of Refugio might indicate El Copano as the point of the objective. The augmented expedition proceeded for the Nueces via the 'lower road' to San Patricio, as originally planned. The Centralists appear to have been caught off-guard." Perhaps, but it is more likely that Westover simply rode to his hometown to recruit more troops before proceeding to Lipantitlán. In this campaign, as in others of the Revolution, "dumb luck" seemed to be with the Texians.

9. Dan Kilgore, "Texans Ousted Mexicans from Nueces County Fort," *Corpus Christi Caller-Times*, January 18, 1959; Dimitt to Austin, October 30, 1835, in Barker, ed., *Austin Papers*, III, 221–223; Austin to Bowie and Fannin, November 1, 1835, in Jenkins, ed., *Papers*, II, 287–288; Huson, *Dimmitt's Commandancy of Goliad*, 81.

10. Westover to Houston, November 15, 1835, in Jenkins, ed., *Papers*, II, 431–432.

11. Linn, *Reminiscences*, 119–120.

12. Westover to Sam Houston, November 15, 1835, in Jenkins, ed., *Papers*, II, 431–432; Huson, *Dimmitt's Commandancy of Goliad*, 107.

13. Kilgore, "Texans Ousted Mexicans from Nueces County Fort," *Corpus Christi Caller-Times*, January 18, 1959.

14. Westover to Houston, November 15, 1835, in Jenkins, ed., *Papers*, II, 431–432; Linn, *Reminiscences*, 120.

15. Westover to Houston, November 15, 1835, in Jenkins, ed., *Papers*, II, 431–432.

16. Linn, *Reminiscences*, 120; Westover to Houston, November 15, 1835, in Jenkins, ed., *Papers*, II, 431–432.

17. Ibid.

18. Dimitt to Austin, November 13, 1835, in Barker, ed., *Austin Papers*, III, 249–251.

19. Westover to Houston, November 15, 1835, in Jenkins, ed., *Papers*, II, 431–432; Linn, *Reminiscences*, 120; James McGloin, "No. 1658. Historical Notes," in Gulick et al., *Papers of Mirabeau Buonaparte Lamar*, V, 380.

20. A. H. Jones to Fannin, November 12, 1835, in Jenkins, ed., *Papers*, II, 384–385.

21. Westover to Houston, November 15, 1835, in Jenkins, ed., *Papers*, II, 431–432; Linn, *Reminiscences*, 121.

22. Linn, *Reminiscences*, 121–122.

23. Ibid., 122.

24. Dimitt to Austin, November 13, 1835, in Jenkins, ed., *Papers*, II, 389–392; Huson, *Dimmitt's Commandancy of Goliad*, 100; Ira Ingram to R. R. Royal, October 31, 1835, in Jenkins, ed., *Papers*, II, 275–277. Although no copy of the orders remains, Ingram in the above-cited letter, written just after the expedition left Goliad, claimed: "adjutant Westover, with 37 men took up the line of march for [Lipantitlán], with orders to take that post, raze the works, and burn the buildings, securing the public caballardo, bringing off the arms and ammunition, and all other public property in their power to remove &c. &c." If such were his orders, Westover seems to have fulfilled them. Westover to

Houston, November 15, 1835, in Jenkins, ed., *Papers*, II, 431–432. The rift between Dimitt and Westover may have created a hardship for those caught up in the conflict, but the consequent letter to Houston has been a boon to historians. It is, by far, the best primary account of the fall of Lipantitlán and the Battle of Nueces Crossing.

25. Huson, *Dimmitt's Commandancy of Goliad*, 106–107.

26. Ibid., 108–109.

27. John Turner to Dimitt, November 30, 1835, in Jenkins, ed., *Papers*, III, 51.

28. Houston to Governor and Council, November 20, 1835, in Jenkins, ed., *Papers*, II, 475.

4. *"The Spectacle Becomes Appalling"*

1. For a lucid background to political aspects of the revolt, see Paul D. Lack, *The Texas Revolutionary Experience: A Political and Social History, 1835 – 1836*. Also useful are more traditional studies such as William C. Binkley, *The Texas Revolution*; David M. Vigness, *The Revolutionary Decades*; and Weber, *Mexican Frontier*.

2. Austin to Bowie and Fannin, November 1, 1835, in Jenkins, ed., *Papers*, II, 287–288.

3. Ibid.

4. Austin to Dimitt, November 2, 1835, in Yoakum, *History of Texas*, II, 16.

5. Bowie to Austin, November 2, 1835, in Jenkins, ed., *Papers*, II, 297.

6. Rena Maverick Green, ed., *Samuel Maverick, Texan, 1803–1870: A Collection of Letters, Journals, and Memoirs*, 35.

7. W. T. Austin, "Campaign of 1835," 313–315; Austin to Andrew Briscoe, November 6, 1835, in "Austin's Order Book," 34–35; Travis to Austin, November 16, 1835, in Jenkins, ed., *Papers*, II, 442–443.

8. Travis to Austin, November 16, 1835, in Jenkins, ed., *Papers*, II, 442–443.

9. W. T. Austin, "Campaign of 1835," 313; Thomas J. Rusk to Houston, November 14, 1835, in Jenkins, ed., *Papers*, II, 413.

10. General Order, November 12, 1835, in "Austin's Order Book," 39.

11. Smither to Austin, November 4, 1835, in Barker, ed., *Austin Papers*, III, 236–238.

12. DeShields, *Tall Men with Long Rifles*, 51–52.

13. Austin to the President of Consultation, November 5, 1835, in Jenkins, ed., *Papers*, II, 320–322; "Austin's Order Book," 39; William H. Wharton to Austin, November 8, 1835, in Barker, ed., *Austin Papers*, III, 247.

14. Eugene C. Barker, "The Texas Revolutionary Army," *Quarterly of the Texas State Historical Association* 9 (April 1906): 227–229.

15. Webb, Carroll, and Branda, eds., *Handbook of Texas*, II, 382; see also Raymond Estep, "Lorenzo de Zavala and the Texas Revolution," *Southwestern Historical Quarterly* 57 (January 1954): 328.

16. Binkley, *Texas Revolution*, 77–81; Henry Smith to Council, November 16, 1835, in Jenkins, ed., *Papers*, II, 438–442.

17. Yoakum, *History of Texas*, II, 13; Anson Jones, *Memoranda and Official Correspondence Relating to the Republic of Texas, its History and Annexation, Including a Brief Autobiography of the Author*, 12–13; Elgin, "Uncle Frank Sparks' Story," *San Antonio Express*, December 8, 1935; [Charles Edwards Lester], *The Life of Sam Houston: The Only Authentic Memoir of him Ever Published*, 76–77.

18. Austin to President of Consultation, November 3, 1835, in Barker, ed., *Austin Papers*, III, 234; Barker, "Texan Revolutionary Army," 228; Yoakum, *History of Texas*, II, 13–14. Although temporary ranging companies had protected settlers against Indian raids for several years, this was the first formal organization of the force that was to become the renowned Texas Rangers.

19. Barker, "Texan Revolutionary Army," 230.

20. Ibid.; Ralph W. Steen, "Analysis of the Work of the General Council, Provisional Government of Texas, 1835–1836," *Southwestern Historical Quarterly* 41 (April 1938): 337.

21. Johnson, *History of Texas and Texans*, I, 326; Pohl and Hardin, "The Military History of the Texas Revolution," 274; Steen, "Work of the General Council," 324.

22. Austin to President of Consultation, November 4, 1835, in Jenkins, ed., *Papers*, II, 310–311.

23. Eugene C. Barker, *Life of Stephen F. Austin, Founder of Texas, 1793–1836: A Chapter in the Westward Movement of the Anglo-American People*, 370–394; Austin to President of Consultation, November 8, 1835, in Barker, ed., *Austin Papers*, III, 247.

24. "Austin's Order Book," 45.

25. Austin to Provisional Executive, November 18, 1835, in Jenkins, ed., *Papers*, II, 450–451.

26. Yoakum, *History of Texas*, II, 22–23; "Austin's Order Book," 47; Austin to Committee, November 18, 1835, in Jenkins, ed., *Papers*, II, 450–451.

27. Johnson, *History of Texas and Texans*, I, 351; Herman Ehrenberg, *With Milam and Fannin: Adventures of a German Boy in Texas' Revolution*, 49–50.

28. Joseph E. Field, *Three Years in Texas, Including a View of the Texan*

Revolution, and an Account of the Principal Battles, Together With Descriptions of the Soil, Commercial and Agricultural Advantages, &c., 18. Field further described how the Texian artillerymen were aided by local *tejanos:* "Our balls were generally returned to us as good as they were sent, by friendly Mexicans in the town, but not exactly in the way that theirs were delivered back to them." "Austin's Order Book," 51; W. T. Austin, "Campaign of 1835," 317; Austin to James F. Perry, November 22, 1835, in Barker, ed., *Austin Papers,* III, 262–263.

29. W. T. Austin, "Campaign of 1835," 319; J. W. Wilbarger, *Indian Depredations in Texas, Reliable Accounts of Battles, Wars, Adventures, Forays, Murders, Massacres, Etc., Together With Biographical Sketches of Many of the Most Noted Indian Fighters and Frontiersmen of Texas,* 34; "Austin's Order Book," 54–55.

30. Houston to Fannin, November 13, 1836, in Jenkins, ed., *Papers,* II, 396–397; W. T. Austin, "Campaign of 1835," 396–397, 319–320.

31. W. T. Austin "Campaign of 1835," 320; Fannin to Houston, November 18, 1835, in Jenkins, ed., *Papers,* II, 457–459; Marquis James, *The Raven: A Biography of Sam Houston,* 215; "Austin's Order Book," 54; Guy M. Bryan, "The Campaign of the Texas Army in 1835, under Austin and Burleson, Ending in the Capture of Bexar," in Wooten, ed., *Comprehensive History of Texas,* I, 557; George Huff and Spencer H. Jack to Council, October 28, 1835, in Jenkins, ed., *Papers,* II, 248–249. I am indebted to Thomas Ricks Lindley for calling this last letter to my attention.

32. Wharton to Branch T. Archer, November 26, 1835, in Jenkins, ed., *Papers,* II, 518–520; John S. Rutland to John H. Moore, November 26, 1835, in Jenkins, ed., *Papers,* II, 517.

33. Yoakum, *History of Texas,* II, 17–18; Johnson, *History of Texas and Texans,* I, 517.

34. DeShields, *Tall Men with Long Rifles,* 53–54.

35. Ibid., 54.

36. Ibid.

37. Edward Burleson to Government, November 27, 1835, in Jenkins, ed. *Papers,* III, 5–6; William H. Jack to Burleson, November 27, 1835, in Jenkins, ed., *Papers,* III, 7–8; Wooten, ed., *Comprehensive History of Texas,* I, 193.

38. Yoakum, *History of Texas,* II, 18.

39. W. H. Jack to Burleson, November 27, 1835, in Jenkins, ed., *Papers,* II, 7–8; Robert Hancock Hunter, *Narrative of Robert Hancock Hunter,* 25; Johnson, *History of Texas and Texans,* I, 347.

40. W. H. Jack to Burleson, November 27, 1835, in Jenkins, ed., *Papers,* III, 7–8.

41. Burleson to Government, November 27, 1835, in Jenkins, ed., *Papers*, III, 5–6.

42. W. H. Jack to Burleson, November 27, 1835, in Jenkins, ed., *Papers*, II, 7–8.

43. DeShields, *Tall Men with Long Rifles*, 55; Brown, *History of Texas*, I, 408–409; William Kennedy, *Texas: The Rise, Progress, and Prospects of the Republic of Texas*, 496.

44. Burleson to Government, November 27, 1835, in Jenkins, ed., *Papers*, III, 5–6; Yoakum, *History of Texas*, II, 18; DeShields, *Tall Men with Long Rifles*, 55.

45. DeShields, *Tall Men with Long Rifles*, 56.

46. Ibid.; Johnson, *History of Texas and Texans*, I, 349.

47. James B. Patrick and William Pettus to Provisional Government, November 30, 1835, in Jenkins, ed., *Papers*, III, 49–50.

48. Barker, "Texan Revolutionary Army," 235–236; Robert C. Morris to Houston, November 29, 1835, in Jenkins, ed., *Papers*, III, 31–32.

49. Morris to Houston, November 29, 1835, in Jenkins, ed., *Papers*, III, 31–32.

50. Green, ed., *Samuel Maverick, Texan*, 43; Yoakum, *History of Texas*, II, 24.

51. Mirabeau Buonaparte Lamar, *The Papers of Mirabeau Buonaparte Lamar*, ed. Charles A. Gulick, Katherine Elliot, Winnie Allen, and Harriet Smither, V, 513–514; John H. Jenkins and Kenneth Kesselus, *Edward Burleson: Texas Frontier Leader*, 71.

52. DeShields, *Tall Men with Long Rifles*, 60; Elgin, "Uncle Frank Sparks' Story, *San Antonio Express*, December 8, 1935; Green, ed., *Samuel Maverick, Texan*, 44; Yoakum, *History of Texas*, I, 24–25.

53. Yoakum, *History of Texas*, II, 25.

54. Ibid.; for more on Hendrick Arnold, see Harold Schoen, "The Free Negro in the Republic of Texas," *Southwestern Historical Quarterly* 41 (July 1937): 89, 92.

55. Yoakum, *History of Texas*, II, 25; A. H. Jones to William E. Jones, January 15, 1836, in "Notes and Fragments," *Quarterly of the Texas State Historical Association* 10 (October 1906): 181–182. Both Johnson and Wooten attack Yoakum for his description of the disorder that ensued upon Burleson's cancellation of the attack order. To them, the Texian volunteers offered a model of soldierly bearing. Wooten alleges that Yoakum "substitutes his imaginings for facts," and Johnson labels the account a "gross slander." They hold that the "orders were received without any 'burst of indignation' nor did a single com-

pany refuse to 'turn out,' and no occasion was given for thinking or 'fearing that the camp would become a theatre of blood.'" Even so, reliable participants such as Creed Taylor, Samuel Maverick, A. H. Jones, and Herman Ehrenberg all reported the chaos those orders generated, and their accounts should not be discounted.

5. *"Crude Bumpkins, Proud and Overbearing"*

1. Brown, *History of Texas*, I, 415; Johnson, *History of Texas and Texans*, I, 352.

2. DeShields, *Tall Men with Long Rifles*, 62; Johnson, *Texas and Texans*, I, 353.

3. Ibid.

4. Johnson, *Texas and Texans*, I, 352.

5. Yoakum, *History of Texas*, I, 25; J. M. Morphis, *History of Texas From its Discovery and Settlement, With a Description of its Principal Cities and Counties, and the Agricultural, Mineral, and Material Resources of the State*, 115; Kennedy, *Texas*, 509; Ehrenberg, *With Milam and Fannin*, 68.

6. DeShields, *Tall Men with Long Rifles*, 63.

7. Burleson to Henry Smith, December 14, 1835, in Jenkins, ed., *Papers*, III, 186–188; Yoakum, *History of Texas*, I, 26; Kennedy, *Texas*, 509.

8. Johnson, *Texas and Texans*, I, 352–353; Louis J. Wortham, *A History of Texas from Wilderness to Commonwealth*, III, 53.

9. Moses Austin Bryan to Cordelia V. Fisk, May 26, 1880, copy at the Daughters of the Republic of Texas Library at the Alamo; see also Cleburn Huston, *Deaf Smith: Incredible Texas Spy*, 1, 24; for a short biography of Smith, see Webb, Carroll, and Branda, *The Handbook of Texas*, II, 622–623; Frederick C. Chabot, *With the Makers of San Antonio, Genealogies of the Early Latin, Anglo-American, and German Families with Occasional Biographies, Each Group Being Prefaced with a Brief Historical Sketch and Illustrations*, 274; Johnson, *Texas and Texans*, I, 353. Johnson, as well as others, mistakenly refer to Maverick as "Norwich." Huson, *Dimmitt's Commandancy of Goliad*, 172.

10. Burleson to Henry Smith, December 14, 1835, in Jenkins, ed., *Papers*, III, 186–188; Yoakum, *History of Texas*, II, 26; *Biographical Directory of the Texan Conventions and Congresses, 1832–1845*, 145.

11. Yoakum, *History of Texas*, II, 26; Ehrenberg, *With Milam and Fannin*, 70–71.

12. Ehrenberg, *With Milam and Fannin*, 71; A. J. Houston, *Texas Independence*, 82.

13. Ehrenberg, *With Milam and Fannin*, 71; Yoakum, *History of Texas*, II, 26–27.

14. Green, ed., *Samuel Maverick, Texan*, 46; Elgin, "Uncle Frank Sparks' Story," *San Antonio Express*, December 8, 1935; DeShields, *Tall Men with Long Rifles*, 66–67.

15. For a discussion of the relative merits of the Brown Bess musket and the Kentucky long rifle, see Pohl and Hardin, "Military History of the Texas Revolution," 280–285; DeShields, *Tall Men with Long Rifles*, 67.

16. Ehrenberg, *With Milam and Fannin*, 74; Johnson, *Texas and Texans*, I, 354.

17. Ehrenberg, *With Milam and Fannin*, 74; DeWitt Clinton Baker, *A Texas Scrap-Book, Made Up of the History, Biography, and Miscellany of Texas and its People*, 38; Johnson, *Texas and Texans*, 354; DeShields, *Tall Men with Long Rifles*, 74–75.

18. Baker, *Texas Scrap-Book*, 38.

19. Johnson, *Texas and Texans*, I, 354–355.

20. "Austin's Order Book," 24; John C. Duval, *Early Times in Texas; or, The Adventures of Jack Dobell*, 47–48; Hardin, "A Vatir y Perseguir," in Davis, ed., *Essays in History*, 161–162; see also George Coalson, "Texas Mexicans in the Texas Revolution," in Ronald Lora, ed., *The American West: Essays in Honor of W. Eugene Hollon*, 216, 226. For a partial list of those *tejanos* who participated in the storming of Béxar, see Ruben Rendon Lozano, *Viva Tejas: The Story of the Mexican-born Patriots of the Republic of Texas*, 47–49. For a good background to the *tejanos*, see Andrew Anthony Tijerina, "Tejanos and Texas: The Native Mexicans of Texas, 1820–1850" (Ph.D. diss., University of Texas at Austin, 1977).

21. Weber, *Mexican Frontier*, 209; W. T. Austin, "Campaign of 1835," 321.

22. Johnson, *Texas and Texans*, I, 355; Yoakum, *History of Texas*, II, 28.

23. Field, *Three Years in Texas*, 20; Green, ed., *Samuel Maverick, Texan*, 47.

24. Johnson, *Texas and Texans*, I, 355; Yoakum, *History of Texas*, II, 28.

25. Johnson, *Texas and Texans*, I, 355; A. J. Houston, *Texas Independence*, 82.

26. Ibid.

27. Garver, "Benjamin Rush Milam," 196–197; Morphis, *History of Texas*, 120; DeShields, *Tall Men with Long Rifles*, 74–75.

28. Garver, "Benjamin Rush Milam," 197; Yoakum, *History of Texas*, 29; DeShields, *Tall Men with Long Rifles*, 74–75.

29. Johnson, *Texas and Texans*, I, 355; Yoakum, *History of Texas*, II, 28;

DeShields, *Tall Men with Long Rifles*, 69–70; for more on the gallant Henry Wax Karnes, see R. M. Potter, "Escape of Karnes and Teal from Matamoros," *Southwestern Historical Quarterly*, 4 (October 1900): 71–84.

30. Field, *Three Years in Texas*, 21; DeShields, *Tall Men with Long Rifles*, 72.

31. Huson, *Dimmitt's Commandancy of Goliad*, 189; Johnson, *Texas and Texans*, I, 356; A. J. Houston, *Texas Independence*, 82.

32. Baker, *Texas Scrap-Book*, 38.

33. Johnson, *Texas and Texans*, I, 356; Morphis, *History of Texas*, 120–121.

34. Huson, *Dimmitt's Commandancy of Goliad*, 189; Burleson to Henry Smith, December 14, 1835, in Jenkins, ed., *Papers*, III, 186–188.

35. "Account of the Taking of San Antonio by Henry C. Dance," in Gulick et al., eds., *Papers of Mirabeau Buonaparte Lamar*, V, 97; W. T. Austin, "Campaign of 1835," 321.

36. W. T. Austin, "Campaign of 1835," 321; Huson, *Dimmitt's Commandancy of Goliad*, 189.

37. Kennedy, *Texas*, 511; José Juan Sánchez-Navarro account, trans. by Ralph Umbarger, in Huson, *Dimmitt's Commandancy of Goliad*, 192.

38. Huson, *Dimmitt's Commandancy of Goliad*, 189.

39. Johnson, *Texas and Texans*, I, 357; Sánchez-Navarro account, in Huson, *Dimmitt's Commandancy of Goliad*, 191.

40. Yoakum, *History of Texas*, II, 31; Vigness, *Revolutionary Decades*, 166; Miguel A. Sánchez Lamego, *The Siege and Taking of the Alamo*, trans. Consuelo Velasco, 11; Sánchez-Navarro account, in Huson, *Dimmitt's Commandancy of Goliad*, 192, 190.

41. Sánchez-Navarro account, in Huson, *Dimmitt's Commandancy of Goliad*, 193.

42. Johnson, *Texas and Texans*, I, 157; Sánchez-Navarro account, in Huson, *Dimmitt's Commandancy of Goliad*, 193.

43. Burleson to Henry Smith, December 14, 1835, in Jenkins, ed., *Papers*, III, 186–188; Sánchez-Navarro account, in Huson, *Dimmitt's Commandancy of Goliad*, 194; Dance account, in Gulick et al., eds., *Papers of Mirabeau Buonaparte Lamar*, V, 95; "A Letter from San Antonio de Bexar in 1836," *Southwestern Historical Quarterly*, 62 (April 1959): 515.

44. "Capitulation, Entered into by Gen. Martin Perfecto de Cos, of the Mexican Troops, and General Edward Burleson, of the Colonial Troops of Texas," December 11, 1835, in Johnson, *Texas and Texans*, I, 359–360; Camilla Davis Trammell, *Seven Pines: Its Occupants and Their Letters, 1825–1872*, 29.

45. Frank W. Johnson to Burleson, December 11, 1835, in Jenkins, ed., *Papers*, II, 160–164. The Texians continued the long-standing U.S. militia tradition of heading home the instant that it appeared the shooting was over. As Yoakum explained: "On the 14th [of December 1835], General Cos left the town with eleven hundred and five troops, the remainder having abandoned his flag. . . . General Burleson, who, although opposed to the attack, when it was begun did all that he could to contribute to its success, on the 15th retired to his home, leaving Colonel Johnson in command at the Alamo, with a sufficient force to maintain it. The remainder of the army dispersed." Yoakum, *History of Texas*, II, 32, 31.

46. Fellow Citizens to General Edward Burleson, Colonel F. Johnson, and all brave officers and soldiers of the citizen volunteer army in Baxar, December 15, 1835, in Jenkins, ed., *Papers*, III, 199–200; Ehrenberg, *With Milam and Fannin*, 95. On December 25, a mere eleven days after Cós's departure, Johnson was able to inform Lieutenant Governor James W. Robinson: "The expedition which you propose against Matamoras can be undertaken speedily with every rational prospect of success and every man in this garrison would willingly Volunteer to proceed to the interior." Perhaps Johnson should have added "every man" who had not already headed for home. Johnson to James W. Robinson, December 25, 1835, in Jenkins, ed., *Papers*, III, 325–327.

47. Ehrenberg, *With Milam and Fannin*, 99.

6. *"Scoundrels Abroad and Scoundrels at Home"*

1. The best English biography of Santa Anna remains Wilfred Hardy Callcott, *Santa Anna: The Story of an Enigma Who Once Was Mexico*. Also useful are Clarence R. Wharton, *El Presidente: A Sketch of the Life of General Santa Anna*, and Antonio López de Santa Anna, in Ann Fears Crawford, ed., *The Eagle: The Autobiography of Santa Anna*. A short, but well-executed, sketch of the career of Santa Anna is found in Robert J. Turkovic, "The Antecedents and Evolution of Santa Anna's Ill-Fated Texas Campaign" (M.A. thesis, Florida Atlantic University, 1973), 1–8. In a more popular vein, see Frank C. Hanigen, *Santa Anna: The Napoleon of the West*. For serviceable works in Spanish, see José C. Valades, *Mexico, Santa Anna y la guerra de Texas*, and the biographical sketch in *Diccionario Porrua de historia, biografía y geografía de Mexico*, 1433–1440.

2. Antonio López de Santa Anna, "Manifesto Which General Antonio López de Santa Anna Addresses to his Fellow Citizens Relative to His Operations During the Texas Campaign and His Capture, 10 of May, 1837," in Carlos E. Castañeda, ed., *The Mexican Side of the Texas Revolution*, 8; Michael P.

Costeloe, "The Mexican Press of 1836 and the Battle of the Alamo," *Southwestern Historical Quarterly* 91 (April 1988): 534; Juan N. Almonte, "Statistical Report on Texas," trans. Carlos E. Castañeda, *Southwestern Historical Quarterly* 27 (January 1925): 211; José María Tornel y Mendivil, quoted in Walter Lord, *A Time to Stand*, 68.

3. Santa Anna, "Manifesto," in Castañeda, ed., *Mexican Side*, 9; Richard G. Santos, *Santa Anna's Campaign against Texas, 1835–1836, Featuring the Field Commands Issued to Major General Vicente Filisola*, 13–14.

4. Pohl and Hardin, "Military History of the Texas Revolution," 277; José Enrique de la Peña, *With Santa Anna in Texas: A Personal Narrative of the Revolution*, trans. and ed. Carmen Perry, 8–9.

5. The following section is greatly improved by numerous conversations with my colleague Kevin R. Young, chief of historical interpretation at San Antonio's Alamo IMAX Theatre, who was unselfish with his time and his encyclopedic knowledge of the Mexican army. See also Haythornthwaite, *The Alamo and the War of Texas Independence*, 23–34; Martin Windrow and Richard Hook, *The Footsoldier*, 45, 48, 50–51; Steven Ross, *From Flintlock to Rifle: Infantry Tactics, 1740–1866*, 40, 128.

6. De la Peña, *With Santa Anna in Texas*, 8–9.

7. Kevin R. Young, "Understanding the Mexican Army," unpublished manuscript in author's possession. Again, I am indebted to Young for sharing the fruits of his research. Haythornthwaite, *The Alamo and the War of Texas Independence*, 23–34; de la Peña, *With Santa Anna in Texas*, 8–9.

8. Nieto, Brown, and Hefter, *El Soldado Mexicano*, 55; Hardin, "Long Rifle and Brown Bess," 46.

9. Pohl and Hardin, "Military History of the Texas Revolution," 281; de la Peña, *With Santa Anna in Texas*, 79; Michael Robert Green, "El Soldado Mexicano, 1835–1836," *Military History of Texas and the Southwest* 13 (1975): 7.

10. Vicente Filisola, *Memoirs for the History of the War in Texas*, trans. Wallace Woolsey, II, 152.

11. Santos, *Santa Anna's Campaign against Texas*, 17.

12. Pohl and Hardin, "Military History of the Texas Revolution," 288–289. The authors argue that, in choosing Béxar as his strategic base, Santa Anna violated some of the most fundamental principals of war. De la Peña, *With Santa Anna in Texas*, 9–10; José María Tornel y Mendivil, "Relations between Texas, the United States, and the Mexican Republic," in Castañeda, ed., *Mexican Side*, 360.

13. Filisola, *History of the War in Texas*, II, 152; James Presley, "Santa Anna

in Texas: A Mexican Viewpoint," *Southwestern Historical Quarterly* 62 (April 1959): 497.

14. Filisola, *History of the War in Texas*, II, 156; Presley, "Santa Anna in Texas," 494.

15. Lord, *A Time to Stand*, 70–71.

16. Green, "El Soldado Mexicano," 10; Filisola, quoted in Presley, "Santa Anna in Texas," 498; Filisola, *History of the War in Texas*, 153; de la Peña, *With Santa Anna in Texas*, 60.

17. Filisola, *History of the War in Texas*, 154; Presley, "Santa Anna in Texas," 479.

18. Filisola, *History of the War in Texas*, 157.

19. José Urrea, "Diary of the Military Operations of the Division under the Command of General José Urrea Campaigned in Texas," in Castañeda, ed., *Mexican Side*, 360.

20. Holley, *Texas*, 336; Tornel, "Relations," in Castañeda, ed., *Mexican Side*, 360.

21. Dimitt to [?], December 2, 1835, in Jenkins, ed., *Papers*, III, 77–78.

22. Baker, *Texas Scrap-Book*, 61–65; Wortham, *History of Texas*, II, 87–89; Huson, *Dimmitt's Commandancy of Goliad*, 198–217.

23. Eugene C. Barker, "The Tampico Expedition," *Quarterly of the Texas State Historical Association* 6 (January 1903): 169–186; Vigness, *Revolutionary Decades*, 176–177; Webb, Carroll, and Branda, eds., *Handbook of Texas*, II, 704–705.

24. James, *The Raven*, 219; Houston to Henry Smith, January 6, 1836, in Jenkins, ed., *Papers*, III, 425–426.

25. Webb, Carroll, and Branda, eds., *Handbook of Texas*, I, 717–718; *Biographical Directory of the Texan Conventions and Congresses, 1832–1845*, 89; Johnson, *History of Texas and Texans*, I, 382–383.

26. James, *The Raven*, 220.

27. A. J. Houston, *Texas Independence*, 97–103; Neill to [?], January [?], 1836, in Jenkins, ed., *Papers*, III, 412–413.

28. Neill to Governor and Council, January 6, 1836, in Jenkins, ed., *Papers*, III, 424–425.

29. Proclamation of the Federal Volunteer Army of Texas, January 10, 1836, in Jenkins, ed., *Papers*, III, 467–468.

30. Henry Smith to Council, January 9, 1836, in Jenkins, ed., *Papers*, III, 458–460; for an in-depth study, see W. Roy Smith, "The Quarrel between Governor Smith and the Council of the Provisional Government of the Republic,"

Quarterly of the Texas State Historical Association" 5 (April 1902): 269–346.

31. Vigness, *Revolutionary Decades*, 179; Neill to Henry Smith, January 27, 1836, in Jenkins, ed., *Papers*, III, 160; Neill to Provisional Government, January 28, 1836, in William C. Binkley, *Official Correspondence of the Texan Revolution, 1835–1836*, 349–351.

32. James, *The Raven*, 221; Houston to Henry Smith, January 17, 1836, in Jenkins, ed., *Papers*, IV, 46–47.

33. James, *The Raven*, 222; Houston to Henry Smith, January 30, 1836, in Jenkins, ed., *Papers*, IV, 195; [Lester], *Life of Sam Houston*, 85.

34. James, *The Raven*, 223; Webb, Carrol, and Branda, eds., *Handbook of Texas*, I, 158–159.

35. Neill to the Governor and Council, January 23, 1836, in Binkley, *Official Correspondence*, I, 328; Lord, *A Time to Stand*, 80–81.

36. Green Jameson to Houston, January 18, 1836, in Jenkins, ed., *Papers*, IV, 58–61.

37. Bowie to Henry Smith, February 2, 1836, in Jenkins, ed., *Papers*, IV, 236–238.

38. John Holland Jenkins, *Recollections of Early Texas: The Memoirs of John Holland Jenkins*, ed. John Holmes Jenkins III, 155; Stephen L. Hardin, "Concepción: The Forgotten Battle of the Texas Revolution," *Heritage of the Great Plains* 20 (Spring 1987): 16; Bowie to Henry Smith, February 2, 1836, in Jenkins, ed., *Papers*, IV, 236–238.

39. Travis to Henry Smith, January 29, 1836, in Jenkins, ed., *Papers*, IV, 185; Lord, *A Time to Stand*, 80–81.

40. Travis to Henry Smith, February 13, 1836, in Jenkins, ed., *Papers*, IV, 327–328; Travis to Henry Smith, February 16, 1836, in Jenkins, ed., *Papers*, IV, 368; Lord, *A Time to Stand*, 81.

41. David Crockett, *A Narrative of the Life of David Crockett*, ix, xiii.

42. Crockett, quoted in Stephen L. Hardin, "The Texian Soldiers of the Texas Revolution," a paper presented before the annual meeting of the Texas State Historical Association, Dallas, Texas, 1991. Copy in possession of author.

43. Crockett, *Narrative*, 135, xii.

44. Stephen L. Hardin, "Gallery: David Crockett," *Military Illustrated, Past and Present* 23 (February–March 1990): 28–30; Hutton, Introduction, in Crockett, *Narrative*, xxix.

45. Hardin, "Gallery: David Crockett," 28–30.

46. Crockett, quoted in Lord, *A Time to Stand*, 54; Crockett, quoted in Gary L. Foreman, *Crockett, the Gentleman from the Cane: A Comprehensive View of*

the Folkhero Americans Thought They Knew, 41, 44. Its title notwithstanding, Foreman's brief volume, while useful, is far from comprehensive.

47. John Sutherland, *The Fall of the Alamo*, 11–12. While rather stolid in style, James Atkins Shackford, *David Crockett: The Man and the Legend*, remains the best biography. Also useful are Richard B. Hauck, *Crockett: A Bio-Bibliography*, and Michael A. Lofaro, ed., *Davy Crockett: The Man, the Legend, the Legacy*. Paul Andrew Hutton's forthcoming treatment promises to emerge as the best Crockett biography in print.

48. Jameson to Henry Smith, February 11, 1836, in Jenkins, ed., *Papers*, IV, 303; Lord, *A Time to Stand*, 84.

49. For reasons unknown, some historians have taken a dislike to Neill, and many accept their view. See Lord, *A Time to Stand*; see also Tom W. Gläser, "'Victory or Death,'" in Susan Prendergast Schoelwer, *Alamo Images: Changing Perceptions of a Texas Experience*, 69.

50. Lon Tinkle, *13 Days to Glory: The Siege of the Alamo*, 84; Ben H. Procter, *The Battle of the Alamo*, 16.

51. Travis to Henry Smith, February 12, 1836, in Jenkins, ed., *Papers*, IV, 317–318; Travis to Henry Smith, February 13, 1836, in Jenkins, ed., *Papers*, IV, 327–328.

52. Travis and Bowie to Henry Smith, February 14, 1836, in Jenkins, ed., *Papers*, IV, 339; the two commanders informed the governor: "By an understanding of to day Col. J. Bowie has command of the volunteers of the garrison, and Col. W. B. Travis of the regulars and volunteer cavalry. All general orders and correspondence will henceforth be signed by both until Col. Neill's return." Phil Rosenthal and Bill Groneman, *Roll Call at the Alamo*, 64.

53. Sutherland, *Fall of the Alamo*, 2–14; James, *The Raven*, 221.

54. Santos, *Santa Anna's Campaign against Texas*, 20, 24.

55. Ibid., 53–54.

56. Lord, *A Time to Stand*, 87–88; Juan N. Seguín folder, Unpaid Claims Collection, Archives Division, Texas State Library. Several *tejanos* in Seguín's company later made claims against the Republic of Texas for their service during the Revolution. Although they claimed to have entered service at differing times, all elected to conclude their service on the same two dates: February 20 and 21, 1836. It is not surprising, therefore, that their claims went unpaid. Yet we should not judge these men too harshly; they abandoned ranks for the same reason Anglo-Celtic volunteers later did during the Runaway Scrape—to provide for the safety of their families. The *tejanos* in question: Domingo Dias (20th), Antonio Hernández (21st), Francisco Díaz (20th), Gregorio Hernández (20th),

Luis Castañón (21st), Agapito Cervantes (21st), Pablo Mansolo (21st), Carlos Chacón (21st), Jesús García (21st), Clemente García (21st), Clemente Bustillo (21st).

57. Travis to Henry Smith, February 13, 1836, in Jenkins, ed., *Papers*, IV, 327–328; Lord, *A Time to Stand*, 88; Sutherland, *Fall of the Alamo*, 21; Travis to Andrew Ponton, February 23, 1836, in Jenkins, ed., *Papers*, IV, 420.

7. "Determined Valor and Desperate Courage"

1. Sutherland, *Fall of the Alamo*, 15; José Batres to Bowie, February 23, 1836, in Jenkins, ed., *Papers*, IV, 415; Travis to Public, February 24, 1836, Jenkins, ed., *Papers*, IV, 423.

2. Juan Almonte, "The Private Journal of Juan Nepomuceno Almonte," *Southwestern Historical Quarterly* 47 (July 1944): 17; Jameson to Sam Houston, January 18, 1836, in Jenkins, ed., *Papers*, IV, 58–61.

3. Henry Guerlac, "Vauban: The Impact of Science on War," in Edward Mead Earle, ed., *Makers of Modern Strategy*, 39–42.

4. Pohl and Hardin, "The Military History of the Texas Revolution," 293–294; Barnard, "Fannin at Goliad," in Wooten, ed., *Comprehensive History*, I, 615.

5. Webb, Carroll, and Branda, eds., *Handbook of Texas*, II, 546; Weber, *Mexican Frontier*, 53.

6. Travis and Bowie to Fannin, February 23, 1836, in Jenkins, ed., *Papers*, IV, 419.

7. Filisola, *Memoirs*, 172–173.

8. Santa Anna, "Manifesto," in Castañeda, ed., *Mexican Side*, 13; de la Peña, *With Santa Anna in Texas*, 45; Filisola, *History of the War in Texas*, 180.

9. Filisola, *History of the War in Texas*, 174; Almonte, "Journal," 18; Walter Lord, "Myths and Realities of the Alamo," in Oates, ed., *Republic of Texas*, 21.

10. Sutherland, *Fall of the Alamo*, 13; Lord, *A Time to Stand*, 106. For a critical examination of the tale concerning Bowie's alleged fall from the gun platform, see Schoelwer with Gläser, *Alamo Images*, 144.

11. January 8, the anniversary of the Battle of New Orleans, was celebrated as a national holiday in the South. Virginia lawyer, William Fairfax Gray was impressed by the festivities in Louisiana, which included a reenactment of the battle: "About 1,000 men were under arms, and the din was tremendous." Texian volunteers who hailed from the South—and that was the vast majority of them—had grown up hearing about Jackson's famous defensive victory over the British, and several of the older ones were themselves veterans of the battle. William Fairfax Gray, *From Virginia to Texas, 1835: Diary of Col. Wm. S.*

Gray, Giving Details of His Journey to Texas and Return in 1835–1836 and Second Journey to Texas in 1837, 70–71.

12. Nieto, Brown, and Hefter, *El Soldado Mexicano*, 53.

13. Sutherland, *Fall of the Alamo*, 20.

14. Neill to Governor and Council, January 6, 1836, in Jenkins, ed., *Papers*, III, 424–425; Sutherland, *Fall of the Alamo*, 22. The original Sánchez-Navarro diagram is housed at the Barker Texas History Center, University of Texas at Austin; for a clear reproduction see Schoelwer with Gläser, *Alamo Images*, 71.

15. Charles J. Long, *1836: The Alamo*, 8–9. Long is the emeritus curator of the Alamo. His booklet details the construction of the fort and the placement of the guns, primarily for model makers and students of historic structures.

16. Sutherland, *Fall of the Alamo*, 30; David Nevin, *The Texans*, 94. See also Tom Gläser's study, "'Victory or Death,'" in Schoelwer with Gläser, *Alamo Images*, 83; Harold L. Peterson, *Round Shot and Rammers*, 80–82.

17. Almonte, "Journal," 17.

18. Travis to Public, February 24, 1836, in Jenkins, ed., *Papers*, IV, 423; Almonte, "Journal," 17–18.

19. Almonte recorded on February 26, 1836, "firing from our cannon was continued. The enemy did not reply, except now and then." Almonte, "Journal," 18.

20. Ibid., 17.

21. Suzanna Dickenson Hanning, in Morphis, *History of Texas*, 174–175; Travis to Houston, February 25, 1836, in Jenkins, ed., *Papers*, IV, 433; Lord, *A Time to Stand*, 117–118.

22. Michael R. Green, "'To the People of Texas & All Americans in the World,'" *Southwestern Historical Quarterly* 91 (April 1988): 493, 498–500.

23. Lord, *A Time to Stand*, 125–127.

24. Ibid., 127–128.

25. Almonte, "Journal," 19.

26. Travis to Convention, March 3, 1836, in Jenkins, ed., *Papers*, IV, 502–504. In this letter, Travis reported the progress of the Mexican entrenchments:

> From the twenty-fifth to the present date the enemy have kept up a bombardment from two howitzers, one a five and a half inch, and the other an eight inch,—and a heavy cannonade from two long nine-pounders, mounted on a battery of the opposite side of the river, at a distance of four hundred yards from our wall. During this period the enemy have been busily employed in encircling us in with entrenched encampments on all sides, at the following distances, to wit: In Bexar,

four hundred yards west; in La villita [La Villita], three hundred yards south; at the powder house, one thousand yards east of south; on the ditch, eight hundred yards north."

27. Ibid.

28. Ibid.

29. Travis to Jesse Grimes, March 3, 1836, in Jenkins, ed., *Papers*, IV, 504–506.

30. Vigness, *Revolutionary Decades*, 187; Barnard, "Fannin at Goliad," in Wooten, *Comprehensive History*, I, 616.

31. Fannin to Robinson, February 28, 1836, in Jenkins, ed., *Papers*, IV, 455–456.

32. Ibid.

33. Almonte, "Journal," 20; John S. Brooks to James Hagarty, March 9, 1836, in Jenkins, ed., *Papers*, V, 30–32. Brooks, a member of Fannin's Goliad command, wrote that an Alamo courier had arrived the day before and reported that the Mexicans had "erected a battery within 400 yards of the Alamo, and every shot goes through it, as the walls are weak." Lord, *A Time to Stand*, 144.

34. Filisola, *History of the War in Texas*, II, 174; de la Peña, *With Santa Anna in Texas*, 42.

35. Santa Anna, "Manifesto," in Castañeda, ed., *Mexican Side*, 13; de la Peña, *With Santa Anna in Texas*, 43.

36. For a critical analysis of the Travis line legend, see Lord, *A Time to Stand*, 201–204; see also Schoelwer with Gläser, *Alamo Images*, 135–138.

37. De la Peña, *With Santa Anna in Texas*, 44. The Negro mentioned by de la Peña was Travis's body servant known to history only as "Joe." Although Joe was seemingly illiterate, he told his story to President David G. Burnet's cabinet on March 20, 1836. The slave's accounts of the battle were recorded by William Fairfax Gray and George Childress, but in neither of their versions did Joe mention that his master was contemplating surrender. Perhaps Gray and Childress neglected to record that unpleasant detail.

38. Filisola, *History of the War in Texas*, II, 176–177. Mrs. Dickenson confirmed the woman's role: "A Mexican woman deserted us one night, and going over to the enemy informed them of our very inferior numbers, which Col. Travis said made them confident of success and emboldened them to make the final assault." The question is raised, of course, how did Travis know that the woman had deserted to the enemy unless he had been in communication with them. Suzanna Dickenson Hanning account, in Morphis, *History of Texas*, 177.

39. De la Peña, *With Santa Anna in Texas*, 45.

40. Santa Anna Order, March 5, 1836, in Jenkins, ed., *Papers*, IV, 518-519.

41. Almonte, "Journal," 22-23; Santa Anna Order, March 5, 1836, in Jenkins, ed., *Papers*, IV, 518-519.

42. Joe's account, in Gray, *Diary*, 137; Lord, *A Time to Stand*, 153-155.

43. Santa Anna Order, March 5, 1836, in Jenkins, ed., *Papers*, IV, 518-519.

44. De la Peña, *With Santa Anna in Texas*, 46.

45. Santa Anna Order, March 5, 1836, in Jenkins, ed., *Papers*, IV, 153-155; Joe's account, in Gray, *Diary*, 137.

46. De la Peña, *With Santa Anna in Texas*, 46. De la Peña recorded: "The moon was up, but the density of the clouds that covered it allowed only an opaque light in our direction, seeming thus to contribute to our designs." Filisola, *History of the War in Texas*, II, 173; Santa Anna, "Manifesto," in Castañeda, ed., *Mexican Side*, 14.

47. Joe's account, in Gray, *Diary*, 137.

48. Gläser, "'Victory or Death,'" in Schoelwer with Gläser, *Alamo Images*, 83.

49. De la Peña, *With Santa Anna in Texas*, 47-49; Filisola, *History of the War in Texas*, II, 177; Ramón Martínez Caro, "A True Account of the First Texas Campaign and the Events Subsequent to the Battle of San Jacinto," in Castañeda, ed., *Mexican Side*, 105.

50. Filisola, *History of the War in Texas*, II, 178; Joe's account, in Gray, *Diary*, 137; George Campbell Childress account, in *Columbia* (Tennessee) *Observer*, April 14, 1836. For more on Travis's death, see Stephen L. Hardin, "A Volley from the Darkness: Sources Regarding the Death of William Barret Travis," *Alamo Journal* 59 (December 1987): 3-10.

51. Lord, *A Time to Stand*, 156-157.

52. Reuben M. Potter, *The Fall of the Alamo*, 31.

53. De la Peña, *With Santa Anna in Texas*, 48-50; Lord, *A Time to Stand*, 159-161; A. J. Houston, *Texas Independence*, 140-141.

54. De la Peña, *With Santa Anna in Texas*, 48.

55. Ibid.; Lord, *A Time to Stand*, 159-160.

56. Pohl and Hardin, "Military History of the Texas Revolution," 294, 296; Gläser, "'Victory or Death,'" in Schoelwer with Gläser, *Alamo Images*, 85.

57. De la Peña, *With Santa Anna in Texas*, 51.

58. Sutherland, *Fall of the Alamo*, 40.

59. Tinkle, *13 Days to Glory*, 214, 220; N. D. Labadie, "San Jacinto Campaign," in Day, comp., *Texas Almanac*, 174. After the Battle of San Jacinto,

Labadie interviewed Fernando Urissa and included his account of the Battle of the Alamo, which related the story of the Mexicans killing the cat. Labadie's article originally appeared in the 1859 *Texas Almanac*.

60. De la Peña, *With Santa Anna in Texas*, 53; for an erudite examination of the sources concerning Crockett's death, see Kilgore, *How Did Davy Die?*

61. Crockett, *Narrative*, 206.

62. Hauck, *Crockett: A Bio-Bibliography*, 44; Lofaro, ed., *Davy Crockett*, 7; Foreman, *Crockett, the Gentleman from the Cane*, 40; Hutton, Introduction, in Crockett, *Narrative*, xix, xx, xxvi-xxvii.

8. *"We Are in a Critical Situation"*

1. De la Peña, *With Santa Anna in Texas*, 52.

2. Carlos Sánchez-Navarro, *La Guerra de Tejas: Memorias de un Soldado* 85; Lord, *A Time to Stand*, 209–210; Martínez Caro, "True Account," in Castañeda, ed., *Mexican Side*, 105; Labadie, "San Jacinto Campaign," in Day, ed., *Texas Almanac*, 174.

3. Filisola, *History of the War in Texas*, 181; Martínez Caro, "True Account," in Castañeda, ed., *Mexican Side*, 106.

4. Santa Anna to José María Tornel, March 6, 1836, in Jenkins, ed., *Papers*, V, 11–12. For more about the New Orleans Greys and their standard, see Cox, *Romantic Flags of Texas*, 200–207.

5. For backgrounds and a demographic breakdown of the Alamo defenders, see Rosenthal and Groneman, *Roll Call at the Alamo*.

6. Typical is the view presented in Rupert Norval Richardson, *Texas: The Lone Star State*, 94. John H. Jenkins calls this work the "standard single-volume history of Texas." Because the book was used extensively as a text for Texas history courses, Richardson's interpretations were widely read and accepted. In describing the significance of the Alamo, the late Professor Richardson wrote: "[The Alamo defenders] had not died in vain; their sacrifices delayed Santa Anna and gave their countrymen a few precious days to prepare to meet the advancing horde." The 1960 John Wayne film, *The Alamo*, also included a scene wherein General Houston (portrayed by Richard Boone) tells his officers to remind Texian soldiers in training that Travis and his men were "buying them this precious time." Granted, the Texians could and should have used the "days to prepare." They did declare independence, prepare a constitution, establish a provisional government, and name Sam Houston commanding general. Militarily, however, the defense of the Alamo hardly seemed to qualify as an example of a successful holding action.

7. Pohl and Hardin, "Military History of the Texas Revolution," 296, 306–308.

8. Travis to Henry Smith, February 12, 1836, in Jenkins, ed., *Papers*, IV, 317–319.

9. James Sowers Brooks to Father, December 23, 1836, in Jenkins, ed., *Papers*, III, 295–297; Brooks to Sister, February 25, 1836, in Jenkins, ed., *Papers*, IV, 424–426; Brooks to James Hagarty, March 9, 1836, in Jenkins, ed., *Papers*, V, 30–32; Fannin to Robinson, February 7, 1836, in Jenkins, ed., *Papers*, IV, 279–283. For a good article dealing with the military career of John Sowers Brooks, incorporating many of his letters, see John E. Roller "Capt. John Sowers Brooks," *Quarterly of the Texas State Historical Association* 9 (January 1906): 157–209.

10. De la Peña noted that Santa Anna did not depart Béxar until March 31; see de la Peña, *With Santa Anna in Texas*, 96.

11. Ibid., 67; Urrea, "Diary," in Castañeda, ed., *Mexican Side*, 222. De la Peña greatly admired Urrea, especially in comparison to Santa Anna:

> Santa Anna did nothing but sacrifice our soldiers at the Alamo, while he ordered useless executions, inviting the enmity of the army as well as that of his military family, dishonoring it and consummating his errors by allowing himself to be surprised at four in the afternoon. General Urrea was marching rapidly from victory to victory, provisioning the soldiers abundantly, even in the nonessential items, and acquiring glory more by his generous and humane actions, which attracted the admiration and respect of the enemy, than by the brilliancy of his victories.

12. Urrea, "Diary," in Castañeda, ed., *Mexican Side*, 223. Urrea's entry for March 1, 1836, reads: "Still in San Patricio. Received news that Dr. Grant was returning from the Rio Bravo with a party of forty or fifty picked riflemen and I marched that night, with eighty dragoons, to meet him. The north wind was very strong and the cold was extreme for which reason I decided to wait for the enemy ten leagues from San Patricio, at the port of Los Cuates de Agua Dulce where he would have to pass. I divided my force into six groups and hid them in the woods."

13. The main (in fact, only) Texian source for the ambush at Agua Dulce is Ruben R. Brown, "Expedition under Johnson and Grant," in Day, comp., *Texas Almanac*, 218–224.

14. From *Red River Herald*, n.d., 1835, in Gaddy, comp., *Texas in Revolt*, 26; see also D. W. Meinig, *Imperial Texas: An Interpretive Essay in Cultural Geography*, 36–37.

15. Fane Downs, "The History of Mexicans in Texas, 1820–1845" (Ph.D. diss., Texas Tech University, 1970), 243; Hardin, "A Vatir y Perseguir," in Davis, ed., *Essays in History*, 166; for added perspective, see Arnoldo De Leon, "Tejanos and the Texas War for Independence: Historiography's Judgement," *New Mexico Historical Review* 61 (April 1986): 137–146; Urrea, "Diary," in Castañeda, ed., *Mexican Side*, 230.

16. Fannin to Francis Desauque and John Chenworth [Chenoweth], March 1, 1836, in Jenkins, ed., *Papers*, IV, 477–478; Webb, Carrol, and Branda, eds., *Handbook of Texas*, I, 700. The *Handbook* entry, "Goliad Campaign of 1836," was written by Harbert Davenport, whom the late Hobart Huson called "the outstanding authority on the history of Fannin's command." The scope of the article goes far beyond most *Handbook* entries, providing both analysis and interpretation, and is in some ways even better than his groundbreaking 1939 article. See also Harbert Davenport, "The Men of Goliad," *Southwestern Historical Quarterly* 43 (January 1939): 21. See also Thomas L. Miller, "Fannin's Men: Some Additions to Earlier Rosters," *Southwestern Historical Quarterly* 61 (April 1958): 522–532.

17. Fannin to Robinson, February 22, 1836, in Jenkins, ed., *Papers*, IV, 398–401.

18. Ibid.

19. Davenport, "Men of Goliad," 22.

20. Gray, *Diary*, 123–124; Vigness, *Revolutionary Decades*, 184.

21. James, *The Raven*, 226–227.

22. Ibid., 227.

23. Kathryn Stoner O'Connor, *The Presidio La Bahia del Espiritu Santo de Zuniga, 1721 to 1846*, 124.

24. W. W. Thompson affidavit, December 1, 1840, in Home Papers, Box 2–9/6, folder 3, Archives Division, Texas State Library.

25. Houston to Henry Raguet, March 13, 1836, in Jenkins, ed., *Papers*, V, 71–72; Houston to James Collinsworth, March 15, 1836, in Jenkins, ed. *Papers*, V, 82–84; John Sharpe account, in Foote, *Texas and the Texans*, II, 268.

26. Jeff Parson, quoted in I. T. Taylor, *The Cavalcade of Jackson County*, 80.

27. DeShields, *Tall Men with Long Rifles*, 120.

28. [Lester], *Life of Sam Houston*, 94–95.

29. Brown, *History of Texas*, I, 599–600; Jewel Davis Scarborough, "The Georgia Battalion in the Texas Revolution: A Critical Study," *Southwestern His-*

torical Quarterly 62 (April 1960): 511–532. The Scarborough article is not a military history but rather examines the battalion's personnel.

30. Webb, Carroll, and Branda, eds., *Handbook*, I, 702.

31. Urrea, "Diary," in Castañeda, ed., *Mexican Side*, 225.

32. Pohl and Hardin, "Military History of the Texas Revolution," 283–285.

33. Webb, Carroll, and Branda, eds., *Handbook*, I, 702.

34. Barnard, "Fannin at Goliad," in Wooten, *Comprehensive History*, I, 618.

35. Webb, Carroll, and Branda, eds., *Handbook*, I, 702.

36. Shackelford account, in Foote, *Texas and the Texans*, II, 229–230.

37. Abel Morgan, "An Account of the Battle of Goliad and Fanning's Massacre: And the Capture and Imprisonment of Abel Morgan Written by Himself," in O'Conner, *Presidio La Bahia*, 203.

38. Shackelford account, in Foote, *Texas and the Texans*, II, 231.

39. Ehrenberg, *With Milam and Fannin*, 169.

40. Morgan, "Account of Goliad and Fanning's Massacre," in O'Connor, *Presidio La Bahia*, 204; Ehrenberg, *With Milam and Fannin*, 170, 169.

41. Barnard, "Fannin at Goliad," in Wooten, ed., *Comprehensive History*, I, 620; Ehrenberg, *With Milam and Fannin*, 170–171.

42. Shackelford account, in Foote, *Texas and the Texans*, II, 231–232.

43. Barnard, "Fannin at Goliad," in Wooten, ed., *Comprehensive History*, I, 622.

44. Shackelford account, in Foote, *Texas and the Texans*, II, 232.

45. Barnard, "Fannin at Goliad," in Wooten, ed., *Comprehensive History*, I, 621–622; Ehrenberg, *With Milam and Fannin*, 171.

46. Shackelford account, in Foote, *Texas and the Texans*, II, 233.

47. Webb, Carroll, and Branda, eds., *Handbook*, I, 703; Barnard, "Fannin at Goliad," in Wooten, ed., *Comprehensive History*, I, 621; Duval, *Early Times in Texas*, 64.

48. Ehrenberg, *With Milam and Fannin*, 172; O'Connor, *Presidio La Bahia*, 151; Barnard, "Fannin at Goliad," in Wooten, ed., *Comprehensive History*, I, 621.

49. W. N. T. Thorne, "Narrative of Dr. W. N. T. Thorne," in Kennedy, *Texas*, 570–571. The Thorne account was originally published in the *Mississippi Free Trader*, November 29, 1838.

50. Barnard, "Fannin at Goliad," in Wooten, ed., *Comprehensive History*, I, 622.

51. Shackelford account, in Foote, *Texas and the Texans*, II, 234.

52. Duval, *Early Times in Texas*, 66–67.

53. Shackelford account, in Foote, *Texas and the Texans*, II, 234; Urrea, "Diary," in Castañeda, ed., *Mexican Side*, 232.

54. Shackelford account, in Foote, *Texas and the Texans*, II, 234; Thorne narrative, in Kennedy, *Texas*, 572. Thorne recalled that "the wounded suffered agonies for want of water, and by their moans and petitions for it made the situation of those who had escaped unhurt even more distressing."

55. Ehrenberg, *With Milam and Fannin*, 179, 176.

56. Duval, *Early Times in Texas*, 72.

57. Barnard, "Fannin at Goliad," in Wooten, ed., *Comprehensive History*, I, 622.

58. Urrea, "Diary," in Castañeda, ed., *Mexican Side*, 234–235; Barnard, "Fannin at Goliad," in Wooten, ed., *Comprehensive History*, I, 622.

59. Shackelford account, in Foote, *Texas and the Texans*, II, 238. Shackelford reported how he and other officers told Fannin that they "would not oppose a surrender, provided we could obtain an honourable capitulation; one on which he could rely: that if he could not obtain such,—come back—our graves are already dug—let us all be buried together. To these remarks the men responded in a firm and determined manner; and the Colonel assured us, that he would never surrender on any other terms."

60. Urrea, "Diary," in Castañeda, ed., *Mexican Side*, 235; James M. Day, "The Battle of Goliad," in *Battles of Texas*, 47–48. Texian survivors always insisted that Urrea had offered them terms but later cravenly reneged on his word of honor. Professor Eugene C. Barker, however, discovered the original surrender document in the Archives of the War Department in Mexico City. This document, signed by both Urrea and Fannin, clearly stated that the surrender was unconditional, as Urrea had always maintained.

61. Webb, Carroll, and Branda, eds., *Handbook*, I, 703.

62. Ibid.

63. Shackelford account, in Foote, *Texas and the Texans*, II, 240; Urrea, "Diary," in Castañeda, ed., *Mexican Side*, 242.

64. Bancroft, *History of the North Mexican States and Texas*, II, 234–236; R. C. Smith, "James W. Fannin, Jr.," 282; Davenport, "Men of Goliad," 28–38. Davenport provides a breakdown of Fannin's command, giving the name of each man and where he was killed, as well as a list of survivors.

65. Yoakum, *History of Texas*, II, 101. Yoakum's bombast is typical of most early Texas historians: "Deliberately and in cold blood [Santa Anna] caused three hundred and thirty of the sternest friends of Texas—her friends while living and dying—to tread the winepress for her redemption. He chose the Lord's day

for this sacrifice. It was accepted; and God waited his own good time for retribution—a retribution to the feet of the Texas victors, whose magnanimity prolonged his miserable life to waste the land of his birth with anarchy and civil war!"

9. *"The Enemy Are Laughing You to Scorn"*

1. Houston to James Collinsworth, March 15, 1836, in Jenkins, ed., *Papers*, V, 82–84.

2. Ibid.

3. "John W. Hunter Literary Effort," Archives Division, Texas State Library. Hunter interviewed Creed Taylor, and the "Literary Effort" is a manuscript that tells the story of the revolt through Taylor's reminiscences. Later Hunter fell upon hard times and was forced to sell the manuscript and all rights to it to Dallas businessman and Texas history buff James T. DeShields for $200. The agreement, now housed in the James T. DeShields Papers at the Daughters of the Republic of Texas Library at the Alamo specified, "All copyright privliges are to be transferred to James T. DeShields." The Hunter manuscript was later the source for *Tall Men with Long Rifles*, with no mention of Hunter's contribution. Yet there is much informative material in the original Hunter manuscript that DeShields failed to include in *Tall Men with Long Rifles*. Nana Smithwick Donaldson, the compiler of *Evolution of a State: Recollections of Old-Time Texas*, appears to have also borrowed heavily from the Hunter manuscript during the preparations of her father's "recollections."

4. "John W. Hunter Literary Effort."

5. Jenkins, *Recollections of Early Texas*, 40.

6. For characteristics of early Texians, see William Ransom Hogan, *The Texas Republic: A Social and Economic History*; also useful is T. R. Fehrenbach, *Seven Keys to Texas*, 1–10.

7. Houston to James Collinsworth, March 17, 1836, in Jenkins, ed., *Papers*, V, 122–124.

8. Seymour V. Connor, "The Battle of San Jacinto," in *Battles of Texas*, 57.

9. Ibid.; Clarence Wharton, *San Jacinto: The Sixteenth Decisive Battle*, 14–20; Santos, *Santa Anna's Campaign against Texas*, 92.

10. Connor, "Battle of San Jacinto," in *Battles of Texas*, 58.

11. Ibid.

12. Sam Houston to Thomas J. Rusk, March 23, 1836, in Jenkins, ed., *Papers*, V, 168–170.

13. Frank X. Tolbert, *The Day of San Jacinto*, 51; [Robert M. Coleman],

Houston Displayed; or, Who Won the Battle of San Jacinto? By a Farmer in the Army, Reproduced From the Original, 4.

14. Houston, quoted in Tolbert, *Day of San Jacinto*, 50–51.

15. Ibid.; Archie P. McDonald, *The Trail to San Jacinto*, 17.

16. Houston to Rusk, March 29, 1836, in Jenkins, ed., *Papers*, V, 234–235.

17. Presley, "Santa Anna in Texas," 506; Santos, *Santa Anna's Campaign against Texas*, 92.

18. Charles W. Hayes, *Galveston: History of the Island and the City*, 146–147; Houston to Rusk, March 29, 1836, in Jenkins, ed., *Papers*, V, 234–235.

19. For more on Santa Anna's faulty strategy, see Pohl and Hardin, "The Military History of the Texas Revolution," 290–292.

20. Santos, *Santa Anna's Campaign against Texas*, 92–93.

21. Connor, "Battle of San Jacinto," in *Battles of Texas*, 59–60; Tolbert, *Day of San Jacinto*, 51–52.

22. J. H. Kuykendall, "Recollections of the Campaign," Eugene C. Barker, ed., *Quarterly of the Texas State Historical Association* 4 (April 1901): 300. As a supplement to his groundbreaking 1901 article, Dr. Barker printed for the first time some of the more important primary accounts of the San Jacinto campaign. Today it still remains one of the best places to begin research on the campaign and battle.

23. James, *The Raven*, 239; Robinson to Burnet, January 4, 1847, quoted in Mirabeau B. Lamar, Jesse Billingsley, et al., *Defence of Gen. Sidney Sherman Against the Charges Made by Gen. Sam Houston, in His Speech Delivered in the United States Senate, February 28th, 1859*, 19.

24. Connor, "Battle of San Jacinto," in *Battles of Texas*, 61.

25. Tolbert, *Day of San Jacinto*, 68; Santos, *Santa Anna's Campaign against Texas*, 94–95.

26. McDonald, *Trail to San Jacinto*, 22.

27. Santa Anna, "Manifesto," in Castañeda, ed., *Mexican Side*, 29–30; Tolbert, *Day of San Jacinto*, 68–69.

28. David G. Burnet, quoted in Tolbert, *Day of San Jacinto*, 81. Burnet criticized Houston for taking the army into the "Foul and turbid lagoons of the Brazos bottoms," yet it was those exact conditions that kept the Mexicans from pursuing and made Groce's plantation a haven for the Texian army. Connor, "Battle of San Jacinto," in *Battles of Texas*, 62.

29. Labadie, "San Jacinto Campaign," in Day, comp., *Texas Almanac*, 150.

30. George Bernard Erath, "The Memoirs of Major George Bernard Erath, 1813–1891," *Southwestern Historical Quarterly* 26 (April 1923): 255; Labadie, "San Jacinto Campaign," in Day, comp., *Texas Almanac*, 151.

31. Burnet to Houston, April 7, 1836, in Connor, "Battle of San Jacinto," in *Battles of Texas*, 62.

32. Wooten, ed., *Comprehensive History*, I, 268; Tolbert, *Day of San Jacinto*, 84–85.

33. Tolbert, *Day of San Jacinto*, 85; Labadie, "San Jacinto Campaign," in Day, comp., *Texas Almanac*, 151.

34. Houston Orders, April 12, 1836, in Jenkins, ed., *Papers*, V, 449; Connor, "Battle of San Jacinto," in *Battles of Texas*, 63.

35. Tolbert, *Day of San Jacinto*, 91.

36. Pedro Delgado, *Mexican Account of the Battle of San Jacinto*, 5–6; Wharton, *San Jacinto*, 64–66.

37. Santa Anna to Vicente Filisola, April 15 [?], 1836, in Jenkins, ed., *Papers*, V, 485–486; English trans. in Santos, *Santa Anna's Campaign against Texas*, 98.

38. Hayes, *Galveston*, 143–145.

39. Santa Anna, "Manifesto," in Castañeda, ed., *Mexican Side*, 31–32; Connor, "Battle of San Jacinto," in *Battles of Texas*, 65–66.

40. Foote, *Texas*, II, 291–292. Many Mexicans and northeastern Yankees speculated at the time that President Andrew Jackson had plotted with Houston and other agents of the "slaveocracy" to wrest Texas from Mexico and, while publicly proclaiming neutrality, that he had secretly promised assistance if Houston got into trouble. While documents to support such a conspiracy have never been found, there were several factors giving the appearance of collusion. Although there was not an immediate Indian threat in Louisiana, General Edmund P. Gaines and a large U.S. army stood poised along the Sabine River. Gaines, furthermore, wryly turned his back while many of his soldiers "deserted" to fight with Houston's army. To avoid diplomatic embarrassment, they were instructed not to be captured wearing the uniform of the United States army. Many, nonetheless, were reported to have worn at least partial U.S. uniforms while serving with the Texians. In July 1836, upon the invitation of Stephen F. Austin, Gaines led a force of U.S. troops to Nacogdoches and occupied the town until the Texian government could be organized. Houston spoke confidently of raising five thousand troops in the United States, and perhaps Jackson had told him that if the Mexican dictator could be lured near the border Jackson could use that fact as an excuse to declare war on Mexico. All this is, of course, speculation. But it would explain Houston's constant desire to retreat toward the Redlands. For a cogent exposition of the slavery thesis, see Frederick Merk, *Slavery and the Annexation of Texas*.

41. Labadie, "San Jacinto Campaign," in Day, comp., *Texas Almanac*, 153.

42. Ibid.; [Coleman], *Houston Displayed*, 18.

43. Robert Hancock Hunter, *Narrative of Robert Hancock Hunter*, 14–15.

44. Ibid., 20–21.

45. Connor, "Battle of San Jacinto," in *Battles of Texas*, 65.

10. *"Nock There Brains Out"*

1. Tolbert, *Day of San Jacinto*, 94.

2. W. P. Zuber, "Zuber's Account of the Camp at Harrisburg," ed. Eugene C. Barker, *Quarterly of the Texas State Historical Association* 4 (April 1901): 284–285; Foote, *Texas and the Texans*, II, 293–294; Bancroft, *History of the North Mexican States and Texas*, II, 253–254.

3. Sam Houston to Henry Raguet, April 19, 1836, in Jenkins, ed., *Papers*, V, 504.

4. Labadie, "San Jacinto Campaign," in Day, comp., *Texas Almanac*, 154–155.

5. Bancroft, *North Mexican States and Texas*, 253–254.

6. James, *The Raven*, 245.

7. Connor, "Battle of San Jacinto," in *Battles of Texas*, 67–68.

8. Delgado, *Mexican Account*, 7.

9. Sam Houston to James Collinsworth, March 17, 1836, in Jenkins, ed. *Papers*, V, 122–124; for more concerning the Anglo-American woodlands–Hispanic prairie hypothesis, see Meinig, *Imperial Texas*, 36–37; see also Pohl and Hardin, "The Military History of the Texas Revolution," 299; Travis to Henry Smith, January 29, 1836, in Jenkins, ed., *Papers*, IV, 185.

10. Meinig, *Imperial Texas*, 35; de la Peña, *With Santa Anna in Texas*, 6.

11. Delgado, *Mexican Account*, 9.

12. Ibid., 7–8.

13. Labadie, "San Jacinto Campaign," in Day, comp., *Texas Almanac*, 157–159; Urizza's account, in Labadie, "San Jacinto Campaign," 173–174; Delgado, *Mexican Account*, 8–9.

14. Conner, "Battle of San Jacinto," in *Battles of Texas*, 69.

15. Labadie, "San Jacinto Campaign," in Day, comp., *Texas Almanac*, 158–161; Santa Anna, quoted in Tolbert, *Day of San Jacinto*, 117.

16. Typescript, Jesse Billingsley, "Retreat of the Texas Army Previous to the Battle of San Jacinto," *Galveston News* (tri-weekly), September 19, 1857, v. 16, no. 30, p. 3, in Billingsley (Jesse) Papers, Barker Texas History Center, Box #3H52, "letters 1843–1889" folder.

17. Walter P. Lane, *The Adventures and Recollections of General Walter P. Lane, a San Jacinto Veteran, Containing Sketches of the Texan, Mexican, and*

Late Wars with Several Indian Fights Thrown In, 12–13; Tolbert, *Day of San Jacinto*, 118.

18. James W. Pohl, *Battle of San Jacinto*, 30; Foote, *Texas and the Texans*, 302–305; Delgado, *Mexican Account*, 9.

19. Tolbert, *Day of San Jacinto*, 119.

20. Delgado, *Mexican Account*, 9.

21. "Extracts from Mosely Baker's Letter to Houston," ed. Eugene C. Barker, *Quarterly of the Texas State Historical Association* 4 (April 1901): 284–285; Connor, "Battle of San Jacinto," in *Battles of Texas*, 69.

22. James, *The Raven*, 248; "R. J. Calder's Recollections of the Campaign," ed. Eugene C. Barker, *Quarterly of the Texas State Historical Association* 4 (April 1901): 337; Connor, "Battle of San Jacinto," in *Battles of Texas*, 70. Connor claims that Houston himself beat reveille on the morning of April 21.

23. John A. Wharton, quoted in [Coleman], *Houston Displayed*, 24; James, *The Raven*, 249.

24. Tolbert, *Day of San Jacinto*, 128–131; Lane, *Adventures and Recollections*, 11–12. Lane recorded that this incident happened on April 20 before Sherman's cavalry charge. His memory was undoubtedly faulty, for at 10:00 A.M.—when he claims the reconnaissance took place—the Mexican army had not yet arrived on the field. Lane, however, did not pen his memoirs until forty years later, after a full military career that saw him achieve a general's rank in the Confederate army. Tolbert, *Day of San Jacinto*, also placed this event on April 21.

25. [Lester], *The Life of Sam Houston*, 126; Wharton, *San Jacinto*, 99.

26. [Coleman], *Houston Displayed*, 24–25; Foote, *Texas and the Texans*, II, 304–305.

27. Connor, "Battle of San Jacinto," in *Battles of Texas*, 70; [Coleman], *Houston Displayed*, 25–26.

28. [Lester], *Life of Sam Houston*, 124, 123; James, *The Raven*, 250.

29. For an erudite discussion of the controversy surrounding Houston's conduct at San Jacinto, see John H. Jenkins's introduction to Coleman's *Houston Displayed*, i–xvii; see also his further comments in John H. Jenkins, *Basic Texas Books: An Annotated Bibliography of Selected Works for a Research Library*, 340–345.

30. Tolbert, *Day of San Jacinto*, 140–142.

31. Bancroft, *North Mexican States and Texas*, II, 261.

32. L. W. Kemp and Ed Kilman, *The Battle of San Jacinto and the San Jacinto*

Campaign, 13. For the uniforms and civilian garb of the Texian soldiers, see Haythornthwaite, *The Alamo and the War of Texas Independence*; see also the Joseph Hefter illustrations in Gaddy, comp., *Texas in Revolt*, 60–61.

33. Antonio Menchaca, *Memoirs*, 26; Hardin, "A Vatir Y Persequir," in Davis, ed., *Essays in History*, 168.

34. Santa Anna, "Manifesto," in Castañeda, ed., *Mexican Side*, 31–32; Connor, "Battle of San Jacinto," in *Battles of Texas*, 70. There is not a scintilla of primary evidence to support the oft-repeated myth that Santa Anna was engaged in a tryst with mulatto slave girl Emily Morgan. For a thorough debunking of the tale, see Kent Biffle, "Yellow Rose Story Loses Its Bloom," *Dallas Morning News*, November 17, 1985, sec. A, 45.

35. Delgado, *Mexican Account*, 9.

36. Ibid.

37. Houston to Burnet, April 25, 1836, in Jenkins, ed. *Papers*, VI, 72–76.

38. Connor, "Battle of San Jacinto," in *Battles of Texas*, 72; Labadie, "San Jacinto Campaign," in Day, comp., *Texas Almanac*, 163; Tolbert, *Day of San Jacinto*, 142.

39. Delgado, *Mexican Account*, 10.

40. For a discussion of the Texians as light infantrymen, see Pohl and Hardin, "Military History of the Texas Revolution," 283–284.

41. Lane, *Adventures and Recollections*, 14; Foote, *Texas and the Texans*, II, 309.

42. W. C. Swearingen to [?] Swearingen, April 23, 1836, in Jenkins, ed., *Papers*, VI, 33–36. In this letter to his brother describing the events of San Jacinto, Swearingen wrote: "To see the number, the position and the termination and the time in which it was done, (time 18 minutes) it at once shows that the hand of Providence was with us." Moses Bryan, quoted in Tolbert, *Day of San Jacinto*, 150.

43. Foote, *Texas and the Texans*, II, 310.

44. Delgado, *Mexican Account*, 11; Labadie, "San Jacinto Campaign," in Day, comp., *Texas Almanac*, 163; Connor, Battle of San Jacinto," in *Battles of Texas*, 73–74.

45. Labadie, "San Jacinto Campaign," in Day, comp., *Texas Almanac*, 164; Hunter, *Narrative of Robert Hancock Hunter*, 16; Connor, "Battle of San Jacinto," in *Battles of Texas*, 74.

46. Tolbert, *Day of San Jacinto*, 152.

47. Moses Austin Bryan Papers, Barker Texas History Center. In Bryan's narrative, the belligerent private was identified as "Joe Dickson." But as Tolbert

discovered, there was no one by that name listed on company rosters. He believed (as do I) that the man was probably J. H. T. Dixon.

48. Connor, "Battle of San Jacinto," in *Battles of Texas*, 74.

49. S. F. Sparks, "Recollections of S. F. Sparks," *Quarterly of the Texas State Historical Association* 12 (July 1908): 71.

50. Ibid., 75; Bancroft, *North American States and Texas*, II, 263–265; [Lester], *Life of Sam Houston*, 145–150.

51. Amasa Turner, "Amasa Turner's Account of the Battle," ed. Eugene C. Barker, *Quarterly of the Texas State Historical Association* 4 (April 1901): 341–342.

52. Labadie, "San Jacinto Campaign," in Day, comp., *Texas Almanac*, 168; James, *The Raven*, 255; Bancroft, *North Mexican States and Texas*, II, 268–269.

53. Santa Anna to Filisola, April 22, 1836, in Jenkins, ed., *Papers*, VI, 15; Presley, "Santa Anna in Texas," 508–509.

54. Horace Greeley, quoted in Lord, *A Time to Stand*, 190; Presley, "Santa Anna in Texas," 509–512; Pohl and Hardin, "Military History of the Texas Revolution," 303–306.

55. Wharton to Austin, November 8, 1835, in Barker, ed., *Austin Papers*, III, 247.

Epilogue

1. De la Peña, *With Santa Anna in Texas*, 144–148; Gene M. Brack, *Mexico Views Manifest Destiny, 1821–1846: An Essay on the Origins of the Mexican War*, 54–55, 74–79.

2. Presley, "Santa Anna in Texas," 508–512; Urrea, "Diary," in Castañeda, ed., *Mexican Side*, 253–260.

3. The best one-volume study of the Mexican War remains K. Jack Bauer, *The Mexican War, 1846–1848*.

4. Theodore Frederic Gaillardet, *Sketches of Early Texas and Louisiana*, trans. and intro. James L. Shepherd III, 14; Theodore Sedgwick, *Thoughts on the Proposed Annexation of Texas to the United States*, 6.

5. Robert Hall, *Life of Robert Hall*, 26. A veteran of several frontier skirmishes, Hall perceptively acknowledged the importance that terrain had played in the San Jacinto campaign, but grossly overstated the significance of Houston's "brilliant military maneuvers."

6. Billingsley to Sidney Sherman, June 19, 1859, quoted in Lamar, Billingsley, et al., *Defence of Gen. Sidney Sherman*, 9; David G. Burnet, *Review of the Life*

of *Gen. Sam Houston, as Recently Published in Washington City, by J. T. Towers*, 6, 15. I am indebted to Thomas Ricks Lindley for calling these rare anti-Houston pamphlets to my attention. Traditionally, Texas historians have dismissed Houston's critics as spiteful subordinates, covetous of their commander's renown. Discussing Coleman's acidic polemic, *Houston Displayed; or, Who Won the Battle of San Jacinto? By a Farmer in the Army* (1837), the late John H. Jenkins asserts:

> The volume was issued, without doubt, as a political maneuver, but it must be remembered that Sam Houston himself seldom wrote a word that was not. Scurrilous and biased as it is, there is truth to at least some of the accusations, and it was undoubtedly believed to be literal truth by scores of veterans of the campaign. Many of its accusations were substantiated by some of Texas' most highly revered heroes of that era. One finds, in fact, that a considerable majority of the officers in Houston's army were severely critical of Houston's actions in the campaign. These men sincerely felt that his laurels were too easily won and too lightly granted by the thousands of post-revolution immigrants who, fed by a pro-Houston press in the United States, came to Texas thinking of Houston as Texas' savior. General Edward Burleson, second in command, despised Houston till the day he died because of the campaign, as did Col. Sidney Sherman, third in command. David G. Burnet, President of Texas, was even more fanatical than Coleman in his denunciation of Houston's part. Gen. Thomas J. Rusk, Adj. Gen. John A. Wharton, Lt. Col. J. C. Neill, Lt. Col. Mirabeau B. Lamar, Lt. Col. John Forbes, Maj. J. H. Perry, Maj. James Collinsworth, Maj. Lysander Wells, Captains Turner, Moreland, Fisher, Gillespie, and Surgeons Anson Jones and William [*sic*] Labadie all criticized some of Houston's actions in the campaign. Only three officers—Henry Millard, Alexander Somervell, and J. L. Bennett—appear to have unceasingly supported Houston.

Houston's descendants have been determined defenders of "Old Sam's" public image. When noted Texas historian Eugene C. Barker presumed to edit and publish a number of primary accounts, some of which were mildly critical of Houston's conduct of the campaign, the general's family demanded—and received—a public apology in the pages of the *Quarterly of the Texas State Historical Association*.

Objective historians can no longer ignore the sheer mass of Houston criticism. To those familiar with the events of the San Jacinto campaign, much of the condemnation appears well founded. The time has come for scholars to set aside the hagiography penned by political hacks and hero worshipers in order to gain a fresh perspective on the "Sword of San Jacinto" and his role in the campaign.

7. Travis to Henry Smith, January 9, 1836, in Jenkins, ed., *Papers*, V, 185; B. H. Duval to William P. Duval, March 9, 1836, in Jenkins, ed., *Papers*, V, 33–35; Jack Jackson, *Los Mesteños: Spanish Ranching in Texas, 1721–1821*, 610–617.

8. Stephen L. Hardin, *The Texas Rangers*, 3–4; for aspects of Anglo cultural borrowing, see Tijerina, "Tejanos and Texas."

9. Gene Brack, "Mexican Opinion and the Texas Revolution," *Southwestern Historical Quarterly* 72 (October 1968): 170–171.

10. *El Mosquito Mexicano* (Mexico, D.F.), June 14 and 17, 1836.

11. Wharton, *San Jacinto*; the inscription is quoted in Pohl, *Battle of San Jacinto*, 48.

SELECTED BIBLIOGRAPHY

ARCHIVAL COLLECTIONS
Center for American History, University of Texas at Austin
Barker, Eugene C. Papers.
Bennet, Valentine. Papers.
Bexar Archives.
Brooks, John Sowers. Letters.
Burkett, Nathan Boon. Reminiscences.
Duval, John C. Papers.
Filisola, Vicente. Papers.
Hale, Philip Smith. Papers.
Hatch, James. Papers.
Hatch, Sylvanus. Narrative.
Huson, Hobart. Narratives.
Kuykendall Family Papers.
Looscan, Adele Lubbock Briscoe. Papers.
Mitchell, Nathan. Papers.
Muster Rolls.
Raguet, Henry. Family Papers.
Reams, Sherwood. Letter.
Rees, Thomas B. Letter.
Rogers, Samuel C. A. Reminiscences.
Rusk, Thomas Jefferson. Papers.
Sinks, Julia. Papers.
Sparks, S. F. Papers.
Texas Veterans Association. Papers.

Thomas, Anne Raney. Papers.

Travis, William Barret. Papers.

Turner, Amasa. Papers.

Archives and Library Division, Texas State Library

Army Papers.

Audited Military Claims, Comptroller of Public Accounts.

Home Papers.

Houston, A. J. Collection.

Lamar, Mirabeau B. Papers.

Memorials and Petitions.

Seguín, Juan N. Papers.

PUBLISHED PRIMARY MATERIALS

Books and Pamphlets

Austin, Stephen F. *The Austin Papers*. Compiled and edited by Eugene C. Barker. 3 vols. Washington, D.C., and Austin: American Historical Association and University of Texas, 1919–1926.

Becerra, Francisco. *A Mexican Sergeant's Recollections of the Alamo and San Jacinto . . . as Told to John S. Ford in 1875*. Introduction by Dan Kilgore. Austin: Jenkins Publishing Co., 1980.

Binkley, William C., ed. *Official Correspondence of the Texan Revolution, 1835–1836*. 2 vols. New York: D. Appleton–Century Co., 1936.

Burnet, D[avid] G. *Review of the Life of Gen. Sam Houston, as Recently Published in Washington City, by J. T. Towers*. Galveston: News Power Press Print, 1852.

[Coleman, Robert M.] *Houston Displayed; or, Who Won the Battle of San Jacinto? By a Farmer in the Army, Reproduced From the Original*. Introduction by John H. Jenkins. 1837; reprint, Austin: Brick Row Book Shop, 1964.

Crockett, David. *A Narrative of the Life of David Crockett of the State of Tennessee*. Introduction by Paul Andrew Hutton. 1834; reprint, Lincoln: University of Nebraska Press, 1987.

de la Peña, José Enrique. *With Santa Anna in Texas: A Personal Narrative of the Revolution*. Translated and edited by Carmen Perry. College Station: Texas A&M University Press, 1975.

de la Teja, Jesús F., ed. *A Revolution Remembered: The Memoirs and Selected Correspondence of Juan N. Seguín*. Austin: State House Press, 1991. Dr. de la Teja's incisive annotations make this the best edition of Seguín's *Personal Memoirs*, listed herein separately.

Delgado, Pedro. *Mexican Account of the Battle of San Jacinto.* Deepwater, Tex.: W. C. Day, 1919.

DeShields, James T., comp. *Tall Men with Long Rifles: Set Down and Written Out by James T. DeShields as Told to Him by Creed Taylor, Captain during the Texas Revolution.* San Antonio: Naylor Co., 1935.

Duval, John C. *Early Times in Texas; or, The Adventures of Jack Dobell.* 1892; reprint, Lincoln: University of Nebraska Press, 1986.

Edward, David Barnett. *The History of Texas; or, The Emigrant's, Farmer's, and Politician's Guide to the Character, Climate, Soil and Productions of That Country; Geographically Arranged From Personal Observation and Experience.* Cincinnati: J. A. James & Co., 1836.

Ehrenberg, Herman. *With Milam and Fannin: Adventures of a German Boy in Texas' Revolution.* Translated by Charlotte Churchill. Edited by Henry Smith. Foreword by Herbert Gambrell. Dallas: Tardy Publishing Co., 1935.

Field, Joseph E. *Three Years in Texas, Including a View of the Texan Revolution, and an Account of the Principal Battles, Together With Descriptions of the Soil, Commercial and Agricultural Advantages, etc.* 1836; reprint, Austin: Steck Co., 1935.

Filisola, Vicente. *Evacuation of Texas: Translation of the Representation Addressed to the Supreme Government by Gen. Vicente Filisola, in Defence of his Honor, and Explanation of his Operations as Commander-in-Chief of the Army Against Texas.* Columbia, Tex.: G. & T. H. Borden, Public Printers, 1837.

———. *Memoirs for the History of the War in Texas.* 2 vols. Translated by Wallace Woolsey. 1849; reprint, Austin: Eakin Press, 1986, 1987.

Gaddy, Jerry J., comp. and ed. *Texas in Revolt: Contemporary Newspaper Account of the Texas Revolution.* Fort Collins, Colo.: Old Army Press, 1973.

Gammel, Hans Peter Nielson, comp. *The Laws of Texas, 1822–1897.* 10 vols. Austin: Gammel Book Co., 1898.

Gray, William Fairfax. *From Virginia to Texas, 1835: Diary of Col. Wm. S. Gray, Giving Details of His Journey to Texas and Return in 1835–1836 and Second Journey to Texas in 1837.* 1909; reprint, Houston: Fletcher Young Publishing Co., 1965.

Green, Rena Maverick, ed. *Samuel Maverick, Texan, 1803–1870: A Collection of Letters, Journals, and Memoirs.* San Antonio: Privately printed, 1952.

Hall, Robert. *Life of Robert Hall.* 1898; reprint, Austin: State House Press, 1992. Introduction to new edition by Stephen L. Hardin.

Helm, Mary Sherwood. *Scraps of Early Texas History, By Mrs. Mary S. Helm Who, With Her First Husband, Elias R. Wightman, Founded the City of*

Matagorda, in 1828–9. Austin: Printed for the author at the Office of B. R. Warmer & Co., 1884.

Holley, Mary Austin. *Texas.* 1836; reprint, Austin: Texas State Historical Association, 1985.

Houston, Sam. *The Writings of Sam Houston, 1813–1863.* 8 vols. Edited by Amelia Williams and Eugene C. Barker. Austin: University of Texas Press, 1938–1943.

Hunter, Robert Hancock. *Narrative of Robert Hancock Hunter.* Introduction by William D. Wittlif. 1936; reprint, Austin: Encino Press, 1966.

Jenkins, John H., ed. *The Papers of The Texas Revolution, 1835–1836.* 10 vols. Austin: Presidial Press, 1973.

Jenkins, John Holland. *Recollections of Early Texas: The Memoirs of John Holland Jenkins.* Edited by John Holmes Jenkins III. Austin: University of Texas Press, 1958.

Johnson, Frank W. *A History of Texas and Texans.* 5 vols. Edited by Eugene C. Barker. Chicago and New York: American Historical Association, 1914.

Jones, Anson. *Memoranda and Official Correspondence Relating to the Republic of Texas, its History and Annexation, Including a Brief Autobiography of the Author.* 1859; reprint, Chicago: Rio Grande Press, 1966.

Lamar, Mirabeau Buonaparte. *The Papers of Mirabeau Buonaparte Lamar.* 6 vols. Edited by Charles A. Gulick, Katherine Elliot, Winnie Allen, and Harriet Smither. Austin: Pemberton Press, 1968.

Lamar, Mirabeau Buonaparte, Jesse Billingsley, et al., *Defence of Gen. Sidney Sherman Against the Charges Made by Gen. Sam Houston, in His Speech Delivered in the United States Senate, February 28th, 1859.* Galveston: Printed at the "News" Book and Job Office, 1859; reprint, Houston: Smallwood, Dealy & Baker, 1885.

Lane, Walter P. *The Adventures and Recollections of General Walter P. Lane, a San Jacinto Veteran, Containing Sketches of the Texan, Mexican, and Late Wars with Several Indian Fights Thrown In.* 1928; reprint, Austin: Pemberton Press, 1970.

Linn, John J. *Reminiscences of Fifty Years in Texas.* New York: D. & J. Sadlier & Co., 1886.

Lockhart, John Washington. *Sixty Years on the Brazos: The Life and Letters of Dr. John Washington Lockhart, 1824–1900.* Los Angeles: Press of Dunn Bros., 1930.

McLean, Malcolm D., comp. and ed. *Papers Concerning Robertson's Colony in Texas.* 13 vols. Fort Worth: Texas Christian University Press (vols. I–III), and Arlington: UTA Press, University of Texas at Arlington, 1974–1993.

Menchaca, Antonio. *Memoirs.* San Antonio: Yanaguana Society Publications, 1937.

Morrell, Zachariah Nehemiah. *Flowers and Fruits From the Wilderness; or, Thirty-Six Years in Texas and Two Winters in Honduras.* Dallas: W. G. Scarff & Co., Publishers, 1886.

Newell, Chester. *History of the Revolution in Texas, Particularly of the War of 1835 & 36, Together With the Latest Geographical, Topographical and Statistical Accounts of the Country, From the Most Authentic Sources, Also, an Appendix.* New York: Wiley & Putnam, 1838.

Sánchez-Navarro, Carlos. *La Guerra de Tejas: Memorias de un Soldado.* Mexico, D.F.: Editoral Jus, 1960.

Santa Anna, Antonio López de. *The Eagle: The Autobiography of Santa Anna.* Edited by Ann Fears Crawford. Austin: Pemberton Press, 1967.

Santa Anna, Antonio López de, et al. *The Mexican Side of the Texas Revolution.* Translated and edited by Carlos E. Castañeda. Dallas: Graphic Ideas, 1970.

Seguín, Juan N. *Personal Memoirs of John N. Seguin, From the Year 1834 to the Retreat of General Woll From the City of San Antonio, 1842.* San Antonio: Ledger Book and Job Office, 1858.

Smithwick, Noah. *The Evolution of a State; or, Recollections of Old Texas Days.* Compiled by Nanna Smithwick Donaldson. 1900; reprint, Austin: University of Texas Press, 1983.

Sutherland, John. *The Fall of the Alamo.* San Antonio: Naylor Co., 1936.

Travis, William B. *The Diary of William Barret Travis, August 30, 1833–June 26, 1835.* Edited by Robert E. Davis. Waco: Texian Press, 1966.

A Visit to Texas, Being the Journal of a Traveller Through Those Parts Most Interesting to American Settlers, With Descriptions of Scenery, Habits, &c. &c. New York: Van Nostrand and Dwight, 1836.

Articles

Almonte, Juan Nepomuceno. "The Private Journal of Juan Nepomuceno Almonte." Introduction by Samuel E. Asbury. *Southwestern Historical Quarterly* 47 (July 1944): 10–32.

———. "Statistical Report on Texas [1835]." Translated by Carlos E. Castañeda. *Southwestern Historical Quarterly* 27 (January 1925): 177–222.

Austin, Stephen F. "General Austin's Order Book for the Campaign of 1835." *Quarterly of the Texas State Historical Association* 11 (July 1907): 1–56.

Austin, William T. "Account of the Campaign of 1835 by William T. Austin, Aid[e] to Gen. Stephen F. Austin & Gen. Ed Burleson." *Texana* 4 (Winter 1966): 287–322.

Baker, Mosely. "Extracts from Mosely Baker's Letter to Houston." Edited by Eugene C. Barker. *Quarterly of the Texas State Historical Association* 4 (April 1901): 272–287.

[Bannister, Charles B.]. "The Storming of San Antonio de Bexar in 1835." Edited by M. L. Crimmins. *West Texas Historical Association Yearbook* 22 (1946): 95–117.

Bennet, Miles S. "The Battle of Gonzales, the 'Lexington' of the Texas Revolution." *Quarterly of the Texas State Historical Association* 2 (April 1899): 313–316.

Bostick, Sion. "Reminiscences of Sion Bostick." *Quarterly of the Texas State Historical Association* 5 (October 1901): 85–95.

Boyle, Andrew A. "Reminiscences of the Texas Revolution." *Quarterly of the Texas State Historical Association* 13 (April 1910): 285–291.

Calder, R. J. "R. J. Calder's Recollections of the Campaign." Edited by Eugene C. Barker. *Quarterly of the Texas State Historical Association* 4 (April 1901): 334–338.

Erath, George Bernard. "The Memoirs of Major George Bernard Erath 1813–1891." Edited by Lucy A. Erath. *Southwestern Historical Quarterly* 26, 27 (January 1923, April 1923, July 1923, October 1923): 207–233, 255–279, 27–51, 120–139.

Kuykendall, J. H. "Recollections of the Campaign." Edited by Eugene C. Barker. *Quarterly of the Texas State Historical Association* 4 (April 1901): 291–306.

Kuykendall, J. H., ed. "Reminiscences of Early Texans." *Quarterly of the Texas State Historical Association* 6, 7 (January 1903, April 1903, July 1903): 236–253, 311–330, 29–64.

"A Letter from San Antonio de Bexar in 1836." *Southwestern Historical Quarterly* 62 (April 1959): 513–518.

Nuñez, Félix. "Notes and Documents—The Félix Nuñez Account and the Siege of the Alamo: A Critical Appraisal." Edited by Stephen L. Hardin. *Southwestern Historical Quarterly* 94 (July 1990): 65–84. While this purports to be a primary account, it is severely flawed and should be employed with caution.

Potter, R. M. "Escape of Karnes and Teal from Matamoros." *Southwestern Historical Quarterly* 4 (October 1900): 71–84.

Smith, Henry. "Reminiscences of Henry Smith." *Quarterly of the Texas State Historical Association* 14 (July 1910): 24–73.

Sparks, S. F. "Recollections of S. F. Sparks." *Quarterly of the Texas State Historical Association* 12 (July 1908): 61–79.

Turner, Amasa. "Amasa Turner's Account of the Battle." Edited by Eugene C.

Barker. *Quarterly of the Texas State Historical Association* 4 (April 1901): 340–343.

Winters, James Washington. "An Account of the Battle of San Jacinto." *Quarterly of the Texas State Historical Association* 6 (October 1902): 139–144.

Zuber, W. P. "Zuber's Account of the Camp at Harrisburg." Edited by Eugene C. Barker. *Quarterly of the Texas State Historical Association* 4 (April 1901): 338–339.

SECONDARY MATERIALS

Books

Adair, A. Garland, and M. H. Crockett, eds. *Heroes of the Alamo: Accounts and Documents of William B. Travis, James Bowie, James B. Bonham, and David Crockett, and Their Texas Memorials.* New York: Exposition Press, 1957.

Alessio Robles, Vito. *Coahuila y Texas desde la consumación de la independencia hasta el Tratado de Paz de Guadalupe Hidalgo.* 2d ed. Mexico, D.F.: Editorial Porrua, 1979.

Baker, DeWitt Clinton. *A Texas Scrap-Book, Made Up of the History, Biography, and Miscellany of Texas and its People.* New York: A. S. Barnes & Co., 1875.

Bancroft, Hubert Howe. *History of the North Mexican States and Texas.* 2 vols. 1889; reprint, New York: Arno Press, n.d.

Barker, Eugene C. *The Life of Stephen F. Austin, Founder of Texas, 1793–1836: A Chapter in the Westward Movement of the Anglo-American People.* 1925; reprint, Austin: Texas State Historical Association, 1949.

———. *Mexico and Texas, 1821–1835: University of Texas Research Lectures on the Causes of the Texas Revolution.* Dallas: P. L. Turner Co., Publishers, 1928.

Barr, Alwyn. *Black Texans: A History of Negroes in Texas, 1528–1971.* Austin: Jenkins Publishing Co., 1973.

———. *Texas in Revolt: The Battle for San Antonio, 1835.* Austin: University of Texas Press, 1990.

Battles of Texas. Waco: Texian Press, 1967.

Bauer, K. Jack. *The Mexican War, 1846–1848.* New York: Macmillan, 1974.

Baugh, Virgil E. *Rendezvous at the Alamo: Highlights in the Lives of Bowie, Crockett, and Travis.* New York: Pageant Press, 1960.

Beers, Henry Putney. *The Western Military Frontier, 1815–1846.* 1935; reprint, Philadelphia: Porcupine Press, 1975.

Benavides, Adán, ed. *The Bexar Archives (1717–1836): A Name Guide.* Austin: University of Texas Press, 1989.

Bennett, Leonora. *Historical Sketch and Guide to the Alamo.* San Antonio: Privately printed, 1902.

Billington, Ray A. *The Far Western Frontier, 1830–1860.* New York: Harper & Row, 1956.

Binkley, William C. *The Texas Revolution.* Baton Rouge: Louisiana State University, 1952.

Biographical Directory of the Texan Conventions and Congresses, 1832–1845. Austin: Book Exchange, 1941.

Brack, Gene M. *Mexico Views Manifest Destiny, 1821–1846: An Essay on the Origins of the Mexican War.* Albuquerque: University of New Mexico Press, 1975.

Brinckerhoff, Sidney B., and Odie B. Faulk. *Lancers for the King: A Study of a Frontier Military System of Northern New Spain, with a Translation of the Royal Regulations of 1772.* Phoenix: Arizona Historical Foundation, 1965.

Brown, John Henry. *History of Texas from 1685 to 1892.* 2 vols. St. Louis: L. E. Daniell, Publisher, 1892–1893.

———. *Indian Wars and Pioneers of Texas.* Austin: L. E. Daniell, Publisher, 1896.

Butterfield, Jack C. *Men of the Alamo, Goliad, and San Jacinto: An Analysis of the Motives and Actions of the Heroes of the Texas Revolution.* San Antonio: Naylor Co., 1936.

Callcott, Wilfred Hardy. *Santa Anna: The Story of an Enigma Who Once Was Mexico.* Norman: University of Oklahoma Press, 1936.

Campbell, Randolph B. *An Empire for Slavery: The Peculiar Institution in Texas, 1821–1865.* Baton Rouge: Louisiana State University Press, 1989.

———. *Sam Houston and the American Southwest.* New York: HarperCollins College Publishers, 1993.

Canales, José Thomas, ed. *Bits of Texas History in the Melting Pot of America: Native Latin American Contribution to Colonization and Independence of Texas.* San Antonio: Artes Graficas, 1957.

Castañeda, Carlos E. *Our Catholic Heritage in Texas, 1519–1936.* 6 vols. Austin: Von Boeckmann–Jones Company, 1936–1958.

Chabot, Frederick C. *The Alamo, Altar of Texas Liberty.* San Antonio: Privately printed, 1931.

———. *With the Makers of Old San Antonio, Genealogies of the Early Latin, Anglo-American, and German Families with Occasional Biographies, Each Group Being Prefaced with a Brief Historical Sketch and Illustrations.* San Antonio: Privately printed, 1937.

Chariton, Wallace O. *Exploring the Alamo Legends*. Plano, Tex.: Wordware Publishing, 1990.

———. *One Hundred Days in Texas: The Alamo Letters*. Plano, Tex.: Wordware Publishing, 1990.

Coalson, George. "Texas Mexicans in the Texas Revolution." In *The American West: Essays in Honor of W. Eugene Hollon*. Edited by Ronald Lora. Toledo: University of Toledo, 1980.

Connor, Seymour V., et al. *Battles of Texas*. Waco: Texian Press, 1967.

Corner, William. *San Antonio de Bexar: A Guide and History*. San Antonio: Bainbridge and Corner, 1890.

Cox, Mamie Wynne. *The Romantic Flags of Texas*. Dallas: Banks Upshaw and Co., 1936.

Day, James M., comp. and ed. *The Texas Almanac, 1857–1873: A Compendium of Texas History*. Waco: Texian Press, 1967.

De Leon, Arnoldo. *The Tejano Community, 1836–1900*. Albuquerque: University of New Mexico Press, 1982.

———. *They Called Them Greasers: Anglo Attitudes towards Mexicans in Texas, 1821–1900*. Austin: University of Texas Press, 1983.

Diccionario Porrua de historia, biografía, y geografía de Mexico. 3 vols. 5th ed. Mexico, D.F.: Editorial Porrua, 1986.

Dixon, Sam Houston, and Louis Wiltz Kemp. *The Heroes of San Jacinto*. Houston: Anson Jones Press, 1932.

Dobie, J. Frank, Mody C. Boatright, and Harry H. Ransom, eds. *In the Shadow of History*. Dallas: Southern Methodist University Press, 1980.

Douglas, Claude L. *Jim Bowie: The Life of a Bravo*. Dallas: Bank Upshaw and Co., 1944.

Drossaerts, Arthur J. *The Truth about the Burial of the Remains of the Alamo Heroes*. San Antonio: Privately printed, 1938.

Earl, Edward Mead. *Makers of Modern Strategy*. Princeton: Princeton University Press, 1971.

Fehrenbach, T. R. *Lone Star: A History of Texas and the Texans*. New York: Macmillan Co., 1968.

———. *Seven Keys to Texas*. El Paso: Texas Western Press, 1983.

Foote, Henry Stuart. *Texas and the Texans; or, Advance of the Anglo-Americans to the Southwest Including a History of Leading Events in Mexico, From the Conquest of Fernando Cortes to the Termination of the Texas Revolution*. 2 vols. Philadelphia: Thomas, Cowperthwait & Co., 1841.

Foreman, Gary L. *Crockett, the Gentleman from the Cane: A Comprehensive*

View of the Folkhero Americans Thought They Knew. Dallas: Taylor Publishing Co., n.d.

Friend, Llerena Beaufort. *Sam Houston: The Great Designer*. Austin: University of Texas Press, 1954.

Fuentes Mares, José. *Santa Anna: Aurora y Ocaso de un Comediande*. Mexico, D.F.: Editorial Jus, 1956.

Gaillardet, Theodore Frederic. *Sketches of Early Texas and Louisiana*. Austin: University of Texas Press, 1966.

Gambrell, Herbert Pickens. *Anson Jones: The Last President of Texas*. Austin: University of Texas Press, 1964.

Gouge, William M. *The Fiscal History of Texas, Embracing An Account of its Revenues, Debts, and Currency, From the Commencement of the Revolution in 1834 to 1851–52, with Remarks on American Debts*. Philadelphia: Lippincott, Grambo, and Co., 1852.

Gould, Stephen. *The Alamo City Guide. San Antonio, Texas. Being a Historical Sketch of the Ancient City of the Alamo, and Business Review; With Notes of Present Advantages, Together With a Complete Guide to All the Prominent Points of Interest About the City, and a Compilation of Facts of Value to Visitors and Residents*. New York: MacGowan & Slipper, Printers, 1882.

Hanigen, Frank C. *Santa Anna: The Napoleon of the West*. New York: Coward-McCann, 1934.

Hardin, Stephen L. *The Texas Rangers*. London: Osprey Publishing, 1991.

Hauck, Richard B. *Crockett: A Bio-Bibliography*. Westport, Conn.: Greenwood Press, 1982.

Hayes, Charles W. *Galveston: History of the Island and the City*. 2 vols. Austin: Jenkins Garrett Press, 1974.

Haythornthwaite, Philip. *The Alamo and the War of Texas Independence*. London: Osprey Publishing, 1986.

Hill, James Michael. *Celtic Warfare, 1595–1763*. Edinburgh: John Donald Publishers, 1986.

Hill, Jim Dan. *The Minute Man in Peace and War: A History of the National Guard*. Harrisburg, Pa.: Stackpole, 1964.

Hogan, William Ransom. *The Texas Republic: A Social and Economic History*. Norman: University of Oklahoma Press, 1946.

Holman, David, and Billie Persons. *Buckskin and Homespun: Texas Frontier Clothing, 1820–1870*. Austin: Wind River Press, 1979.

Houston, Andrew Jackson. *Texas Independence*. Houston: Anson Jones Press, 1938.

Huson, Hobart. *Captain Phillip Dimmitt's Commandancy of Goliad, 1835–*

1836: An Episode of the Mexican Federalist War in Texas Usually Referred to as the Texian Revolution. Austin: Von Boeckmann–Jones Co., 1974.

Huson, Hobart. *Refugio: A Comprehensive History of Refugio County from Aboriginal Times to 1953.* 2 vols. Woodsboro, Tex.: Rooke Foundation, 1953–1955.

Huston, Cleburn. *Deaf Smith: Incredible Texas Spy.* Waco: Texian Press, 1973.

Jackson, Jack. *Los Tejanos.* Stamford: Fantagraphics Books, 1982.

———. *Los Mesteños: Spanish Ranching in Texas, 1721–1821.* College Station: Texas A&M University Press, 1986.

James, Marquis. *The Raven: A Biography of Sam Houston.* Indianapolis: Bobbs-Merrill Co., 1929.

Jenkins, John H. *Basic Texas Books: An Annotated Bibliography of Selected Works for a Research Library.* Austin: Jenkins Publishing Co., 1983.

Jenkins, John H., and Kenneth Kesselus. *Edward Burleson: Texas Frontier Leader.* Austin: Jenkins Publishing Co., 1990.

Jomini, Antoine Henri. *Jomini and His Summary of the Art of War.* Edited by J. D. Hittle. Harrisburg, Pa.: Stackpole Books, 1947.

Jones, Oakah L., Jr. *Santa Anna.* New York: Twayne Publishers, 1968.

Kemp, Louis Wiltz. *The Signers of the Texas Declaration of Independence.* Houston: Anson Jones Press, 1944.

Kemp, D. W., and Ed Kilman. *The Battle of San Jacinto and the San Jacinto Campaign.* Houston: Webb Printing Co., 1947.

Kennedy, William. *Texas: The Rise, Progress, and Prospects of the Republic of Texas.* Fort Worth: Molyneaux Craftsmen, 1925.

Kesselus, Kenneth. *History of Bastrop County, Texas, before Statehood.* Austin: Jenkins Publishing Co., 1986.

Kilgore, Dan. *How Did Davy Die?* College Station: Texas A&M University Press, 1978.

King, C. Richard. *Susanna Dickinson, Messenger of the Alamo.* Austin: Shoal Creek Publishers, 1976.

Lack, Paul D. *The Texas Revolutionary Experience: A Political and Social History, 1835–1836.* College Station: Texas A&M University Press, 1992.

Lamego, Miguel A. Sánchez. *The Siege and Taking of the Alamo.* Translated by Consuelo Velasco. Santa Fe: Blue Feather Press for the Press of the Territorian, 1968.

Lanza, Conrad H., comp. *Napoleon and Modern War: His Military Maxims Revised and Annotated.* Harrisburg, Pa.: Military Service Publishing Company, 1943.

Leach, Joseph. *The Typical Texan: Biography of an American Myth*. Dallas: Southern Methodist University Press, 1952.

Leclerc, Frederic. *Texas and Its Revolution*. Translated by James L. Shepard. Houston: Anson Jones Press, 1950.

[Lester, Charles Edwards]. *The Life of Sam Houston: The Only Authentic Memoir of Him Ever Published*. New York: J. C. Derby, 1855.

Lofaro, Michael A. *Davy Crockett: The Man, the Myth, the Legacy*. Knoxville: University of Tennessee Press, 1985.

Long, Charles J. *1836: The Alamo*. San Antonio: Daughters of the Republic of Texas, 1981.

Lord, Walter. *A Time to Stand*. New York: Harper & Brothers, 1961.

Lowrie, Samuel H. *Culture Conflict in Texas, 1821–1835*. New York: Columbia University Press, 1932.

Lozano, Reuben Rendon. *Viva Tejas: The Story of the Mexican-born Patriots of the Republic of Texas*. San Antonio: Southern Literary Institute, 1936.

Lukes, Edward A. *DeWitt Colony of Texas*. Austin: Jenkins Publishing Co., 1979.

McDonald, Archie P. *The Trail to San Jacinto*. Boston: American Press, 1982.

———. *Travis*. Austin: Jenkins Publishing Co., 1976.

McWhiney, Grady. *Cracker Culture: Celtic Ways in the Old South*. Tuscaloosa: University of Alabama Press, 1988.

Meinig, D. W. *Imperial Texas: An Interpretive Essay in Cultural Geography*. Austin: University of Texas Press, 1969.

Merk, Frederick. *Slavery and the Annexation of Texas*. New York: Alfred A. Knopf, 1972.

Miller, Thomas Lloyd. *Bounty and Donation Land Grants of Texas, 1835–1888*. Austin: University of Texas Press, 1967.

Montejano, David. *Anglos and Mexicans in the Making of Texas, 1836–1986*. Austin: University of Texas Press, 1987.

Moorehead, Max L. *The Presidio: Bastion of the Spanish Borderlands*. Norman: University of Oklahoma Press, 1975.

Morphis, J. M. *History of Texas From its Discovery and Settlement, With a Description of its Principal Cities and Counties, and the Agricultural, Mineral, and Material Resources of the State*. New York: Van Nostrand, 1874.

Muñoz, Rafael F. *Santa Anna*. Mexico, D.F.: Editorial "Mexico Nuevo," 1937.

Myers, John Myers. *The Alamo*. New York: E. P. Dutton and Co., 1948.

Neito, Angelina, Joseph Hefter, and Mrs. John Nicholas Brown. *El Soldado Mexicano, 1837–1847: Organización, Vestuario, Equipo*. Mexico, D.F.: Privately printed, 1958.

Nevin, David. *The Texans*. New York: Time-Life Books, 1975.

Nixon, Patrick Ireland. *The Medical Story of Early Texas, 1528–1853*. Lancaster, Pa.: Mollie Bennett Lupe Memorial Fund, 1946.

Oates, Stephen B., ed., *The Republic of Texas*. Palo Alto: American West Publishing Co. and Texas State Historical Association, 1968.

Oberste, William Herman. *Texas Irish Empresarios and Their Colonies: Power and Hewetson, McMullen & McGloin, Refugio–San Patricio*. Austin: Von Boeckmann–Jones Co., 1953.

O'Connor, Kathryn Stoner. *The Presidio La Bahia del Espiritu Santo de Zuniga, 1721 to 1846*. Austin: Von Boeckmann–Jones Co., 1966.

Pereyra, Carlos. *Tejas, la Primera Desmembración de Mejico*. Madrid: Editorial-America, 1917.

Peterson, Harold L. *Ramshot and Rammers*. New York: Bonanza Books, 1969.

Pickrell, Annie Doom. *Pioneer Women in Texas*. Austin: E. L. Steck Co., 1929.

Pohl, James W. *The Battle of San Jacinto*. Austin: Texas State Historical Association, 1989.

Potter, Reuben M. *The Fall of the Alamo*. 1878; reprint, Hillsdale, N.J.: Otterden Press, 1977.

Procter, Ben H. *The Battle of the Alamo*. Austin: Texas State Historical Association, 1986.

Prucha, Francis Paul. *The Sword of the Republic: The United States Army on the Frontier, 1783–1834*. New York: Macmillan, 1969.

Ratcliffe, Sam DeShong. *Painting Texas History to 1900*. Austin: University of Texas Press, 1992.

Reichstein, Andreas V. *Rise of the Lone Star: The Making of Texas*. College Station: Texas A&M University Press, 1989.

Renatus, Flavius Vegetius. *Military Institutions of the Romans*. Translated by John Clark. Edited by Thomas R. Phillips. Harrisburg, Pa.: Stackpole Books, 1944.

Richardson, Rupert Norval. *Texas: The Lone Star State*. Englewood Cliffs, N.J.: Prentice-Hall, 1958.

Rives, George Lockhart. *The United States and Mexico, 1821–1848: A History of the Relations between the Two Countries from the Independence of Mexico to the Close of the War with the United States*. New York: Charles Scribner's Sons, 1913.

Rosenthal, Phil. *Alamo Soldiers: An Armchair Historian's Guide to the Defenders of the Alamo*. N.p.: Privately printed, 1989.

Rosenthal, Phil, and Bill Groneman. *Roll Call at the Alamo*. Fort Collins, Colo.: Old Army Press, 1985.

Ross, Steven. *From Flintlock to Rifle: Infantry Tactics, 1740–1866.* London: Associated University Presses, 1979.

Ryan, William M. *Shamrock and Cactus: The Story of the Catholic Heroes of Texas Independence.* San Antonio: Southern Literary Institute, 1936.

Santos, Richard G. *Santa Anna's Campaign against Texas, 1835–1836, Featuring the Field Commands Issued to Major General Vicente Filisola.* Waco: Texian Press, 1968.

Schoelwer, Susan Prendergast, with Tom W. Gläser. *Alamo Images: Changing Perceptions of a Texas Experience.* Dallas: De Golyer Library and Southern Methodist University Press, 1985.

[Sedgwick, Theodore]. *Thoughts on the Proposed Annexation of Texas to the United States.* New York: D. Fanshaw, 1844.

Shackford, James Atkins. *David Crockett: The Man and the Legend.* Edited by John B. Shackford. Chapel Hill: University of North Carolina Press, 1956.

Sowell, Andrew Jackson. *Early Settlers and Indian Fighters of Southwest Texas . . . Facts Gathered from Survivors of Frontier Days.* Austin: Ben C. Jones & Co., Printers, 1900.

———. *Rangers and Pioneers of Texas, With a Concise Account of Early Settlements, Hardships, Massacres, Battles, and Wars by Which Texas Was Rescued From the Rule of the Savage and Consecrated to the Empire of Civilization.* San Antonio: Shepard Bros. & Co., Printers and Publishers, 1884.

Taylor, I. T. *The Cavalcade of Jackson County.* San Antonio: Naylor Co., 1938.

Thorp, Raymond W. *Bowie Knife.* Albuquerque: University of New Mexico Press, 1948.

Tinkle, Lon. *13 Days to Glory: The Siege of the Alamo.* 1958; reprint, College Station: Texas A&M University Press, 1985.

Tolbert, Frank X. *The Day of San Jacinto.* New York: McGraw-Hill Book Co., 1959.

Trammell, Camilla Davis. *Seven Pines: Its Occupants and Their Letters, 1825–1872.* Dallas: SMU Press, 1986.

Trujillo, Rafael. *Olvidate de El Alamo.* Mexico, D.F.: Populibros "La Prensa," 1965.

Turner, Martha Anne. *William Barret Travis: His Sword and His Pen.* Waco: Texian Press, 1972.

Valades, José C. *Mexico, Santa Anna y la guerra de Texas.* Mexico, D.F.: Imprenta Mundial, 1936.

Vigness, David M. *The Revolutionary Decades.* Austin: Steck Vaughn, 1965.

Walraven, Bill, and Marjorie K. Walraven. *The Magnificent Barbarians: Little-told Tales of the Texas Revolution.* Austin: Eakin Press, 1993.

Webb, Walter Prescott. *The Texas Rangers: A Century of Frontier Defense.* Boston: Houghton Mifflin Co., Riverside Press, 1935.

Webb, Walter P., H. Bailey Carroll, and Eldon Stephen Branda, eds. *The Handbook of Texas.* 3 vols. Austin: Texas State Historical Association, 1952, 1976.

Weber, David J. *The Mexican Frontier, 1821–1846: The American Southwest under Mexico.* Albuquerque: University of New Mexico Press, 1982.

———. *Myth and the History of the Southwest: Essays by David J. Weber.* Albuquerque: University of New Mexico Press, 1988.

Weigley, Russell F. *The American Way of War: A History of the United States Military Strategy and Policy.* New York: Macmillan, 1973.

Wharton, Clarence R. *El Presidente: A Sketch of the Life of General Santa Anna.* Houston: C. C. Young Printing Co., 1924.

———. *San Jacinto: The Sixteenth Decisive Battle.* Houston: Lamar Book Store, 1930.

Wilbarger, J. W. *Indian Depredations in Texas, Reliable Accounts of Battles, Wars, Adventures, Forays, Murders, Massacres, etc., Together With Biographical Sketches of Many of the Most Noted Indian Fighters and Frontiersmen of Texas.* Austin: Hutchings Printing House, 1889.

Williams, Alfred M. *Sam Houston and the War of Independence in Texas.* Boston: Houghton, Mifflin and Co., 1895.

Windrow, Martin, and Richard Hook. *The Footsoldier.* Oxford: Oxford University Press, 1982.

Wisenhunt, M. K. *Sam Houston: American Giant.* Washington, D.C.: Robert B. Luce, 1962.

Wooten, Dudley G., ed. *A Comprehensive History of Texas, 1685 to 1897.* 2 vols. 1898; reprint, Austin: Texas State Historical Association, 1986.

Wortham, Louis J. *A History of Texas from Wilderness to Commonwealth.* 5 vols. Fort Worth: Wortham-Molyneaux Co., 1924.

Yoakum, Henderson King. *History of Texas From its First Settlement in 1655 to its Annexation to the United States in 1846.* 2 vols. New York: Redfield, 1855.

Articles

Barker, Eugene C. "Declaration of Causes for Taking Up Arms against Mexico." *Quarterly of the Texas State Historical Association* 15 (January 1912): 173–185.

———. "James H. C. Miller and Edward Gritten." *Quarterly of the Texas State Historical Association* 13 (October 1909): 145–152.

———. "Land Speculation as a Cause of the Texas Revolution." *Quarterly of the Texas State Historical Association* 10 (July 1906): 76–95.

———. "Native Latin American Contribution to the Colonization and Independence of Texas." *Southwestern Historical Quarterly* 46 (April 1943): 317–335.

———. "Stephen F. Austin and the Independence of Texas." *Quarterly of the Texas State Historical Association* 13 (April 1910): 257–284.

———. "The Tampico Expedition." *Quarterly of the Texas State Historical Association* 6 (January 1903): 169–186.

———. "The Texas Revolutionary Army." *Quarterly of the Texas State Historical Association* 9 (April 1906): 227–261.

Barton, Henry W. "The Anglo-American Colonists under Mexican Militia Laws." *Southwestern Historical Quarterly* 65 (July 1961): 61–71.

———. "The Problem of Command in the Army of the Republic." *Southwestern Historical Quarterly* 62 (January 1959): 299–311.

Brack, Gene. "Mexican Opinion and the Texas Revolution." *Southwestern Historical Quarterly* 72 (October 1968): 170–182.

Cleaves, W. S. "Lorenzo De Zavala in Texas." *Southwestern Historical Quarterly* 36 (July 1932): 29–40.

Costeloe, Michael P. "The Mexican Press of 1836 and the Battle of the Alamo." *Southwestern Historical Quarterly* 91 (April 1988): 533–543.

Crane, R. C. "Santa Anna and the Aftermath of San Jacinto." *West Texas Historical Association Year Book* 11 (1935): 56–61.

Crimmins, M. L. "American Powder's Part in Winning Texas Independence." *Southwestern Historical Quarterly* 52 (July 1948): 109–111.

———, ed. "John W. Smith, the Last Messenger from the Alamo and the First Mayor of San Antonio." *Southwestern Historical Quarterly* 54 (January 1951): 344–346.

Crisp, James E. "Sam Houston's Speechwriters: The Grad Student, the Teenager, the Editors, and the Historians," *Southwestern Historical Quarterly* 97 (October 1993): 203–237.

Davenport, Harbert. "Captain Jesús Cuellar, Texas Cavalry, Otherwise 'Comanche.'" *Southwestern Historical Quarterly* 30 (July 1926): 56–62.

———. "General José María Jesús Carbajal." *Southwestern Historical Quarterly* 55 (April 1952): 475–483.

———. "The Men of Goliad." *Southwestern Historical Quarterly* 43 (January 1939): 1–41.

De Leon, Arnoldo. "Tejanos and the Texas War for Independence: Historiography's Judgement." *New Mexico Historical Review* 61 (April 1986): 137–146.

Dienst, Alex. "Contemporary Poetry of the Texan Revolution." *Southwestern Historical Quarterly* 21 (October 1917): 156–184.

Dobie, J. Frank. "Jim Bowie, Big Dealer." *Southwestern Historical Quarterly* 60 (January 1957): 337–357.

Elliot, Claude. "Alabama and the Texas Revolution." *Southwestern Historical Quarterly* 50 (January 1947): 315–328.

Estep, Raymond. "Lorenzo de Zavala and the Texas Revolution." *Southwestern Historical Quarterly* 57 (January 1954): 322–335.

Garver, Lois. "The Life of Benjamin Rush Milam." *Southwestern Historical Quarterly* 38 (October 1934, January 1935): 79–121, 177–202.

Gilbert, Randal B. "Arms for the Revolution and Republic." *Military History of Texas and the Southwest* 9 (1971): 191–216.

Graham, Don. "Remembering the Alamo: The Story of the Texas Revolution in Popular Culture." *Southwestern Historical Quarterly* 89 (1985): 35–66.

Green, Michael Robert. "Activo Batallon of Tres Villas, February–April, 1836." *Military History of Texas and the Southwest* 14 (1976): 53–58.

———. "El Soldado Mexicano, 1835–1836." *Military History of Texas and the Southwest* 13 (1975): 5–10.

———. "'To the People of Texas & All Americans in the World.'" *Southwestern Historical Quarterly* 91 (April 1988): 483–508.

Greer, James K. "The Committee on the Texan Declaration of Independence." *Southwestern Historical Quarterly* 30, 31 (April 1927, July 1927): 239–251, 33–49.

Hardin, Stephen L. "Concepción: The Forgotten Battle of the Texas Revolution." *Heritage of the Great Plains* 20 (Spring 1987): 10–18.

———. "Gallery: Ben McCulloch." *Military Illustrated, Past and Present* 49 (July 1992): 46–47, 50.

———. "Gallery: David Crockett." *Military Illustrated, Past and Present* 23 (February–March 1990): 28–35.

———. "J. C. Neill: The Forgotten Alamo Commander." *Alamo Journal* 66 (May 1989): 5–11.

———. "A Vatir y Perseguir: Tejano Deployment in the War of Texas Independence, 1835–1836." *Essays in History: The E. C. Barksdale Student Lectures, 1985–1986.* Edited by Lisa C. Davis. Arlington, Tex.: Omicron Kappa Chapter of Phi Alpha Theta, 1986.

———. "A Volley from the Darkness: Sources Regarding the Death of William Barret Travis." *Alamo Journal* 59 (December 1987): 3–10.

———. "'We Flogged Them Like Hell': The Capitulation of Lipantitlán and the Battle of Nueces Crossing." *Journal of South Texas* I (1988): 49–64.

Henderson, H. M. "A Critical Analysis of the San Jacinto Campaign." *Southwestern Historical Quarterly* 59 (January 1956): 344–362.

Hutton, Paul Andrew. "The Alamo: An American Epic." *American History Illustrated* 20 (March 1986): 12–37.

King, C. Richard. "James Clinton Neill." *Texana* 2 (Winter 1964): 231–252.

Koury, Mike. "Cannon for Texas: Artillery in the Revolution and the Republic." *Military History of Texas and the Southwest* 10 (1972): 127–139.

Lindley, Thomas Ricks. "Alamo Artillery: Number, Type, Caliber, and Concussion." *Alamo Journal* 82 (July 1992): 3–10.

———. "Alamo Sources." *Alamo Journal* 74 (December 1990): 3–13.

———. "James Butler Bonham, October 17, 1835–March 6, 1836." *Alamo Journal* 62 (August 1988): 3–11.

Looscan, Adele. "Micajah Autry: A Soldier of the Alamo." *Quarterly of the Texas State Historical Association* 14 (April 1911): 315–324.

McDonald, Archie P. "Lone Star Rising: Texas before and after the Alamo." *American History Illustrated* 20 (March 1986): 48–51.

———. "The Young Men of the Texas Revolution." *Texana* 3 (Winter 1965): 333–346.

Marks, Paula Mitchell. "The Men of Gonzales: They Answered the Call." *American History Illustrated* 20 (March 1986): 46–47.

Miller, Thomas Lloyd. "Fannin's Men: Some Additions to Earlier Rosters." *Southwestern Historical Quarterly* 61 (April 1958): 522–532.

———. "José Antonio Navarro, 1795–1871." *Journal of Mexican American History* 2 (Fall 1972): 71–89.

———. "Mexican-Texans at the Alamo." *Journal of Mexican American History* 2 (Fall 1971): 33–44.

———. "Mexican Texans in the Texas Revolution." *Journal of Mexican American History* 2 (1971): 105–130.

———. "The Roll of the Alamo." *Texana* 2 (Spring 1964): 54–64.

Moorman, Evelyn Buzzo, ed. "A Red Rover's Last Letter." *Texana* 4 (Spring 1966): 14–22.

Nackman, Mark E. "The Making of the Texan Citizen Soldier, 1835–1860." *Southwestern Historical Quarterly* 78 (January 1975): 231–253.

Nance, J. Milton. "Rendezvous at the Alamo: The Place of Bowie, Crockett, and Travis in Texas History." *West Texas Historical Association Year Book* 63 (1987): 5–23.

Pohl, James W., and Stephen L. Hardin. "The Military History of the Texas Revolution: An Overview." *Southwestern Historical Quarterly* 89 (January 1986): 269–308.

Presley, James. "Santa Anna in Texas: A Mexican Viewpoint." *Southwestern Historical Quarterly* 62 (April 1959): 489–512.

Riviere, Wm. T. "Sam Houston's Retreat." *Southwestern Historical Quarterly* 46 (July 1942): 9–14.

Roller, John E. "Capt. John Sowers Brooks." *Quarterly of the Texas State Historical Association* 9 (January 1906): 157–209.

Scarborough, Jewel Davis. "The Georgia Battalion in the Texas Revolution: A Critical Study." *Southwestern Historical Quarterly* 62 (April 1960): 511–532.

Schoen, Harold. "The Free Negro in the Republic of Texas." *Southwestern Historical Quarterly* 41 (July 1937): 83–108.

Shuffler, R. Henderson. "The Signing of Texas' Declaration of Independence: Myth and Record." *Southwestern Historical Quarterly* 65 (January 1962): 310–332.

Sibley, Marilyn McAdams. "The Burial Place of the Alamo Heroes." *Southwestern Historical Quarterly* 70 (October 1966): 272–280.

Siegal, Stanley. "Santa Anna Goes to Washington." *Texana* 7 (Summer 1969): 126–135.

Smith, Ruby Cumby. "James Walker Fannin, Jr., in the Texas Revolution." *Southwestern Historical Quarterly* 23 (October 1919, January 1920, April 1920): 80–90, 171–203, 271–284.

Smith, W. Roy. "The Quarrel between Governor Smith and the Provisional Government of the Republic." *Quarterly of the Texas State Historical Association* 5 (April 1902): 269–346.

Steen, Ralph W. "Analysis of the Work of the General Council, Provisional Government of Texas, 1835–1836." *Southwestern Historical Quarterly* 41 (April 1938): 324–348.

Vernon, Ida S. "Activities of the Seguins in Early Texas History." *West Texas Historical Association Year Book* 25 (1949): 3–11.

Williams, Robert H. "Travis: A Potential Sam Houston." *Southwestern Historical Quarterly* 40 (October 1936): 154–160.

Winkler, E. W. "Membership of the 1833 Convention of Texas." *Southwestern Historical Quarterly* 45 (January 1942): 255–257.

———. "The 'Twin Sisters' Cannon, 1836–1865." *Southwestern Historical Quarterly* 21 (July 1917): 61–68.

Winston, James E. "Mississippi and the Independence of Texas." *Southwestern Historical Quarterly* 21 (July 1917): 36–60.

———. "New York and the Independence of Texas." *Southwestern Historical Quarterly* 17 (April 1915): 368–385.

NEWSPAPERS
Dallas Morning News.
Corpus Christi Caller-Times.
Telegraph and Texas Register.

THESES AND DISSERTATIONS

Adams, Allen F. "The Leader of the Volunteer Grays: The Life of William G. Cooke, 1808–1847." M.A. thesis, Southwest Texas State Teachers College, 1940.

Boyce, Fannie Boyd. "James Bowie." M.A. thesis, Southwest Texas State Teachers College, 1939.

Boyce, Sallie Joy, "James Walker Fannin." M.A. thesis, Southwest Texas State Teachers College, 1939.

Callaway, Carolyn Louise. "'The Runaway Scrape': An Episode of the Texas Revolution." M.A. thesis, University of Texas, 1942.

Curry, Ora Mae. "The Texan Siege of San Antonio, 1835." M.A. thesis, University of Texas, 1927.

Downs, Fane. "The History of Mexicans in Texas, 1820–1845." Ph.D. diss., Texas Tech University, 1970.

Garver, Lois Antoinette. "The Life of Benjamin Rush Milam." M.A. thesis, University of Texas, 1931.

George, Catherine. "The Life of Philip Dimmitt." M.A. thesis, University of Texas, 1937.

Hale, Laura Elizabeth. "The Groces and the Whartons in the Early History of Texas." M.A. thesis, University of Texas, 1942.

Hardin, Stephen L. "Long Rifle and Brown Bess: Weapons and Tactics of the Texas Revolution, 1835–1836." M.A. thesis, Southwest Texas State University, 1985.

———. "Texian Iliad: A Narrative Military History of the Texas Revolution, 1835–1836." Ph.D. diss., Texas Christian University, 1989.

Harris, Helen Willits. "The Public Life of Juan Nepomuceno Almonte." Ph.D. diss., University of Texas, 1935.

Jackson, Lillis Tisdale. "Sam Houston in the Texas Revolution." M.A. thesis, University of Texas, 1932.

McDonald, Johnnie Belle. "The Soldiers of San Jacinto." M.A. thesis, University of Texas, 1922.

Mixon, Marie Ruby. "William Barret Travis, His Life and Letters." M.A. thesis, University of Texas, 1930.

Moore, Robert Lee. "History of Refugio County." M.A. thesis, University of Texas, 1937.

Putman, Lucile. "Washington-on-the-Brazos." M.A. thesis, East Texas State Teachers College, 1952.

Smith, Ruby Cumby. "James W. Fannin, Jr., in the Texas Revolution." M.A. thesis, University of Texas, 1919.

Tijerina, Andrew Anthony. "Tejanos and Texas: The Native Mexicans of Texas, 1820–1850." Ph.D. diss., University of Texas, 1977.

Turkovic, Robert J. "The Antecedents and Evolution of Santa Anna's Ill-fated Texas Campaign." M.A. thesis, Florida Atlantic University, 1973.

Watkins, Willye Ward. "Memoirs of General Antonio López de Santa Anna: Translation with Introduction and Notes." M.A. thesis, University of Texas, 1922.

Webb, Rufus Mac. "Military Campaigns of the Texas Revolution." M.A. thesis, North Texas State College, 1951.

Weiss, August H. "The Texas Revolution." M.A. thesis, Southwest Texas State Teachers College, 1946.

Williams, Amelia. "A Critical Study of the Siege of the Alamo and the Personnel of Its Defenders." Ph.D. diss., University of Texas, 1931.

———. "The Siege and Fall of the Alamo." M.A. thesis, University of Texas, 1926.

Williams, Lawrence Drake. "Deaf Smith: Scout of the Texas Revolution." M.A. thesis, Trinity University, 1964.

Yarbrough, Yancy Parker. "The Life and Career of Edward Burleson." M.A. thesis, University of Texas, 1936.

INDEX